MW00526597

The Damming of
the Presidency

The Damming of the Presidency

How Environmental Factors Impact a Political Campaign

Frederick D. Gordon

LEXINGTON BOOKS
Lanham • Boulder • New York • London

Published by Lexington Books
An imprint of The Rowman & Littlefield Publishing Group, Inc.
4501 Forbes Boulevard, Suite 200, Lanham, Maryland 20706
www.rowman.com

6 Tinworth Street, London SE11 5AL, United Kingdom

Copyright © 2021 by The Rowman & Littlefield Publishing Group, Inc.

All rights reserved. No part of this book may be reproduced in any form or by any electronic or mechanical means, including information storage and retrieval systems, without written permission from the publisher, except by a reviewer who may quote passages in a review.

British Library Cataloguing in Publication Information Available

Library of Congress Cataloging-in-Publication Data

Library of Congress Control Number: 2020944238

ISBN 978-1-7936-0645-7 (cloth)
ISBN 978-1-7936-0646-4 (electronic)

This book is dedicated my late father Judge Nathan W. Gordon who often quoted Cicero's statement that a room without books is like a body without a soul. I hope this book will contribute to enrichment of the soul.

Contents

List of Figures

Acknowledgments

The book *The Damming of the Presidency How Environmental Factors Impact a Political Campaign* took several years to develop. There were two key factors that contributed to this study. First, I taught a course titled River Politics, which examined several interstate riparian conflicts, which included the Great Flood of 1927. This course revealed the link between the 1928 election and the Great Flood. Second, I made my initial presentation on this research at the Mississippi Flood at the 2017 Louisiana Water Policy Conference, which featured keynote speaker John Barry, author or *Rising Tide*. I continued to present chapters at recent regional political science conferences in Austin, Texas, and San Juan, Puerto Rico. I gained valuable insight from responder comments which helped shape my research.

I am very appreciative of Joseph Parry, the Senior Acquisitions editor at Rowman and Littlefield, who offered sound guidance in enabling me to see this project through completion. I am also thankful of Adenike Ajibowu, a graduate student in the Masters of Public Administration Program at East Tennessee State University, who helped collect campaign data, and Grete Scott who assisted with copyediting the manuscript. I also extend thanks to Dr. Liz Skilton of the University of Louisiana Lafayette who accepted my proposal to present at the 2017 Louisiana Water Policy conference. I also would like to thank my brother Dr. Louis Gordon who provided me with the initial lead to apply to the Louisiana Water Policy conference and of course to my parents Nathan and Beatrice Gordon who from an early age laid the foundation for the importance of education. Finally, I extend thanks to Angela Cunningham who provided support as I journeyed through each chapter.

Introduction

This study explores an unusual amalgamation of presidential, environmental, and emergency policy making. It draws upon a series of empirical and theoretical insights that suggest an increasing influence of force majeure events on presidential elections. Policy making is not predictive. However, it can project, and that is the cornerstone of this study. The book makes every attempt to treat its primary case study, the Great Mississippi Flood of 1927, holistically. The hope of this study is to serve as a baseline for future studies exploring the link between environmental and disaster management and the presidency. Good decisions lead to better outcomes, but sometimes, hubris, misinformation, and reductionism make that goal distant.

A significant feature of American government has been the expansion of governmental activity related to emergencies. A condition that evokes extraordinary exercise of governmental power as a necessary means of preserving the existing order is variously labeled as an "emergency," a "crisis," an "exigency," or a "pressing necessity."[1] Recent years have witnessed the use of terms like "emergency" as a justification for the use of unusual powers. In 1933, the national government addressed an economic crisis with direct intervention. On September 8, 1939, President Roosevelt declared "a limited national emergency," and on May 27, 1941, extended it to an "unlimited national emergency." The United States' entry into World War II was accompanied by the use of extraordinary powers that had rarely been seen. Elmer Cornell wrote a half century ago, "It has been the presidency, more than any other part of the system, that has enabled the American democracy to succeed and flourish . . . . And it has been the relationship between President and public that has given this office its power and importance."[2]

Crisis calls for unified action and consistent initiative and leadership. When national security is jeopardized, presidential leadership is paramount.

1

The president can command every source of information, make immediate decisions, and execute them without delay. Alexander pointed this out when he said,

> Energy in the Executive is a leading character in the definition of good government. It is essential to the protection of the community against foreign attacks; it is not less essential to the steady administration of the laws; to the protection of property against those irregular and highhanded combinations which sometimes interrupt the ordinary course of justice; to the security of liberty against the enterprises and assaults of ambition, of faction, and of anarchy.[3]

Disaster policy also fits in the emergency power domain. It impacts presidential decision making, as well as political legacy and image. The U.S. Constitution empowers the president to protect and defend the nation. In addition to their "implied powers," the president has constitutional obligations to address emergencies and disasters that befall the nation. Moreover, since 1950, presidential disaster declaration authority has granted the president emergency management leadership authority.[4]

Roman leader Lucius Quinctius Cincinnatus lived in Rome around 500 BC. He was a farmer with a reputation for being a good and wise man. One day, while working in a field, he was approached by the Roman military. He was informed that his services were needed to help repel enemy soldiers. Rome needed a leader and their Senate selected Cincinnatus. His appointment legally bound him for six months of power, and Cincinnatus completed his mission in only sixteen days. Yet instead of living out the next five-and-a-half months of his appointment in the glory of victory, Cincinnatus immediately surrendered his command and returned to his humble farm. Cincinnatus is remembered for his humility. He was granted absolute power and he accepted it, but only insofar as it allowed him to serve his country. The Cincinnatus story is relevant today not because policy problems can be solved in a matter of days or weeks, but rather because his story displays the honor and conviction required in making earnest attempts towards solving pressing policy concerns.[5]

The story of Cincinnatus is important because it shows selflessness in terms of policy making. Today, policy objectivity can be captured leaving incomplete results. Cincinnatus's example of briefly but heartily embracing absolute power would have benefited the administration following the Great Mississippi Flood. James Madison feared unbridled power and devoted too much time towards balancing and checking ambitions. The U.S. government made demonstrated efforts to check political ambition by imposing presidential term limits and campaign finance to further transparency. These structures remain in place today. But what about the message of Cincinnatus?[6]

Presidents are expected to make good decisions, but questions remain in terms of policy efficiency. Thomas Cronin likened the president to "Superman." Over time, public expectations of the president changed. The president was no longer viewed merely as a constitutional officer with a limited scope in duties. Instead, presidential performance was akin to being ubiquitous, meaning the president was expected to vanquish all foreign and domestic threats while protecting American national interests. A strong president would then serve as the "engine of change for the nation."[7]

Cronin's theme remains relevant today, though it is unclear whether the Founding Fathers would approve of today's presidency. Alexander Hamilton, a leading advocate of a strong presidency, might be daunted by some of the blank check unitary executive power ascribed to the president.[8] But there is more to it than dichotomizing the president as good or evil. The Founding Fathers may have been oracles, but like all of us, they were flawed individuals with limited vision. The *Federalist* warns against a "blind veneration for antiquity."[9] This caution can be interpreted in several ways. First, policy should not be stuck in the past. Even more importantly, society constantly needs to evolve. The best way to safeguard this process is through a society governed by laws and that no individual reigns supreme.[10]

PRESIDENTIAL ELECTIONS

Each presidential election tells its own tale. Some presidential election outcomes can be more easily predicted by public opinion polls than others. However, there have been some incongruities in deciphering modern presidential outcomes. The 1948 election between President Truman and Governor Dewey is most notable. Dewey was predicted to win the presidency, yet due to flawed campaign strategies, he did not aggressively make campaign appearances and lost. American politics is replete with untested assumptions about how presidential campaigns are won and lost. According to Powell, aspiring candidates pay careful attention to the media and other critical public opinion sources.[11] However, there is no guarantee of a political victory.

The memorable picture of Truman holding a copy of the *Chicago Daily Tribune* stating "Dewey Wins" could not be any further from the truth.[12] In more recent times, war, economy, and public confidence in the governing institutions all serve as salient variables and approaches towards deciphering presidential outcomes. The 2016 presidential election garners important introspection because long-term blue states like Pennsylvania, Michigan, and Wisconsin all shifted to vote as red states. However, often overlooked is whether a major environmental event could also impact a national election.

This book advances the idea that environmental events have a subtle impact on the presidency. Whether it be a hurricane, flood, or other force majeure event, presidents and political candidates are under increased pressure and scrutiny. The American public expects cogent policy solutions, the alleviation of pain and suffering, and effective management of the situation. Yet could such transformative events sway public opinion to change an electoral outcome? This query is driven by Farley's Law or the theory of minimal change,[13] which some people might call incremental ideology. It posits that people are generally reluctant to vote for candidates from opposing parties and that they have selected their candidates at least six months prior to the election. Yet could a force majeure event or other disaster-oriented event be a game changer in a national election? Or in other words, do natural disasters help or hurt politicians' electoral fortunes?[14]

This idea has been raised by scholars. Heersink, Peterson, and Jenkins conducted a study on the link between natural disasters and electoral punishment to incumbent politicians. The focus was on the quality of relief efforts. Their study applied retrospective voting principles by attaching natural disaster or random events to past political performance. Their central assumption was the better the disaster response, the greater the likelihood for a more positive outcome at the polls.[15]

Studies of the effects of disaster and relief have come to contradictory conclusions. Achen and Bartels established a foundation for the study of "blind retrospection" by investigating the electoral consequences of shark attacks along the New Jersey shore in 1916, droughts and floods in twenty-six presidential elections across the twentieth century, and droughts and floods in the 2000 presidential election. Across these cases, they found that citizens punish incumbent party candidates for random events outside of their control, which would challenge Farley's Law.[16]

Other research reveals more of a longitudinal approach. Voters represent an "alternative electorate," capable of assigning praise and blame after a natural disaster by incorporating both disaster effects and relief operations in determining vote choice. Healy and Malhotra find no evidence that disaster damage influences presidential vote share but do uncover a relationship between relief spending and support for the incumbent party.[17] Similarly, Healy and Malhotra and Gasper and Reeves find voters punish incumbent presidents for damage from severe weather but that positive electoral effects of disaster declarations overwhelm the negative effects of the disaster itself. A key difference between these findings is the inclusion of relief spending as a variable; studies that account for subsequent relief efforts generally find that voters balance their assessment based on disaster and subsequent relief.[18,19]

The level of relief response is also correlated to the type of government. Highly active governments often have different expectations about providing relief than countries with limited resources and less active governments.[20] The inference that governments with the largest welfare states are the most likely to offer best disaster relief policies is not clear. What is certain is that best disaster relief policies stem from responder training and available technology. Considerable literature also examines natural disaster and relief operations in other countries, revealing that natural disasters can be an electoral boon to incumbent politicians.[21]

Yet differentiation across time is another matter. Achen and Bartels study some cases in the pre–New Deal United States (such as the 1916 shark attacks).[22] Their research also examined retrospection focused exclusively on the post–New Deal era. The federal government's dramatic expansion over time has yielded a normative perception of what the government *should* do. While the federal government has always been involved in disaster relief in some form, national politicians in the pre–New Deal era generally agreed that first responder relief was the responsibility of state and local governments. The post–New Deal era may have come to expect the federal government to provide critical relief, but questions remain today as to who should provide the immediate relief.[23]

CASE STUDY SELECTION

The case of the Great Mississippi Flood of 1927 will be introduced here and further expanded upon in chapter 5 on Hoover and the Great Flood. Our familiarity with the case is important. First, some scholars, policy experts, and the general public might inquire why the 1918 Pandemic was not the main case study of a force majeure event's impact upon a national campaign. The Great Pandemic of 1918 was the fulcrum in changing how the United States addressed widespread disease. However, no political figure wore both admiration and responsibility in how the pandemic was resolved, offering no direct connections to presidential elections. Yet the Great Mississippi Flood of 1927 filled that gap by creating both political opportunity and political demise.

A proper assessment of the connections between the Great Mississippi Flood and Herbert Hoover requires multiple theoretical frameworks. The roles of the media, campaign, electoral college, president, policy process, public opinion, federalism, and force majeure events are integral to offering an in-depth perspective. The 1928 and 1932 elections are unique. They stand back nearly a hundred years, and the role of the federal government has changed significantly.

Yet these two electoral outcomes are significant in the scholarly community, since they are often viewed as the loci for major political party realignment. This is true, but what is their nexus to the 1927 Mississippi Flood? This cataclysmic event showed the internal weakness of federal infrastructure. The flood affected 1 percent of the nation's population and cost thousands of lives. It also served as a political aperture for Herbert Hoover to gain the presidency. Hoover won the 1928 presidential election against Democratic nominee Al Smith. Smith was a popular New York governor, but his Prohibition repeal stance and Catholic identity limited his national appeal. Hoover had national experience. He was touted as a "Great Engineer" for his relief effort in Europe and had served under two presidents. The political climate favored Hoover, but there were cracks. He did not carry the Deep Southern states who were most impacted by the flood.[24]

Hoover was media savvy, even in 1927, and was able to cultivate a favorable media impression. This was important considering the flood's magnitude. The nascent television spectrum revealed the extent of the flood's destruction. Heavy rains drenched tributary valleys in April 1927 and the Mississippi River levee system failed. By May 1, 1927, refugees, loss of life, and property damage became common themes. Thousands of people fled their homes, and the flood deluged more than a million acres of crops.[25]

Governors sought Hoover's help, and Hoover responded by creating a ubiquitous impression that he could address all flood damage needs. Hoover travelled to the flood management headquarters in Memphis. People saw him at the broken Melville levee on the Atchafalaya and in various counties warning citizens of the flood dangers. He completed several inspection tours and people felt better because Mr. Hoover was there.[26]

Herbert Hoover appeared to be the perfect foil for the political times. President Coolidge did not see a clear federal role in flood management. Coolidge believed that natural disasters had been historically managed at the state and local levels. There was much precedent for this. Grover Cleveland stated that the Constitution did not provide for the national government to indulge. However, as deaths mounted, Coolidge was forced to alter his policy approach. On April 22, 1927, Coolidge appointed Hoover as chair of a special cabinet committee to relieve the stricken areas. Hoover's goodwill and reputation seemed to make him the perfect candidate. Will Rogers quipped, "When a man is sick, he calls a doctor. But when the United States of America is sick, they call for Herbert Hoover."[27] And people did, by electing him to become the thirty-second president of the United States. However, like an iceberg, the Mississippi River flood had many jagged edges that would contribute to the unravelling of his presidency.

In fact, the Great Mississippi Flood of 1927 is one of the largest natural disasters in American history. There are countless sources that reveal the extent of the disaster. *Back Water Blues: The Mississippi Flood of 1927 in the African American Imagination* by John Mizelle and John Barry's *Rising*

Tide yield a plethora of information about the event. Both works signify the political acrimony that engulfed the floodplain regions. Three notable factors impacted Hoover's management of the Great Flood. First was the weakness in the levees-only policy approach. In short, better land management strategies needed to be developed. Second, the Red Cross relief agency failed to treat all flood victims equally. Force majeure events like a great flood could provide a political opportunity as well as a political vacuum, leading to long-standing political setbacks. Therefore, the third point was the fluctuant manner of federalism. The federal government was transitioning slowly toward a clear regulatory capacity. Dual federal practices were slowly being supplanted by a more proactive federal government. However, this meant regulatory behavior, which was not always supported by business interests.

Yet signs of federal management were already evident well before the Great Flood. For instance, the Federal Flood Control Act of 1917 offered annual federal appropriations for flood control and supported a basic form of cooperative federalism. Local levee districts managed the right of way and road alteration processes. However, the levees were constructed by the federally based Mississippi River Commission. The actual levees were built from clay and concrete, which translated into a $229 million investment by Congress. But the levees were no match for water moving at a speed of 3 million cubic feet per second. The levees began to crumble on Good Friday, April 12 in Missouri, and six days later, a mile-wide crevasse burst open at Mounds Landing, Mississippi. The levees were breached at 140 points in six weeks stretching from St. Louis to New Orleans.[28]

Force majeure events are rarely asymptomatic. In this case, the structural problem was the dated levees-only policy. In the spring of 1927, a period of unusually heavy rainfall combined with significant deforestation resulted in the bursting of levees along the Mississippi River Valley. This was unprecedented in several ways. First, the swathe of destruction was tremendous. Flood waters traversed over 26,000 square miles of land in 170 counties in Illinois, Kentucky, and in particular, Tennessee, Arkansas, Mississippi, and Louisiana. Flooding was particularly severe in Mississippi and Louisiana, with a considerable number of counties directly along the Mississippi River completely submerged.[29]

Both federal relief and the presidential viewpoint were much different than today. The central relief effort was organized by President Calvin Coolidge. Coolidge held staunch conservative views about federal intervention, and resultingly, his actions were measured and delayed. The lack of executive urgency alienated many lower Mississippi Valley residents and would ultimately be a political deficit for the Republican Party. Coolidge adeptly shifted flood management to his Secretary of Commerce Herbert Hoover. Afterall, Hoover had significant refugee relief expertise during the latter part of World War I. Under Hoover's guidance, more than 120,000 families across the South received Red Cross aid. Relief efforts equaled $32 million or in 2015, $438 million.[30] Hoover was not subjected to the social media scrutiny of today, but newspaper and magazines documented his visits to relief sites. And Hoover capitalized on this. His campaign team created a documentary titled "Herbert Hoover, Master of Emergencies," which showcased his prowess for addressing national calamities.[31] However, river management was complex.

The Mississippi River means numerous things to people. Southern Reconstruction left an indelible impression in the South and contributed to southern economic stagnation. Bitter resentment existed between the North and South over the economic progress. The South felt contemptuous because Civil War wounds remained decades after Lee's surrender at the Appomattox Court House in Virginia. The Mississippi River, an indelible reminder of slavery, also served as a unifying force. The South lay prone after the war and struggled even after post-Reconstruction society. A healthy Mississippi River signified a vibrant economy, and for some, this was a way to heal the deep rift from the Civil War. The Mississippi River served as a conduit of political forces, meaning it not only impacted southern and midwestern states. Western states sought political leverage by supporting Mississippi River Valley legislation as well.[32]

Mississippi River management was a long-standing political issue. According to Barry, river management was also a long-standing legislative problem. In 1850, the Congress authorized a survey of the lower valley from Cairo, Illinois to the Gulf. Barry writes, "The aim was to discover the laws governing the Mississippi River, and determine how to tame it."[33] The *American Journal of Science* recommended a "single channel theory," which tied together flood control and navigation interests.[34]

By the 1880s, army engineers were building flood control levees all along the lower Mississippi River. However, the "levees-only" approach created a catch-22. The initial levees caused the river to carry a greater volume of water. This in turn forced engineers to construct taller levees. Another option would have been to exercise eminent domain over private property, but this was met with resistance. Hence, "levees only" became a natural political compromise.[35]

Either way, during the winter and spring months of 1927, the Mississippi River well surpassed record flood stages. In April 1927, waters began to rise precipitously, approaching sixty feet above mean sea level. By May, floods had devastated thirty-two towns and cities and pushed the Ohio tributary backward. Political wrangling soon emerged. The breach panicked New Orleans authorities, who convinced the Corps of Engineers and Mississippi River Commission to divert flooding in order to save their city. When it was over, 20 percent of the river's volume poured through a 3,200 feet wide breach into St. Bernard and Plaquemines Parishes.[36]

The exact number of casualties remains uncertain. The American Red Cross reported 246 deaths, but the actual toll may have been several times higher. An estimated 700,000 people were rendered homeless, and more than 300,000 victims spent several months in Red Cross camps. Another 300,000 people received food and other assistance outside the camps. Approximately 200,000 buildings were damaged or destroyed, and at least 20,000 square miles of land (or as much as 27,000 square miles, by some accounts) were flooded. The Association of State Floodplain Managers called the 1927 flood of the Mississippi River "the greatest natural disaster to befall the United States in terms of human suffering and misery."[37]

What was the level of federal intervention at that time? Kosar states, "It was a mixture of pre–New Deal minimalist and 'governing by network.'"[38] The federal government would make no immediate appropriations to the affected area. Instead, federal resources would coordinate networks of federal, state, private, and not-for-profit organizations to deliver relief services. The president's cabinet would direct the relief effort in close consultation with the American National Red Cross. Thus, "flood response policy was centralized, but its execution was decentralized."[39]

This process mixing centralized and decentralized responses mirrored dual federalism. There was national centralized power, but significant decision making remained with the states. Dual federalism was known for racial inequality. Barry demonstrates stark levels of inequity by comparing Greenville, Mississippi, to New Orleans. Each city's flood outcomes demonstrated different levels of racial equality. In Greenville, African Americans were compelled, sometimes at gunpoint, to maintain the levees. More than 13,000 African Americans around Greenville were stranded for days without food or clean water. The National Guard patrolled the levees and refused to allow anyone access without a pass. Yet in Greenville itself, whites stayed on the upper floors of offices and hotels. A Colored Advisory Commission report states, "We found numerous instances where the colored people, were living under a semi-peonage system." Further many communities were afraid to ask for their entitlements under the Red Cross.[40]

Downstream, other inequities occurred. The city of New Orleans detonated thirty tons of dynamite to breach a downriver levee to avert flooding. New Orleans oligarchs promised to compensate the trappers and other rural inhabitants inundated by the breach, but in the end paid no reparations to local residents. Ironically, the breach was unnecessary, as earlier upstream breaks had already relieved flood pressure.[41]

Since cooperative federalism was still in a nascent stage, the American Red Cross absorbed much of the financial relief effort. The Red Cross had elevated status and was part of a a quasi-governmental commission that included cabinet members. Hoover's team coordinated the largest disaster relief effort in U.S. history. In other words, dual federalism was slowly being supplanted by cooperative federalism. The response blended federal, state, local, and private resources.

However, the relief resources proved to be controversial. First, they were inadequately distributed amongst African American sharecroppers. Second, relief and recovery supplies contributed to the debt peonage system. White landowners received the aid and then charged black sharecroppers for supplies. It was a classic debt peonage system. Hoover faced a dilemma. He understood the level of racial tension inside refugee camps. He was also concerned about securing the Republican Party nomination for the 1928 election. Hoover sought to minimize these problems by influencing African American community leaders to keep the deplorable situation in the refugee camps quiet from the media. And it worked, to some extent. His 1928 presidential election victory was due in part to positive media publicity garnered from managing the flood. Yet his failure to the African American community would be one of several factors resulting in later political realignment. As a result, black allegiance would soon shift from the Republican to the Democratic Party.[42]

A paradigm shift occurred following the flood. Barry argues that the flood penetrated to the core of the nation and revealed the nation's character. Then it tested that character and changed it. The flood marked the end of a way of seeing the world, says Barry, and possibly an end of that world itself. It shifted perceptions of the role and responsibility of the federal government, called for a great expansion, and shattered the myth of a quasi-feudal bond between Delta blacks and the southern aristocracy. The great migration of blacks moving north was accelerated. And both southern and national politics were altered.[43]

The Flood Control Act of 1928 abandoned the levees-only approach and provided a federal-local partnership. Yet federal involvement in local affairs would expand further. Congress appropriated $10 million for relief and reconstruction associated with the 1927 flood, but it spent thirty times this amount—$300 million—the following year on flood control projects.[44]

The devastating floods in New England and the Ohio River basin led to the Flood Control Act of 1936. Flood control became a national interest, though there was agency competition. On one side, the Department of Agriculture established plans to reduce runoff and retain rainfall. On the other side, the Corps of Engineers developed engineering plans for downstream projects. In theory, the plan required cooperation, but in fact, there was no specific mechanism to ensure coordination. Ultimately, the major work fell to the Corps.[45]

Congress passed additional flood control acts in 1938 and 1941, authorizing more construction and 100 percent more federal spending for dams and reservoirs. Congress appropriated more than $11 billion for flood control projects between 1936 and 1952. Key actors such as floodplain managers, engineers, and scholars understood the narrowness of the levee-only policy. Critics warned national flood damage potential was growing faster due to urbanization. As one researcher wrote, "Federal flood control projects made matters worse by providing a false send of security that attracted new development to floodplains. A broader policy reach was needed that considered all possible means to mitigate flooding, including land use planning, zoning, restrictions on the use of land in flood zones, flood proofing, and insurance."[46] The levee-only policy was too narrow for effective flood management.

Today, the National Flood Insurance Program, administered by the Federal Emergency Management Agency (FEMA), requires local governments to institute effective floodplain management measures, such as levees and dams, to reduce flood losses. However, deeply entrenched social, economic, and political forces serve as a catalyst for people to remain in vulnerable areas.[47]

Hence, the Great Mississippi Flood of 1927 mirrored social inequalities endemic to the United States. Wealthy white citizens fared far better than African Americans and other poor minorities. Racial inequality was a factor. However, there were other reasons as well. Wealthier residents lived in less vulnerable places and had more resources to escape. There was also a social mobility factor. Wealthier people tended to have friends in distant locations within the state or beyond to offer refuge. Further, people from stable economic units tended to have more secure jobs, savings, insurance, and other resources. Perhaps most revealing is the interconnectivity factor: Financially stable individuals and families understood how government agencies and local banks operated and established close relationships with both. Interconnectivity meant loans could be obtained more easily than people without any discernible credit.[48]

A series of paradoxes surround U.S. emergency management. Policy makers and administrators often seem to craft plans and procedures in response to the latest disaster. Few resources are allocated for forecasting force majeure events and their impact.[49] Despite this reality, the American public wants emergency decision making to be clear and straightforward. This is buttressed by our country's separation of power mantra. As Rubin states, "We correctly think and speak of our government as one based on the 'separation of powers,' but while the institutions and levels of our complex, democratized republic are 'separate' in that they are institutionally distinct from one another, in actuality the Constitution makes their powers shared or overlapped." This then obfuscates both policy design and implementation, making it difficult for emergency management agencies to do their job. Effective emergency management requires nonpartisan, political, and interorganizational administrative and management skills. This is hard to find and even harder to implement.[50]

Further, disasters are hard to label. Each one is categorically different even though they are all tragic and even catastrophic. They catch people by surprise. It is difficult to raise revenue for foreseeable events, but even more challenging when timing is unpredictable.[51] Long-range emergency planning is expensive and not nearly as newsworthy as the damage and suffering that follows. The media has played an important role in shaping the policy agenda. In part, they define what counts as a problem and inform the public what is most salient. The federal government responds to these events and seeks organizational equilibrium and stability. However, sudden environmental events unsettle this framework.[52]

The greatest challenge to federal emergency management is more political than scientific. The failure to achieve an effective disaster response leads to political wrangling. This process is fueled by the myth of "can do," seen in the rational expectations for addressing force majeure events and their impact. Emergency management is complex and there are numerous classifications of disasters. On the surface, this appears positive. However, the higher the expectations, the greater the disappointment. According to Rubin, as public expectations rise, the likelihood of a failure increases. That life and property should be protected is understood. However, who should assume responsibility?[53]

The link between disaster management and elections is in an early phase. It is unclear how and to what extent such events impact elected officials. However, that voters vent their frustration at the polls is certain, as occurred in Florida after Hurricane Andrew in 1992. Voters are quick to shift blame. This makes emergency management more difficult. Unbiased analysis is required to understand disaster response strategies. However, multilevel political forces challenge that objective.[54]

Citizens view efficiency through a national narrative. The United States won World War II, rebuilt Europe through the Marshall Plan, sent men to the moon, and defeated the Soviet Union in the Cold War. This solidified the view that the United States is a nation of "doers"—efficient, effective, and organized. Government should be run like a business. However, this belief ignores the fact that emergency management is much more complicated in safeguarding flood victims.[55]

Yet national consciousness and its pursuit of organizational efficiency often preclude anyone from taking responsibility. According to Rubin, policy makers use reductionist thinking in addressing emergencies. At one level, this satisfies a hierarchy of who is responsible, but at the same time sacrifices system complexity. In turn, policy makers substitute simplistic and convenient answers that are grounded on faulty analysis. This leads to erroneous premises, which inevitably result in system and organizational failure.[56]

Political leaders use science as a means of legitimizing their actions. However, science must be elevated in deciphering natural climactic events while maintaining rationality and objectivity. And science can be co-opted. Political leaders use science to infer that humans have control over unstable environment conditions, even in the face of a random, indifferent natural order.[57]

Governmental reorganization reinforces cultural, social norms that suggest mastery over science and nature is possible. This allows for government agencies to appear as legitimate actors, reinforcing confidence in political leadership. However, reorganization and reform efforts are actually classic examples of "satisficing behavior"; groups make decisions not for the optimal solution, but rather for the immediate preferences or needs of the majority. The end result is incomplete solutions lacking serious reform merit. Those in charge must understand a myriad number of conditions including social, economic, and political contexts. Only then will there be a better future for emergency management.[58]

Perhaps this starts at the helm. Presidents have fought to maintain authority over some if not all facets of emergency management. Presidential authority means that any recommendations for change must keep the president at the apex of the hierarchical system. But this is at odds with emergency management. Emergency management requires a multiplicity of support. This includes but is not limited to presidential attention and non-hierarchical, network-like cooperation across federal, state, and local governments, as well as across public, nonprofit, and private sectors. Only then could emergency management approach effectiveness, saving lives and protecting society.[59]

Presidential opposition to reduced authority over emergency management coupled with indifferent stewardship drives reorganization efforts toward hierarchical centralization. This simplifies the development of a command and control system that can coordinate activities across the multiple and complex levels of government. Rubin explains, "Hierarchy used authority (legitimate power) to create and coordinate a horizontal and vertical division of labor. Under hierarchy, knowledge is treated as a scarce resource and is therefore concentrated, along with the corresponding decision rights, in specialized functional units and at higher levels of the organization."[60]

It is difficult to argue against hierarchy in large organizations with clear missions, such as to deliver the mail to all households and businesses in the United States or to send checks to millions of social security recipients on time. The operations may be incredibly complex and involve large groups of people and machinery, but the tasks are repetitive and routine, and there is clear accountability for decisions and operations. Hierarchy embodies the presumption not only that others will comply with lawful orders, but also that established rules and procedures will be followed. According to Rubin,

"Hierarchy can provide institutional support for the current bundles of routines, informational systems, values, and other key elements that influence production."[61]

But while hierarchy may have its place in institutional or organizational structures, great difficulties remain. Emergency responses require multilevel coordination. This means working across organizations, government agencies, and private sectors under crisis conditions. Today there are more than thirty federal agencies with emergency management responsibilities. The scale of agency coordination in disaster response is overwhelming. These agencies must interact not only with one another but also with state and local government agencies and private and nonprofit organizations. Rigid, hierarchical decision making impedes effective responses. The notion of hierarchy rests on the notion that the organizations to be coordinated have been identified or can be readily identified by the headquarters coordinators, that the relationship of these organizations to each other are well understood, that agreement had been reached about what objectives will be accomplished by altering certain of these interorganizational relationships, and that the authority and means to effectuate desired goals exist to alter the relationships in the desired direction. It short, this means hierarchy will facilitate the implementation.[62]

Yet recent investigations reveal otherwise. The policy response failures during the 2005 hurricane season suggest that centralized, hierarchical systems of response fail to interact with agencies and groups outside the federal government. The federal government fails to communicate effectively with state and local systems because it holds little understanding of the local systems in the affected areas. As the consequences of disasters unfolded, responding organizations were faced with unprecedented problems that they had not considered. In the case of Hurricane Katrina, the hierarchy of the Federal Emergency Management Agency and the Department of Homeland Security had to reprogram their coordination strategies. Or in other terms, policymakers had to think outside the prescribed lines of authority and control, seeking creative solutions to emerging problems. When this happens, the strength of a hierarchy becomes a weakness.[63] With this valuable background, we can progress with our study of how force majeure events impact a presidential campaign.

NOTES

1. Albert L. Sturm, "Emergencies and the Presidency," *The Journal of Politics* 11, no. 1 (1949): 121, https://doi.org/10.2307/2126502.
2. Sturm, "Emergencies," 121.

3. Ibid.

4. Ibid.

5. Ben Chapman, "Americans Have Forgotten the Story of Cincinnatus," *Medium* (2018), https://medium.com/@Ben_Chapman/americans-have-forgotten-the-story-of-cincinnatus-b49728164ce1

6. Chapman, "Americans."

7. Gene Healy, "Our Continuing Cult of the Presidency," in *The Presidency in the Twenty-First Century*, ed. Charles Dunn (University of Kentucky Press, 2011), 145, https://doi.org/10.2307/j.ctt2jchdr.

8. Healy, "Our Continuing Cult," 145.

9. Ibid.

10. Ibid.

11. Richard J. Powell, "The Strategic Importance of State-Level Factors in Presidential Elections," *Publius: The Journal of Federalism* 34, no. 3 (2004): 115–130, www.jstor.org/stable/20184913.

12. Tim Jones, "Dewey Defeats Truman," *Chicago Tribune*, December 19, 2007, https://www.chicagotribune.com/nation-world/chi-chicagodays-deweydefeats-story-story.html

13. James E. Campbell, *The American Campaign U.S. Presidential Campaigns and the National Vote* (Texas A&M Press, 2000), 242.

14. Boris Heersink, Brenton Peterson, and Jeffrey A. Jenkins, "Disasters and Elections: Estimating the Net Effect of Damage and Relief in Historical Perspective," *Political Analysis* 25, no. 2 (Cambridge University Press, April 3, 2017): 260–268, doi: 10.1017/pan.2017.7.

15. Heersink, Peterson, and Jenkins, "Disasters and Elections," 260–268.

16. Christopher Achen and Larry M. Bartels, "Blind Retrospection: Electoral Responses to Drought, Flu and Shark Attacks," Paper presented at the *American Political Science Association*, Boston, 2002, 3–42.

17. Andrew Healy and Neil Malhotra, "Myopic Voters and Natural Disaster Policy," *American Political Science Review* 102, no. 3 (2009): 387–406, https://doi.org/10.1017/S0003055409990104.

18. Andrew Healy and Neil Malhotra, "Random Events, Economic Losses, and Retrospective Voting: Implications for Democratic Competence," *Quarterly Journal of Political Science* 55, no. 2 (2010): 340–355, http://dx.doi.org/10.1561/100.00009057.

19. John T. Gasper and Andrew Reeves, "Make it Rain? Retrospection and the Attentive Electorate in the Context of Natural Disasters," *American Journal of Political Science* 55, no. 2 (2011): 340–355, https://doi.org/10.1111/j.1540-5907.2010.00503.x.

20. Heersink, Peterson, Jenkins, "Disasters and Elections," 260–268.

21. Ibid.

22. Christopher H. Achen and Larry M. Bartels, *Democracy for Realists: Why Elections Do Not Produce Responsive Government* (Princeton, NJ: Princeton University Press, 2016), 1–423.

23. Heersink, Peterson, Jenkins, "Disasters and Elections," 260–268.

24. Harris Gaylord Warren, *Herbert Hoover and the Great Depression* (New York: Norton, 1967), 1–372.

25. Warren, "Herbert Hoover," 1–372.

26. Ibid.

27. Bruce A. Lohoff, "Herbert Hoover: Spokesman of Human Efficiency: The Mississippi Flood of 1927," *American Quarterly* 22, no. 3 (1970): 690–700, doi: 10.2307/2711620.

28. Robert P. Howell, "Society of American Military Engineers," 19, no. 105 (May–June, 1927): 194–195, http://www.jstor.org/stable/44691326.

29. Richard M. Mizelle Jr., *Backwater Blues: The Mississippi Flood of 1927 in the African Imagination* (University of Minnesota Press, 2014), 1–224.

30. Heersink, Peterson, and Jenkins, "Disasters and Elections," 260–268.

31. Ibid.

32. Ned Randolph, "River Activism, 'Levees Only' and the Great Mississippi Flood of 1927," *Media and Communications* 6, no. 1 (2017): 43–51, http://dx.doi.org /10.17645/mac.v6i1.1179.

33. John Barry, *Rising Tide: The Great Mississippi Flood of 1927 and How It Changed America* (Simon & Schuster, 1998), 74.

34. Todd Shallat, "Building Waterways, 1802-1861: Science and the United States Army in Early Public Works," *Technology and Culture* 31, no. 1 (1990): 18–50, http://dx.doi.org/10.2307/3105759.

35. Barry, "Rising Tide," 84.

36. Ibid.

37. Mizelle, "Backwater Blues," 1–22.

38. Kevin R. Kosar, "Disaster Response and Appointment of a Recovery Czar: The Executive Branch's Response to the Flood of 1927," *Congressional Research Service,* October 25, 2005, http://fpc.state.gov/documents/organization/55826.pdf.

39. Kevin R. Kosar, "Disaster Response and Appointment of a Recovery Czar: The Executive Branch's Response to the Flood of 1927," *Congressional Research Service*, October 25, 2005, http://fpc.state.gov/documents/organization/55826.pdf.

40. David Butler, "The Expanding Role of the Federal Government: 1927-1950," in *Emergency Management: The American Experience 1900-2010*, ed. Claire Rubin (New York: Taylor and Francis Group, 2012), 51–57.

41. Butler, "The Expanding Role of the Federal Government: 1927-1950," pp. 51–56.

42. Ibid.

43. Ibid.

44. Ibid.

45. Ibid.

46. Ibid.

47. Ibid.

48. Ibid.

49. Ibid.

50. Ibid.

51. Ibid.

52. Ibid.
53. Ibid.
54. Ibid.
55. Ibid.
56. Ibid.
57. Ibid.
58. Ibid.
59. Ibid.
60. Ibid.
61. Ibid.
62. Ibid.
63. Ibid.

Chapter 1

Emergency Management Overview

Before delving into an emergency management overview we must understand the research pathway. This study hones in on the Hoover administration to gain a better understanding of how a major environmental event could impact a presidential campaign. The available literature suggests that the Great Mississippi was a central locus of impact in both the 1928 and 1932 presidential elections. What is lesser known is that voters, regardless of environmental impact, select their presidential candidates along ideological party lines. This central observation is demonstrated by analyzing the Hoover case study buttressed with relevant theoretical and historical frameworks. The research design seeks to test three central hypotheses. H_1 asks whether larger environmental events lead to greater voter shifts in a national election. H_2 seeks to discover whether increased levels of volunteerism could serve as a viable recovery strategy after a major flood. H_3 queries whether increased levels of federal intervention in force majeure events could influence more voter decisions in a national election. The guiding theory for this study is Farley's Law, which posits that most people have decided whom to vote for at least six months prior to the start of the campaign season. Federalism theory will be applied to ascertain the inherent problem of disaster management and understand how its scope extends beyond the purview of the presidency.

As this study progressed, it became evident that multiple independent variables were needed to enhance proper evaluation. Intense force majeure events are quite complex. The environmental variable, while integral to the study, was interrelated with many other causal factors such as federalism, campaign strategies, rhetoric, public opinion, volunteerism, and the media. All of these elements contribute to the understanding of why Hoover, the Great Engineer, struggled in managing the Great Mississippi Flood of 1927.

Herbert Hoover gained significant fame for handling crisis conditions, noted with his food distribution plan for Belgium during World War I. His scientific management principles and emphasis on volunteerism were plausible policy approaches during the Great War. However, just a decade later, these approaches were inopportune and relatively ineffective. And this is where the title *The Damming of the Presidency* originated. Yes, it is true that Hoover had an overwhelming task of mitigating unprecedented flood damage, but his miscalculations and over-exuded confidence were also contributory factors in his inability to maintain American political support. This phenomenon lends itself to significant lessons from both the 1928 and 1932 elections. Finally, as this study will demonstrate, federalism continues to be a guiding approach in understanding and evaluating disaster relief management strategies. Admittedly, federalism has evolved considerably since 1928. At that time, the level of governmental intervention was severely limited. It would take the Great Depression as well as Roosevelt's New Deal to transform the role of the federal government. However, as one will see in current times, presidents and federal governmental agencies still struggle with major environmental disasters. Delay, confusion, and lack of understanding complex issues all factor into the damming of the presidency.

UNDERSTANDING DISASTER MANAGEMENT POLICY

Disaster policy is quite enigmatic. According to Shugart,[1] disaster relief is perceived as a bad public good. A chronological list of considerations exists when encountering an urgent management event. The immediate task of first responders is to supply private goods. Rescuing survivors from the rooftops of flooded homes and businesses or digging them out of the rubble are rivalrous activities. Everyone in immediate danger cannot be moved to safety simultaneously; when a rescue crew is working to locate survivors at one disaster scene, others necessarily must wait their turn. Emergency relief supplies such as drinking water, meals ready to eat, blankets, and temporary housing are likewise fully private goods, whose consumption by one victim reduces the amount available for all. In essence, Shugart states quite clearly, first responders must mobilize and distribute aid rapidly.[2]

The story of Hurricane Katrina is a contemporary case that resonates with many themes of the Great Mississippi Flood of 1927. It is a story of neglect and incompetence, and at some levels greed and avarice. The Katrina disaster was blamed in large part on the victims. The victims made choices about how to live and how to respond to the event. The Katrina disaster was also blamed on public officials and their respective institutions such as Ray Nagin Jr., the mayor of New Orleans; Kathleen Blanco, the governor of Louisiana; and the Federal Emergency Management Agency (FEMA). Finally, the tragedy was blamed on the belief that the public sector, primarily federal, state, and local governments, was in the best position to prevent such a disaster. Many economists likened better management practices to a businesslike Walmart approach.[3]

In other words, neoclassical economic theory has been offered as a way to manage and mitigate force majeure events. Yet there are problems with this line of thinking. Neoclassical thinking rests on mathematical assumptions to address societal wants and needs. However, it is this overreliance on mathematical models that limits the number of people who can readily be part of the policy process. Further, the system infers that well-off stakeholders may not be accountable to society. The bottom line for individual and group survival is most important, emphasizing the development of an exclusively material incentive-based pathway at any cost.[4]

In parallel reasoning, De Alessi[5] suggests property rights and public choice models need to be considered. He believes that governments like markets can fail to produce ideal results. Public policies fail not because of differences in actor motives—as all are assumed to pursue their self-interests rationally—but rather because public collective action differs from the private sector. In short, there are different incentives and constraints in the public sector. The first implication is that the public sector offers the democratic process. This provides larger political payoffs to new public works projects and real estate development initiatives rather than adhering to a bottom-line profit sharing alternative. The second implication is that well-defined property rights are not as evident in the public sphere. This leads to risk-taking aversion. In other words, public officials should safely do nothing rather than risk being open to criticism. This approach suggests the need for incremental policy thinking, which is in stark contrast to emergency management.[6]

Birkland and Waterman[7] yield analysis also germane to the Katrina disaster. They see the Category 5 hurricane as a failure of federal initiative and organization. Federal management underperformed in terms of disaster preparedness, response, recovery, and mitigation, raising this concern: They state, "If the federal government cannot prepare for something like Katrina, how can it prepare for a major act of terrorism?" Birkland thus infers that force majeure events should not be viewed as individual policy problems. Despite this framework gap, there are positive disaster relief approaches. According to Derthick,[8] pre-storm evacuation and search and rescue are success stories that involved considerable intergovernmental coordination. However, Derthick also notes that the intergovernmental failure of flood protection reveals limitations within federalism.[9]

But where should disaster management responsibility lie? Birkland and Waterman[10] view disaster management as an institutional concern. They argue that the creation of the Department of Homeland Security (DHS) led to substantial federal-state-local policy changes in emergency management. However, these changes were directed against terrorism prevention and did little to strengthen federal response to natural disasters.[11] Two seminal questions arise: first, were the failures in Hurricane Katrina a result of federalism? Or second, did these failures simply reflect the inherent difficulties in preparing for, responding to, and recovering from catastrophes? Disaster management is quite complex, and even the most competent administrator may not have the time to get things right.

Earlier eras of federalism were conceptualized as cooperative or competitive.[12] Over time, more power was concentrated at the national level, which links coercive federalism to opportunistic federalism.[13] Coercive federalism describes how states are compelled to comply with federal standards in the pursuit of a national agenda.[14] Many states felt that post–September 11 policy was coercive by attaching strings to federal preparedness aid.

However, making a strong case for coercion in disaster policy is difficult. There are just too many unknown variables in comparison with education or drinking age policy.[15] The latter are relatively high salience issues with clear linkages between state and local behavior and federal funds. Natural hazard policies portray a much lower salience, which in turn links disaster policy decisions to technical experts rather than political leaders.[16] The failure of local governments to follow mandates related to natural hazards is likely to procure much citizen attention. The one exception may be flood insurance; communities that fail to take certain mitigation steps will make themselves ineligible for highly subsidized federal flood insurance.[17]

After September 11, 2001, there was some coercion in tying various forms of aid to the National Incident Management System (NIMS) and adherence to the National Response Plan (NRP), now known as the National Response Framework Plan (NRF). However, this type of "coercive funding" is basically redistributive (pork) spending rather than spending on risk or needs assessment, making such funding an attractive way to spend federal money locally. Second, while many programs look like coercion, state and local governments have rather willingly ceded leadership and federal funding authority, particularly given the promise of vast funding flowing from Washington to the states under the "homeland security" rubric as well as the desire to be seen as doing their share.[18]

A potentially more explanatory model of federalism is *opportunistic federalism*, which Conlan defines as "a system that allows and often encourages actors in the system to pursue their immediate interests with little regard for the institutional or collective consequences." For example, federal mandates, policy preemptions, and highly prescriptive federal grant programs tend to be driven by opportunistic policy makers who seek to achieve their own policy and political goals regardless of traditional norms of behavior or boundaries of institutional responsibility.[19]

Opportunistic federalism is consistent with the "opportunistic" and episodic nature of nearly all disaster policies, since disaster and crisis policies are almost entirely event-driven. Decisions are made rapidly, and policies are often adopted without long-term considerations. For example, in the process of creating DHS, Congress, with the president's assent, moved FEMA into the new agency without regard for its existing organizational and intergovernmental relationships. Furthermore, homeland security "experts" (many of whom had little experience in this new field) essentially ignored vast amounts of knowledge accumulated by social scientists and practitioners. The homeland security establishment was driven by political and policy goals, or a single verse, double analogy. The single loop treats the cause while the double loop hones in on the source. Rigor was sacrificed in terms of disaster preparedness, response, and recovery.[20]

Davies suggests that presidents or presidential candidates often end up in unenviable positions in disaster management.[21] He cites a more modern case of George W. Bush, who was accused of inadequate presidential leadership in the aftermath of Hurricane Katrina. Davies compares Bush to presidential predecessor Texan Lyndon B Johnson (LBJ) who also had to address a major climactic event in Louisiana with Hurricane Betsy in 1964.[22]

Bush was slow to visit the swathe of destruction left by Katrina. He eventually circled overhead in Air Force One, rather than partaking in symbolic management and inspecting the scene on the ground. Yet according to Davies, Johnson did the opposite. Johnson landed at Moisant Airport (New Orleans International Airport) within hours of Hurricane Betsy, met the victims, and personally directed the federal response. When he acknowledged the shortcomings of his response in his memoir, *Delusion Points*, even Bush seemed to acknowledge that LBJ's activist approach had constituted the proper presidential approach to disaster.[23]

Federal disaster relief protocol was already in place by the 1960s. However, principal responsibility lay with state and local governments, as well as the American Red Cross. Presidents had little to contribute: dealing with disaster was a largely federal bureaucratic task. In fact, according to the Federal Disaster Act of 1950, most natural emergencies were largely delegated to the Army Corps of Engineers, the Bureau of Public Roads, and the Small Business Administration. There were few occasions when a president chose to visit a disaster scene. However, it was done, though often linked to political expediency. Presidential disaster visits were an opportunity to expand a political agenda, promote volunteerism, or simply support a federally funded "pork" project.[24]

Federal response has changed in the past fifty years. First, the number of incidents constituted as major disasters increased from about a dozen per year under Eisenhower to an annual figure of seventy under George W. Bush to more than 200 under President Trump. Federal spending on disaster relief doubled during the 1960s (in inflation-adjusted dollars), doubled again during the Nixon-Ford presidency, and experienced another increase under Clinton and Bush. Presidents used to turn down one-third of gubernatorial requests for disaster aid, but by the early twenty-first century, the figure dropped to 14 percent. The federal share of total disaster spending went from around 6 percent under Eisenhower to nearly 50 percent under Nixon.[25]

Second, consistent with the increasing role of presidential power, modern presidents are expected to take charge during a crisis. They need to provide strong and empathetic leadership to assuage the public. This often entails visiting the scene, sometimes even following modest disasters: In 2007, George Bush visited Greenberg, Kansas, following a tornado that killed eleven people;[26] five years later, Barak Obama went to Colorado following a series of wildfires.[27] Roberts views the modern president as a "responder in chief."[28] A *Washington Post* reporter referred to Bush's role as "consoler in chief" following his visit to Blacksburg after a mass shooting at Virginia Tech.[29] Thus a presidential enigma develops. Symbolic leadership is essential and can enhance a presidential image, as noted with Obama's response to Hurricane Sandy shortly before the 2012 election.[30] Yet it probably takes more than disaster mismanagement to lose a political base as in the case and damage aftermath of Katrina.[31]

Davies's study offers a sobering interpretation of executive disaster management. According to Davies, the Great Society and increased federal responsibility helped champion a greater focus on disaster management. His study was from November 1963 to the fall of 1965. This was the zenith of the Great Society program. Federal focus was vast, including antipoverty, health, criminal justice, minority rights, and environmental protection. And by coincidence, the major natural disasters of his presidency were concentrated here. This created the aperture for disaster response policy as well.[32]

Yet it was two critical events that reveal most about natural disaster response development. The first is the Ohio River Flood, which occurred in March 1964. This flood impacted the Ohio River and a number of its tributaries, caused a dozen deaths, and ruined farmland, overwhelming a number of medium-sized towns in Ohio, including Zanesville and Athens. The Red Cross established refugee camps in Ohio, Indiana, Kentucky, West Virginia, and Pennsylvania to care for some of the estimated 110,000 who had to flee their homes.[33]

While devastating, this event never became more than a regional news story. In all fairness, the flood was relatively modest in comparison to the 1962 Nor'easter or to Hurricanes Carol, Diane, and Connie during Eisenhower's presidency. And it did not impact major cities: Pittsburgh, Cincinnati, Louisville were largely spared. The media did not endeavor to spread the news further. For instance, the *New York Times* relegated the flood to back pages. Johnson's response to the news of the flood was perplexing. Upon learning about the flood, he told his secretary that "every little boy [who] knows how to use the telephone is calling this morning," and instructed her not to put through any more nonurgent calls. However, his callers were not just "little boys"; Johnson was communicating with his defense secretary, national security advisor, and CIA director about political hot spots in Cyprus and South. Yet Johnson made a snap decision for an aerial inspection of the Ohio River Valley, covering 1,700 miles in five hours.[34]

Johnson was under no scrutiny as he flew to the Ohio River Valley. However, his political agenda was evident. Several governors accompanied Johnson on the trip, including the Ohio, Indiana, Kentucky, and West Virginia governors, the heads of the Army Corps of Engineers, the Bureau of Public Roads, the Small Business Administration, the American Red Cross, and reporters from the Associated Press (AP) and the *Washington Post*. Johnson touched down only once in Cincinnati to give a brief statement and sign autographs.[35]

The AP's Frank Cormier, an experienced LBJ watcher, was most struck by the last scene. The trip was more like a campaign tour. And while many governors accompanied Johnson, the one governor who failed to join the president was William Scranton of Pennsylvania, a possible GOP opponent in the forthcoming presidential race. LBJ was governing as well as campaigning when he visited the flood scene. It was politically helpful for him to spend time on Air Force One with a group of influential Midwestern governors at a time when he was reaching out in all possible directions to maximize his political standing. He needed all the political capital that he could muster to force an ambitious political agenda—most especially the passage of a Civil Rights Act and the war on poverty—through a Congress that John F. Kennedy had found "frustratingly recalcitrant."[36]

Other presidents had undertaken aerial flood inspection tours, albeit in response to much larger disasters. Truman had flown over the Missouri River Valley in 1951 to inspect flooding in Kansas City. Eisenhower had inspected the damage wrought by Hurricane Diane in Pennsylvania and New York in 1955. And both presidents, like LBJ, had been motivated not just by the gravity of the disaster but by the opportunity to advance their political agendas. For Eisenhower, this agenda also included the defense of traditional federalism and voluntary giving. For Truman, the agenda included the establishment of the Missouri Valley Authority. Johnson's foray into disaster politics would be challenged further in just a few weeks when the strongest earthquake in U.S. history rocked the state of Alaska.[37]

Due to the remote location and poor telecommunications, initial reports appeared far worse than reality. Rumors circulated that there were several thousand casualties and that tsunamis were headed to both the West Coast and the Gulf of Mexico. The tremblor, rumors said, would also impact major continental cities as far away as Houston. Those stories subsided into a lesser but grim reality: 115 dead, 30 blocks of downtown Anchorage completely destroyed, nearly every harbor ruined (at a time when the state's economy was based on fishing, rather than oil), many small towns utterly wrecked, and the coasts of Oregon and northern California damaged by tsunamis. Where the Ohio floods had barely been noticed outside of the affected region, the earthquake was probably the most dramatic natural disaster to have struck the United States since the New England hurricane of 1938. It received significant coverage accordingly.[38]

Alaska was vulnerable. The damage impacted 60 percent of the new state's economy, which was home to just 250,000 people. Alaska state government was weak and lacked the essential governing agencies other states had. Resultingly, Alaska's dependence was heavy upon the federal government for schooling, housing, road repairs, and policing. Johnson had a multifaceted dilemma to support and lead the recovery effort.[39]

Johnson remained calm during this crisis. He avoided any connection to conspicuous leadership and stayed in the background rather than visit the scene. In fact, he stayed on his ranch, where he had retreated for the long Easter weekend. Instead of embracing panicky demands for relief, he emphasized the need to find out exactly what had happened before developing a federal response. The incident was also much further away, which could explain his reticence toward traveling to Alaska.[40]

Policies are often reactionary to other events. However, in this case, issue framing was not focused to allow for a targeted federal response. As fitting, one reporter asked Johnson whether he intended to visit the scene of the disaster, to which Johnson offered a monosyllabic negative. In the spring of 1964, a president could get away with such a response; no reporter followed up, no one criticized him, no one asked him why not. Politics is inherently intertwined with multiple issues, and in Johnson's case, it was a complex civil rights agenda. Johnson's decision not to visit Alaska was part of a larger political calculus. This was a time when the Senate commenced what promised to be an exhausting and fractious debate over civil rights. Secondary issues had to be sidelined in order to proceed with civil rights discussions on the Senate floor. It was just too risky for another issue to stop the passage of civil rights legislation. "Cloture" had to be obtained, otherwise critical civil rights legislation would not have passed. Hence, a congressional debate over

Alaskan aid had to be avoided at all costs. Johnson knew that civil rights opponents would like nothing better than to shift the conversation to disaster relief in the name of helping Alaska. This would make it more difficult to pass the civil rights bill.[41]

But if the federal response was indeed intractable, where did better measures occur? Birkland[42] mentions that well into the twentieth century, disaster response, relief, and recovery were primarily a state and local responsibility.[43] This was practical. State and local governments are almost always "first" at the scene regardless of the event, whether a house fire or a terrorist attack.[44] The exact role of federal relief is not entirely clear. Many communities in the late nineteenth and early twentieth centuries resisted federal aid to avoid the perception of a lost or severely damaged community.[45] Rather, emphasis was placed on the appearance of resilience and rebuilding. This policy approach was stressed even when the rebuilding meant vulnerability, like San Francisco, where the Marina District was built on a debris dump loose fill from the 1906 earthquake.[46]

By the 1960s, civil defense organizations began to shift greater federal attention to natural hazards. There were other focusing events as well, such as Hurricane Camille, which struck Louisiana and Mississippi. Camille led to the Disaster Relief Act of 1969, while in 1972, Hurricane Agnes led to the Disaster Relief Act of 1974, which provided for relief assistance to local governments and individual victims. The 1964 Alaskan earthquake revealed the extent of damage to communities in sparsely populated places; a "smaller" earthquake on the Richter scale in California would yield a much worse outcome in the 1971 San Fernando quake.[47]

The term *disaster mitigation* surfaced with the 1974 Disaster Relief Act. This 1974 act embodied devolution principles by clearly dictating that ultimate disaster response policy be centered with state and local governments. In essence, "New Federalism," or "shared governance" functioned under the federal mandate guidelines, where states received federal funding but ultimately made specific decisions in order to meet federal guidelines.[48]

Disaster management ebbed during the Carter administration when "big government" was supplanted by deregulation, agency reorganization, and zero-based budgeting. In short, deregulation was viewed as a way to lessen industry restrictions. Agency reorganization reflected an internal desire to make government agencies more accountable. Zero-based budgeting was reactionary to incrementalism, where policy was made in a slow, methodical step-by-step process. ZBB sought to check and evaluate each governmental output from start to finish. If a program was inefficient at any step of the process, it could be terminated or sunset.[49]

The Federal Emergency Management Agency (FEMA) was formed in 1979 to consolidate emergency management agencies. This benefited the

Reagan administration, and greater emphasis was directed toward national security concerns like preparedness and response.[50] However, FEMA lacked a clear agency mandate and performed poorly. It soon became known as a "turkey farm" that was delegated for third-rate political appointees.[51] FEMA largely ignored natural disasters, even though the 1977 National Earthquake Hazards Reduction Act (NEHRA) had indicated that FEMA was the lead director response agency in the case of major earthquakes, hurricanes, and flood programs.[52]

Even with an obfuscated disaster management framework, pertinent legislation was passed. Most notably and relevant today was the Robert T. Stafford Disaster Relief and Emergency Assistance Act of 1988, PL 100-707, hereinafter the Stafford Act.[53] The Stafford Act was a function of shared governance. It established a blueprint for how the federal government cooperated with the states during disaster management. The Stafford Act was amended in 1993 and 2000 to improve performance and stress mitigation. However, these amendments did not alter the fact that the state and local governments were the true "first responders."[54]

There is some confusion regarding the Stafford Act mandate. It should not be viewed as an entirely top-down model. The act states that Congress's aim 42 USC 5121 (b) is "to provide an orderly and continuing means of assistance by the federal government to state and local governments." This passage suggests that shared governance is essential in addressing disaster response.[55] More specifically, disaster response strategies include "encouraging the development of plans by the states and local governments." In the realm of American Exceptionalism and Manifest Destiny, this "encourages individuals, states and local governments to protect themselves," and seek mitigation efforts. The crux of emergency management still lies with the states.[56]

A rational expectation and market interpretation model also exists. Emergency management is inherently tied to market forces. This means that individuals have incentive to protect their property against flood or other cataclysmic events. One way of doing this is by having homeowners purchase flood insurance. This could result in an increase in state and local funds to people in need (Section 322 of the Stafford Act, as amended by the Disaster Mitigation Act of 2000). Disaster management is also based on federal mandates. The Stafford Act is federal based, but each individual state decides how to meet such guidelines.[57]

Title III of the Stafford Act is particularly noteworthy in terms of shared governance and cooperative federalism. It specifically addresses guidelines for state requests of federal aid. This usually means access to food and medicine. The provision specifies how state governors initiate requests for federal aid. While relief is central, mitigation efforts must also be addressed. This policy component was strengthened by amendments in 2000. Most noteworthy is the mitigation provision called the "322 program," codified at 42 USC 5165. Similar to an environmental impact statement, one must consider all options before commencing on a project. The 322 program is a mitigation-based approach that works as follows: In exchange for increased federal funding, the 322 program requires states and localities to submit mitigation plans to FEMA. In short, the greater the level of program implementation and mitigation, the greater the level of federal funding. While the program is incentive based, it is not compulsory. This can prove problematic if states minimize hazard mitigation strategies.[58]

Disaster relief can breed political corruption. More funding does not mean better results. Some have ascribed emergency relief strategies to the Dutch disease or natural resource curse. While predominantly used as an explanatory theory to explain underdevelopment in low gross national product countries, an eerie parallel exists. The Dutch disease is destabilizing because country leaders do not distribute its resource benefits nationally. Instead, corruption, coups, and calamity are often the end product, and the cycle repeats. Peter Boettke and associates as well as Peter Leeson and Russel Sobel argue that the "windfall" of money and other resources that pour into a disaster impact area are prone to maldistribution. The lives at stake create such pressure to "do something" that missteps develop. Evidence suggests that because responses to accountability are conducted with little attention to oversight public officials are more likely to be indicted and convicted of corruption in disaster-prone zones.[59]

Finally, poor disaster management leads to a series of "unintended" consequences. No matter how well intended, the measures to provide "relief" require public funding and in-kind assistance. This includes commitments to spend billions of tax dollars to rebuild and offer grants, tax breaks, and low interest loans for property owners, including those who failed to obtain private or federally subsidized hazard insurance. Moving emergency policies beyond the "levees-only approach" is important. Natural hazards cause significant property damage. Government relief must be both declaratory and regulatory. Anything less can lead to a moral hazard. In short, unmitigated responses will most likely lead to greater catastrophes in the future.[60]

Yet, closer inspection of Katrina reveals deep emergency policy gaps that question whether federalism is an effective management approach. Hurricane Katrina formed in the Bahamas on Thursday, August 25, 2005. It reached Category 3 strength. Two days later, storm surge models at Louisiana State University's (LSU) Center for the Study of the Public Health Impacts of Hurricanes predicted that Katrina would hit New Orleans hard enough to inundate the city. This paralleled LSU's Katrina simulation drills generated by FEMA the previous summer. In that July 2004 exercise, a hypothetical Category 3 storm "produced catastrophic flooding in New Orleans. Still, some of FEMA's own officials and the U.S. Army Corps of Engineers greeted the results of that exercise with skepticism."[61]

Low-lying New Orleans was vulnerable to flooding. The city flooded severely in 1735, 1785, and 1849. Hurricane Betsy flooded 20 percent of New Orleans in 1965. The city narrowly avoided similar fates in 1973, 1997, and possibly in 1927, by levee breaches upriver that diverted rising flood-water produced by months of heavy rains to low-lying areas farther north.[62] Some policy experts believe the city would not have flooded during the Great Mississippi Flood of 1927.

FEMA's mock "Hurricane Pam" was not the first harbinger of vulnerability. Several studies addressed hurricane landfall near New Orleans. In 2002, there was a publicly funded study that concluded a slow-moving Category 3 storm could cause major flooding "in the bowl of New Orleans north of the Mississippi River." Although the 350-mile levee system was designed to withstand such storms, the Corps of Engineers warned state and local officials about the dangers of soil erosion and the flood barrier sinking as much as three feet below sea level.[63]

Katrina packed winds between 125 and 140 miles per hour, and the storm surge caused three major levee breaches, allowing the Mississippi River and Lake Ponchartrain to flood the city. Nearly 80 percent of New Orleans was soon submerged, in some areas as deep as twenty feet. Designating blame on one factor is unfair, but public officials knew of the impending danger. Yet in spite of these warnings, public official efforts were sluggish and inept.[64]

Politicians and bureaucrats are self-interested actors who often make politically expedient decisions. A sense of elite theory pervades in voters' rational ignorance about specific issues. Policymakers recognize this political aperture and may generate considerable efforts towards special interests and reelection campaign strategies. Reelection or reappointment becomes the calculus of decision making. This is the central challenge for public management. Publicly financed infrastructure deteriorates slowly and even invisibly. This pernicious matrix creates an uneasy opening for both politicians and bureaucrats to defer repairs and neglect routine maintenance. The end result of these critical delays creates untold societal impacts.[65]

Katrina reinforced a Balkanization principle: There were so many managing stakeholders that effective communication was inhibited. Most of the levees were federal projects supported by the U.S. Army Corps of Engineers. Daily operations of floodwalls, floodgates, earthen embankments, and pumping stations were overseen by four separate levee district boards. Each of these boards included gubernatorial and political appointees. Both entities wielded broad taxing and borrowing powers for financing levee maintenance and for contributing a share of the cost of major repairs or other flood control projects, usually valued at 30 percent. In fact, New Orleans had an independent water and sewer board that operated and maintained the pumps and canals for low-lying areas.[66]

This bureaucratic fragmentation had foreseeable consequences. The levees were compared to the Maginot Line, a haphazardly constructed border built by the French in the 1930s to deter a resurgent German army. A National Science Foundation report concluded that many of the weak spots breached by the storm resulted from unclear lines of authority and insufficient coordination of the levee system. There was a lack of coordination in materials used. In some locations, floodwalls were built to different heights with varying source material. At one pumping station, at least three separate agencies were responsible for creating an uneven concrete floodwall. Katrina's storm surge overflowed the shorter structure, rendering the more substantial one useless.[67]

In another perspective, public employees' fear of being blamed for doing something wrong (or failing to do something right) produces risk aversion. This leads to micromanagement, where each level of government seeks control by writing and imposing detailed operating rules that restrict discretionary authority. One result of this top-down model is that the people who make decisions are often separated from those on the ground by multiple layers of management. A silo approach soon develops and relevant information is not disseminated. As a result, there is little incentive for sharing information in mutually beneficial ways.[68]

The public response to Katrina was hampered by the Oval Office as well. The White House and Defense Department stalled in whether to "federalize" National Guard units and send them to the high impact areas of the 1992 Los Angeles riots.[69] Political undertones were also evident. Shortly after the hurricane, President Bush visited Louisiana and reportedly asked Louisiana governor Kathleen Babineaux Blanco, a Democrat, to relinquish control of the local law enforcement and National Guard troops, a stark challenge to state and local control. The governor ultimately refused. However, no such request was made to the Republican Mississippi governor whose state was also severely impacted by Katrina.[70]

The link between presidential elections and emergency response is uncertain but warrants inspection. President Bush was a second-term president with less incentive to act. However, President Bush was more active with August 2004 Hurricane Charley. The hurricane hit electoral-college rich Florida during the campaign season. In this case, the president was at the impact zone within two days. Bush waited a full four days before visiting Katrina's impact area.[71]

Bureaucratic paralysis extended to all levels of authority. Governor Blanco was slow to respond. She proclaimed a state of emergency on Friday, August 26, which triggered the state's disaster plan. She then deferred to Mayor

Ray Nagin to order a mandatory evacuation of New Orleans.[72] This in turn was hampered by communication system breakdown. This disruption helps explains why her call to the White House for federal assistance was delayed almost a week after hurricane impact. Yet her symbolic management was evident. One of her first public post-Katrina appearances was to lead a thirty-minute prayer service televised locally from the state's emergency headquarters in Baton Rouge.[73]

But prayers could not assuage flooding and create proper evacuation protocol. New Orleans mayor Nagin essentially panicked. Despite reports from LSU's storm trackers and the director of the National Hurricane Center, he did not issue an immediate order to evacuate the city. He released an evacuation warning when Katrina was within forty-eight hours of making landfall. Mandatory evacuation procedures were released less than twenty-four hours before the storm reached land.

To complicate matters further, Mayor Nagin and his crisis team opted for refuge at the Hyatt Regency hotel rather than taking charge at the city's Mobile Command Center or joining other local and state officials at Louisiana's emergency operations facility in Baton Rouge. As a consequence, Mayor Nagin and his advisors were cut off for two days, spending most of their time warding off looters because of an inoperative telecommunications system.[74]

Still, significant blame lies with FEMA. Garrett and Sobel write that "Katrina exposed FEMA as a dysfunctional organization," labeling it "a parking lot for political allies since its creation in 1979." FEMA has been shown to be more responsive to the political interests of the White House than to disaster victims on the ground. Garrett and Sobel offer key insight into motivating factors for federal disaster relief support: Once a disaster has been declared, they explain, federal emergency relief funds tend to be allocated disproportionately to electoral-vote-rich states important to the sitting president's reelection strategy.[75]

In the end, Hurricane Katrina caused more than $200 billion in economic losses. The storm is blamed for 1,464 deaths in Louisiana alone; it displaced 1.4 million people and destroyed approximately 217,000 homes and 18,000 businesses.[76] More than sixteen-thousand federal employees were dispatched to the Gulf Coast. Congress initially appropriated $88 billion for relief recovery, and another $20 billion was requested for future efforts. The Small Business Administration underwrote $5.8 billion in disaster loans, and the term federal unemployment insurance eligibility was extended for workers displaced by the storm. Congress passed legislation just two weeks after the storm, designating a "Gulf Opportunity Zone" to stimulate revitalization by providing temporary tax reductions, investment incentives, and regulatory relief to "formerly booming neighborhoods that have lost their economic bases" to Mother Nature's wrath.[77]

Pauly coined the term *moral hazard* to describe the behavior of people who have insured themselves against sickness and injury. The simple logic is that becoming fully insured reduces the cost of carelessness. A large portion of health costs include doctor visits, hospitalization, and prescription drugs. Individuals who have purchased health insurance are able to consume more of these goods. This allows the insured to pay less than the full cost of healthcare, but also leads them to demand more extensive diagnostic tests and medical specialists. The overutilization of these scarce health resources raises the costs of medical care for both insured and uninsured.[78]

The same reasoning could apply to the Hurricane Katrina. Meeting immediate survival needs is one level of aid. However, providing billions of tax dollars in the form of outright grants, low-interest loans, and other aid intended to finance a return of pre-storm conditions is cost prohibitive for tight fiscal government budgets. The shift of relief aid to taxpayers encourages people to rebuild, who could not have done so previously. Federal and state reconstruction assistance offers incentives for some to relocate their homes and businesses to inland areas of comparative safety. Yet over the past several decades "the coastal population growth rate has more than doubled the national growth rate"; the percentage of property under development or already developed and the value of real property in coastal zones have risen pari passu, or equal footing.[79]

People who place themselves in harm's way assume additional risk. However, the government has created reimbursement policies to reduce the cost of living in disaster-prone areas. After widespread flooding along the Mississippi River in 1993, FEMA initiated a "mitigation program" and bought vulnerable floodplain property to prevent the rebuilding of homes. However, this preventative attempt was wrought with legal impediments. The Mississippi attorney general responded by filing a lawsuit against three of the affected area's largest insurers—State Farm, Allstate, and Nationwide—in an attempt to force payment claims for flood damage even on policies with rider exclusions. Congress also enacted a $29 billion Gulf Coast hurricane relief package. This included $11.5 billion in nonrepayable "community development block grants" for Alabama, Florida, Louisiana, Mississippi, and Texas providing payment of up to $150,000 for homeowners who wanted to rebuild, whether they were insured or not.[80]

Yet as much as 69 percent of Mississippi's Gulf Coast residents did not have federal flood insurance during Katrina. Federal flood insurance program participation had been low since its inception by the National Flood Insurance Act in 1968. The reluctance of large numbers of property owners to purchase flood insurance suggests risk bias. They treat low-probability, catastrophe-like, zero-probability events: Federal flood insurance is mandatory only for property that is mortgaged and then only for the outstanding balance on the property owner's loan. Hence banks and other lenders, rather than property owners, are the principal beneficiaries. This program, which collects only about $2 billion in premiums annually, also faces solvency issues.[81]

FEMA was depleted by Katrina-related claims and forced to suspend payments temporarily to flood insurance policyholders. Katina reflects a mottled effort to plan, assess, mitigate, and solve a major force majeure event. The data and science were there, but the institutional support was without clear guidance. This extends to the executive office, hinting that disaster events straddle executive decision-making authority. This case also lends itself to the moral hazard principle, which the federal government implicitly supports. The federal government encourages landowners to purchase flood insurance. Landowners who purchase insurance expect their land to be protected. However, this guarantee of protection allows people to remain in the same vulnerable places. This is a cyclical process, and the moral hazard is that people purchase policies and the government has a moral obligation to protect them. People then remain in the same location, thereby extending the hazard. Hence a paradox exists. On the one hand, there may be little incentive for people to participate in the insurance program. On the other hand, it is a human impulse to aid victims of natural disaster. The end result is more lives lost and deeper costs.[82]

Yet there are rational steps towards achieving disaster mitigation. According to Kapucu, disaster management is an interdisciplinary approach. He cites four common elements (1) prevention/mitigation, (2) preparedness, (3) response, and (4) recovery. Mitigation represents activities that prevent a disaster, reduce the chance of it occurring, or reduce its damaging effects. Preparedness represents those actions taken before impact, including plans and preparations for disaster. Response refers to actions taken during the initial impact of a disaster to save lives and prevent further property damage. Recovery includes actions taken after the initial impact, including those directed toward a return to normality.[83]

The president, political challengers, first responders, and collaborative networks all need to provide cogent policy solutions. Each participant's expectations are different. Kapucu et. al. liken response to both public and private sector. They state that private companies' disaster response is similar to an incentives-based approach. This means a return on investment, business continuity, and effective cost/benefit analysis. Nonprofits and government agencies are more motivated by effective service delivery, increased income, and capacity building. However, one cannot overlook political expediency, which could inhibit collective action.[84]

Second, each community approach varies. A customized plan requires "systematic identification of resources and strategies beyond a 'levees only' policy. There are needs for land use, public preparedness, education, and short- and long-term disaster recovery strategies." Flexibility is critical due to uncertainty, and the approach should be built on integrated relationships. If not, loosely connected organizations may not be able to manage effectively.[85]

Third, collaboration should be decentralized. While limited, the U.S. Coast Guard's response to Hurricane Katrina is associated with decentralization. The National Research Council (NRC) defines networks as the interactions between people and organizations. These networks can be affected by natural hazards, as disaster situations disrupt community interactions. Vulnerability of social networks is intrinsically related to community reliance. In rural communities, this progress might be complicated if access to social capital is limited. Disasters then are the result of the intersection of environmental hazards and social systems that impact the ability of communities to anticipate, resist, and recover.[86]

Race, class, and gender must also be considered. Collins's theory of matrix domination explains how race, class, and gender intersect to create varying systems of oppression. Specifically, Collins argues that race, class, and gender create lives that are qualitatively different in opportunity and experience. It is not surprising, then, that disaster researchers have identified race, social class, and gender as barriers to disaster resilience.[87] Ursano, Fullerton, and Terhakopian identified low socioeconomic positions and mistrust of governmental agencies/officials as potential barriers to community resilience.[88] Elliot and Pais found that blacks were less likely to take hurricane warnings seriously and were almost seven times more likely to lose their jobs than whites in the aftermath of a storm.[89]

The twenty-first century has witnessed some of the most devastating events in human history—the terrorist attacks of September 11 (2001), the Indian Ocean tsunami (2004), the catastrophe of Hurricane Katrina (2005), the earthquake tsunami nuclear disaster in Japan (2011), and COVID-19 (2019). The loss of life and property impacts our resilience capacity. These events inextricably transform the physical and social landscape of countless communities. As long as communities continue to build along fault lines, floodplains, tropical coasts, windswept plains, and fertile shadows of volcanoes, hazards will inevitably continue to affect society.[90]

Disasters are viewed as events concentrated in time and space. The common phases of disaster (preparedness, mitigation, response, and recovery) are referred to as the *hazards cycle*. Regardless of the event, the response is constituted by ongoing activities and behaviors over the time following. An individual response has long-term impacts. Disaster management demands adaptation through an assortment of shifts and adjustments. Resiliency is most likely seen during the immediate and long-term recovery phases.[91]

Emergency planning is a response to specific, repetitive events. However, each event must be treated in its own way, despite internal pressures to standardize the recovery process. Communities have plans for floods, hurricanes, earthquakes, and wars. Further, the United States has conducted community-wide risk assessments to determine commonalities among various disaster plans. The goal was to develop individual functional plans. Most communities had a single plan for sheltering, regardless of whether the impetus was flood or war.[92]

As the Cold War waned, FEMA encouraged communities to evaluate natural hazards and create emergency plans that focused on "multiple-use opportunities for personnel, procedures, facilities, and equipment." This led to the creation of integrated emergency operations plans and multi-hazard training. After September 11, there was an "all terrorism all the time" focus for emergency planning. However, after Hurricane Katrina, the National Response Framework (NRF) emphasized a routinized platform for hazard management. FEMA's largest emergency planning guidance is focused on "all levels of government in their efforts to develop and maintain viable, all hazards all threats emergency plans."[93]

Yet a one-size-fits-all plan became problematic. Mileti notes that the United States failed to assess risk before permitting development. This means considering both technological and environmental factors. Philips notes that vulnerabilities are enhanced by human efforts to "engineer" three "major misfits" in the environment: the natural systems, the built environment, and the location of human habitation.[94] Mileti further states "the built environment" contributes directly to natural disasters. There is no paucity of examples of homes and industries located in floodplains, below dams, or near scenic faults. Sometimes, people try to engineer their way out of disasters. Levees give people a false sense of security.[95]

The social system also enhances disaster vulnerability and some population segments bear disproportionate losses. Philips notes that "vulnerable populations bring resources to the table." They have social capital in the form of relationships and organizations that meet their special needs in non-disaster times. Organizations that regularly provide services to people with hearing limitations will have staff members who know American sign language. If such an organization were included in developing a community's disaster plan, it could assist people with hearing limitations during disaster response and recovery. Community-based nonprofit organizations that provide paratransit, language interpretation, or medical procedures like dialysis would contribute knowledge and resources to an effective disaster plan. The question that remains is this: How can American communities better align social capital to not only understand hazards, but to also anticipate response needs and recovery plans?[96]

Philips analyzes recovery in four ways. First, in systems theory, the problem is viewed through the relationship between natural and human environments. Second, vulnerability theory posits the unequal sharing of risk and an opportunity during recovery to "alter differential risks" such as income, development status, gender, race, and disability. Normative theory points out that new threats like terrorism and pandemics often create new needs and groups. Finally, sociopolitical ecology argues that "disasters disrupt social interactions which influences how people recover." As Philips cogently states, "Communities must therefore interact to provide that support and . . . equitable participation . . . should lessen the uneven chance of returning home."[97] Yet there is no guarantee. Flood victim relocation remains difficult even today.

NOTES

1. William F. Shugart II, "Disaster Relief as Bad Public Policy," *The Independent Review* 15, no. 4 (2011): 519–539, https://www.independent.org/pdf/tir/tir_15_04_2_shughart.pdf.

2. Shugart, "Disaster Relief," 519–539.

3. Ibid.

4. Charles R. P. Pouncy, "Hurricane Katrina and the 'Market' for Survival: The Role of Economic Theory in the Construction and Maintenance of Disaster in America's Unnatural Disaster," in *Hurricane Katrina: America's Unnatural Disaster*, eds. Jeremy Levitt and Matthew Whitaker (University of Nebraska Press, 2009), 55–80.

5. Louis De Alessi, "Property Rights: Private and Political Institutions," in *The Elgar Companion to Public Choice*, eds. William Shugart II and Laura Razzolini (Edward Elgar Publishing, 2001), 33–58.

6. Alessi, "Property Rights," 33–58.

7. Thomas Birkland and Sarah Waterman, "Is Federalism the Reason for Policy Failure in Hurricane Katrina?" *The Journal of Federalism* 38, no. 4 (2008): 692–714, https://doi.org/10.1093/publius/pjn020.

8. Martha Derthick, "Where Federalism Didn't Fail," *Public Administration Review* 67 (2007): 36–47, https://doi.org/10.1111/j.1540-6210.2007.00811.x.

9. Derthick, "Where Federalism," 36–47.

10. Birkland and Waterman, "Is Federalism?" 692–714.

11. Kathleen Tierney, Christine Bevc, and Erica Kuligowski, "Metaphors Matter: Disaster Myths, Media Frames, and Their Consequences in Hurricane Katrina," *Annals of the American Academy of Political and Social Science* 604, no. 1 (2006): 57–81, https://doi.org/10.1177/0002716205285589.

12. Morton Grodzins, *The American System: A New View of Government in the United States*, ed. D. J. Elazar (Chicago, IL: Rand McNally, 1966).

13. Tim Conlan, "From Cooperative to Opportunistic Federalism: Reflections on the Half-Century Anniversary of the Commission on Intergovernmental Relations," *Public Administration Review* 66, no. 5 (2006): 663–676, https://doi.org/10.1111/j.1540-6210.2006.00631.x.

14. John Kincaid, "From Cooperative to Coercive Federalism," *Annals of the American Academy of Political and Social Science* 509 (1990): 139–152, https://doi .org/10.1177/0002716290509001013.

15. Dale A. Krane, "The State of American Federalism, 2001-2002: Resilience in Response to Crisis," *Publius: The Journal of Federalism* 32, no. 4 (2002): 1–28.

16. Ibid.

17. Ibid.

18. Paul Posner, "The Politics of Coercive Federalism in the Bush Era," *Publius: The Journal of Federalism* 37, no. 3 (2007): 390–412, https://doi.org/10.1093/publius /pjm014.

19. Conlan, "From Cooperative to Opportunistic Federalism," 663–676.

20. Birkland and Waterman, "Is Federalism?" 692–714.

21. Gareth Davies, "The Historical Presidency: Lyndon Johnson and Disaster Politics," *Presidential Studies Quarterly* 47, no. 3 (September 2017): 529–551, https://doi.org/10.1111/psq.12384.

22. Davies, "The Historical Presidency," 529–551.

23. George W. Bush, *Decision Points* (New York: Crown, 2010).

24. Bush, *Decision Points.*

25. Douglas C. DaCy and Howard Kunreuther, *The Economics of Natural Disaster: Implications for Federal Policy* (New York: Free Press, 1969).

26. David Greenberg, *Republic of Spin: An Inside History of the American Presidency* (New York: Norton, 2016).

27. David Nakamura, "After Aurora Shootings, Obama Again Takes on Role as Healer in Chief Colorado," *Washington Post*, July 7, 2012, https://www.washingt onpost.com/politics/after-aurora-shootings-obama-again-takes-on-role-as-healer-in -chief-in-colorado/2012/07/22/gJQAdEO92W_story.html.

28. Patrick Roberts, "Our Responder in Chief," *National Affairs* 43 (2010): 76–90, https://www.nationalaffairs.com/publications/detail/our-responder-in-chief.

29. Michael Fletcher, "President Again Takes on Role of 'Consoler in Chief'," *Washington Post*, April 18, 2007.

30. John Cassidy, "How Much Did Hurricane Sandy Help Obama?" *New Yorker,* November 4, 2012, https://www.newyorker.com/news/john-cassidy/how-much-did -hurricane-sandy-help-obama.

31. David Remnick, "High Water: How Presidents and Citizens Respond to Disaster," *New Yorker,* September 26, 2005, https://www.newyorker.com/magazine/ 2005/10/03/high-water.

32. Davies, "The Historical Presidency," 529–551.

33. Ibid.

34. Ibid.

35. Ibid.

36. Ibid.

37. Ibid.

38. Ibid.

39. Ibid.

40. Ibid.

41. David Shreve and Robert David Johnson, eds., *The Presidential Records: Lyndon B. Johnson: Toward the Great Society,* V (New York: Norton, 2007).

42. Birkland and Waterman, "Is Federalism?" 692–714.

43. Richard T. Sylves, "Federal Emergency Management Comes of Age: 1979-2001," in *Emergency Management: The American Experience, 1900-2005,* ed. C. B. Rubin (Arlington, VA: Public Entity Risk Institute, 1997).

44. Saundra Schneider, "Who's to Blame: (Mis)Perceptions of the Intergovernmental Response to Disasters," *Publius: The Journal of Federalism* 38, no. 4 (2008): 715–738, https://doi.org/10.1093/publius/pjn019.

45. Theodore Steinberg, *Act of God: The Unnatural History of Natural Disasters in America* (New York: Oxford University Press, 2000).

46. Carl-Henry Geschwind, *California Earthquakes: Science, Risk, and the Politics of Hazard Mitigation* (Baltimore, MD: Johns Hopkins University Press, 2001).

47. Birkland and Waterman, "Is Federalism?" 692–714.

48. Peter J. May and Walter Williams, *Disaster Policy Implementation Managing Programs under Shared Governance, Disaster Research in Practice* (New York: Plennum Press, 1986).

49. May and Williams, *Disaster Policy.*

50. Lee Ben Clarke, *Mission Improbable: Using Fantasy Documents to Tame Disaster* (Chicago, IL: University of Chicago Press, 1999).

51. Mark Murray, "Lessons from a Master of Disaster," *National Journal* 33, no. 2 (2001): 133–135.

52. George Haddow, Jane A. Bullock, and Damon Coppola. *Introduction to Emergency Management,* 3rd ed. (Boston, MA: Elsevier, 2007).

53. Sylves, "Federal Emergency Management."

54. Ibid.

55. Birkland and Waterman, "Is Federalism?", 692–714.

56. Ibid.

57. Ibid.

58. Peter H. Rossi, James D. Wright, and Eleanor Weber-Burdin, *Natural Hazards and Public Choice: The State and Local Politics of Hazard Mitigation* (New York: Academic Press, 1982).

59. Peter J. Boettke, "The Politics, Economics, and Social Aspects of Katrina," *Southern Economic Journal* 74, no. 2 (2007): 363–376, https://doi.org/10.2307/20111972.

60. Mark V. Pauly, "The Economics of Moral Hazard: Comment," *The American Economic Review* 58, no. 3, Part 1 (1968): 531–537, http://static.stevereads.com/papers_to_read/the_economics_of_moral_hazard.pdf.

61. James Carney, et al, "An American Tragedy: Four Places Where the System Broke Down," *Time* 166 (September 19, 2005): 34–41, http://content.time.com/time/magazine/article/0,9171,1103560,00.html.

62. John M. Barry, *Rising Tide: The Great Mississippi Flood of 1927 and How It Changed America* (New York: Simon and Schuster, 1997).

63. Ann Carrns, "Army Corps Faces Scrutiny on Levee Flaws," *Wall Street Journal,* November 2, 2005, https://www.wsj.com/articles/SB113089222733485805.

64. Carrns, "Army Corps."

65. Russell Sobel and Peter Leeson, "Government's Response to Hurricane Katrina: A Public Choice Analysis," *Public Choice* 127 (2006): 55–73, https://doi.org/10.1007/s11127-006-7730-3.

66. Sobel and Leeson, "Government's Response," 55–73.

67. Carrns, "Army Corps."

68. Sobel and Leeson, "Government's Response," 55–73.

69. Evan Thomas, "How Bush Blew It," *Newsweek* 146 (September 19, 2005): 42–52.

70. James Carney, et al., "An American Tragedy," 34–41.

71. "Hurricane Charley: Two Days Later," CNN Live Sunday, CNN, broadcast 4:00 P.M., eastern time, August 15, 2004, http://transcripts.cnn.com/Transcripts/0408/15/sun.02.html.

72. "Excerpts from Brown Hearing," *Wall Street Journal,* September 27, 2005.

73. Carrns, "Army Corps."
Sobel and Leeson, "Government's Response," 55–73.

74. Shugart, "Relief," 519–539.

75. Thomas Garrett and Russell Sobel, "The Political Economy of FEMA Disaster Payments," *Economic Inquiry* 41, no. 3 (2003): 496–509, https://doi.org/10.1093/ei/cbg023.

76. K. Wells, *The Good Pirates of the Forgotten Bayous: Fighting to Save a Life in the Wake of Hurricane Katrina* (New Haven, CT: Yale University Press, 2008).

77. Wells, 204.

78. Pauly, "The Economics," 531–537.

79. Shugart, "Relief," 519–539.

80. Shugart, "Relief," 519–539.

81. Andrew Young, "Replacing Incomplete Markets with a Complete Mess: Katrina and the NFIP," *International Journal of Social Economics* 38, no. 8 (2008): 561–68, https://doi.org/10.1108/03068290810889189.

82. Young, "Replacing Incomplete Markets," 561–68.

83. Naim Kaoucu, Christopher V. Hawkins, and Fernando I. Rivera, *Disaster Resiliency: Interdisciplinary Perspectives* (London: Routledge, 2013).

84. Kaoucu, Hawkins, and Rivera, *Disaster Resiliency.*

85. Kaoucu, Hawkins, and Rivera, *Disaster Resiliency.*

86. Heather Allen and Rebecca Katz, "Demography and Public Health Emergency Preparedness: Making the Connection," *Population Research and Policy Review* 29, no. 4 (2009): 527–539. https://doi.org/10.1007/s11113-009-9158-1.

87. Patricia Hill Collins, *Black Feminist Thought,* 2nd ed. (New York: Routldege, 2009).

88. Robert Ursano, Carol Fullerton, and Artin Terhakopian, "Disasters and Health: Distress, Disorders, and Disaster Behaviors in Communities, Neighborhoods, and

Nations," *Social Research* 75, no. 3 (2008): 1015–1028, https://www.jstor.org/stable /40972101?seq=1.

89. James Elliot and Jeremy Pais, "Race, Alass, and Hurricane Katrina: Social Differences in Human Responses to Disaster," *Social Science Research* 35 (2006): 295–321, https://doi.org/10.1016/j.ssresearch.2006.02.003.

90. Rubin, *Emergency Management*, 197–200.

91. Ibid.

92. Ibid.

93. FEMA (Federal Emergency Management Agency), *Developing and Maintaining Emergency Operations Plans: Community Preparedness Guide (CPG) 101*. Washington, DC: FEMA, 2010, https://www.fema.gov/media-library-data/ 1573581112287-035972e4d26817854c833457863c34cc/201911Listening_CPG_101 _V2_22NOV2010.pdf.

94. Brenda Philips, *Disaster Recovery* (Boca Raton, FL: CRC Press, 2009).

95. Dennis Mileti, *Disasters by Design: A Reassessment of Natural Hazards in the United States* (Washington, DC: Joseph Henry Press, 1999).

96. Brenda Philips, *Disaster Recovery* (Boca Raton, FL: CRC Press, 2009).

97. Philips, *Disaster Recovery*.

Chapter 2

Connecting Environmental Management to Politics

Several critical sources shaped this study. The central areas warranting attention are the roles of floods, the environment, the Great Mississippi Flood of 1927, and Herbert Hoover's decision-making ability. Key collective action principles can also help offer possible mitigating governing strategies. The Great Mississippi Flood was horrific, and more so since it was captured on film. This created a sense of fear and disbelief well beyond the Mississippi Valley region. According to Trexler, great floods have been indelibly seared into the American subconscious. Often unforeseen and hinting of biblical parallels, floods maim and traverse countless communities. The fear of deluge gained prominence after the horrors of World War I and was renewed further by Hiroshima and the threat of nuclear annihilation.[1]

Land, Wood, and Water, though published in 1960, pinpoints to a struggle between economic development and environmental protection. This early but important mid-century work yields insight regarding environmental mismanagement.[2] The case addresses severe flooding and rightfully recognizes significant works that make the connection between water and power. This connection is somewhat misunderstood, because water seems plentiful in some areas of the United States. However, riparian conflicts have pervaded U.S. society throughout history. More recently, interstate conflict has surfaced due to scarcity of resources. The Mississippi Flood of 1927 is known for flood management problems. But there is a story of political power. This was evidenced by New Orleans elites who lobbied to divert raging water from descending on their city to poorer communities.

Willoughby's *Flowing through Time* is a key study because it looks at a tri-state riparian conflict between Florida, Georgia, and Alabama. The book details a protracted interstate water conflict, and as a result sheds light on the role of the federal government in protecting and managing water supplies.

No definitive conclusion is offered except that there will always be a fight over water resources.[3] John Barry's *Rising Tide* is most applicable to this study because it breaks down Hoover's approach towards handling the great flood and offers stunning insight about the Great Mississippi Flood of 1927's permanent effects on both the environmental and the political landscape of the United States. For instance, the flood contributed to the great migration of African Americans to the North, the impact of the 1928 and 1932 presidential elections, and probably most significantly, the changing dynamics of federalism. This shaped how the United States would respond to future disaster events.[4] If Barry's book undertook to reshape the American political landscape in the East, Reisner's *Cadillac Desert* parallels the link between water and political power in the American Southwest. In this noted study, bitter politics envelop scarce water resources.[5] Reisner's work reframes the incessant need for water and the political steps people would take to claim it. Again, in this case, the goal was in how to manage water in order to avert flooding. However, trenchant politics remained.

In terms of key stakeholders, there is none more important than Herbert Hoover. Hoover was the key federal decision maker, and while the Red Cross had prominence in the central decision-making process, Hoover ultimately had the most influence. Several books offer important insights about Hoover's philosophy and decision making. For instance, *Winter War* offers insight about Republican and Democratic strategies in response to the Great Depression.[6] Whyte's *Hoover: An Extraordinary Life in Extraordinary Times* offers an exhaustive study about Hoover's philosophy and general management approach and style.[7] Nash's *Life of Herbert Hoover* may be a stand-alone prototype book that details the development and emergence of Hoover as a key political figure.[8] Though published in 1967, Harris Gaylord Warren's *Herbert Hoover and the Great Depression* offers a keen evaluation of Hoover's early years and time as a statesman. One common theme throughout much of the literature is Hoover's principle of volunteerism.

In short, volunteerism was both a bane and benedict in flood management.[9] Volunteerism was a complement to federalism at the time, arguing that public deficit needed to be shouldered by both public and private institutions. The concept of cooperative federalism was a slowly evolving concept. Much of the power to make decisions remained with state and local government and the general public until the Great Depression. Whether it was flood, fire, or other calamity, the general public was expected to absorb the costs. The idea of regulatory state was at least another decade away. The Great Mississippi Flood of 1927 would chart a new path for a government that was redefining itself.

At the flood's onset, the principal relief agency was the Red Cross. The Red Cross was an established organization that extended back to the 1880s.

However, it was not prepared to manage a refugee situation of this magnitude. Admittedly, both federalism and equal protection were different. Jim Crow policies were firmly embedded in the Deep South and President Coolidge was slow in assessing damage and delivering necessary relief. This pause also alienated many people in the Deep South, which would later impact the 1928 and 1932 presidential elections.

More immediately, Coolidge's inaction led to uneven management practices, which resulted in the Red Cross overseeing quite distinct and disparate relief efforts. Often, white refugees received much better treatment than their black counterparts. A prima facie explanation suggests that the Red Cross was overwhelmed by a lack of clear leadership, which led to racial tensions. This assertion corresponds with a bevy of research detailing these inequities. Spencer's *The Mississippi Flood of 1927 and the Struggle to Control Black Labor* harshly rebukes the Red Cross as being not only ineffective but tacitly allowing discriminatory practices to go unchecked.[10] In *Black Levee Camp Workers, the NAACP, and the Mississippi Flood Control Project, 1927–1933*, Mizelle provides rich details of the horrific and impossible work conditions that black workers faced.[11] In his broader work, *Backwater Blues: The Mississippi Flood of 1927 in the African American Imagination*, Mizelle investigates the relatively unexplored political significance of the Mississippi River from the post–Civil War to the Great Flood, as well as the plight of black Southerners.[12]

The Flood Year 1927: A Cultural History by Susan Scott Parish also serves as an important baseline for understanding the political current with the Mississippi Valley region.[13] Finally, Nash's *Herbert Hoover versus the Great Depression* offers a more apologetic approach by intimating that Hoover's management approach to the Great Flood was positive and that wide-scale relief was extended to all refugees.[14]

ENVIRONMENTALISM

However, beyond the political spectrum and amidst burgeoning racial tension, another vantage point must be recognized. As indicated previously, a central tenet of this book is to plumb the extent of environmentalism and its impact on political campaigns. While modern federalism was in its infancy during the great flood, policy makers did not understand the deeper context of environmentalism. At the time, environmentalism was viewed as a function of the Wise Movement. For many, the main goal was to use the environment in the most productive way. Crops could be rotated, while vast tracts of forests could be harvested for timber. The Wise Movement also encouraged monolithic dams to capture emerging water power from major rivers throughout the country. In many ways this was a "build first approach." There was no federal environmental legislation at the time, nor was there a protective environmental impact statement requiring federal oversight. This allowed the levees-only policy to flourish. The theory was that major riverways could be dammed by creating various levee systems. Little emphasis was placed on environmental impact. Further, a more regulatory form of federalism may have offered better control on levee construction. The Mississippi River flooding breached levees in several locations, contributing to a wider disaster.

In some ways, the Wise Movement underscored the debate between modern development and environmentalism. This clash is clearly evidenced in Commoner's *Making Peace with the Planet*. While written fifty years after the Great Flood, the book explains how limited governmental oversight, in part, contributed to the great deluge. Commoner viewed conflicted as embedded with the ecosphere and technosphere. In essence, he framed the environmental debate in two paths, production and development versus environmental security. He expands on this dichotomy through his principles of ecology. Principle one says, "Everything is connected to everything else." This expresses the elaborateness of the ecosphere's network, in which each component is linked to many others. Thus, in an aquatic ecosystem, a fish is not only a fish, but also the parent of other fish. A fish is also the producer of organic waste that nourishes microorganisms and ultimately, aquatic plants.[15]

The second principle of Commoner's ecology is "Everything has to go somewhere." Together with the first, this idea expresses the fundamental importance of cycles of the ecosphere. In the aquatic ecosystem, for example, participating chemical elements move through closed cyclical processes. The technosphere, in contrast, is dominated by linear processes. The third principle of ecology is "Nature knows best." The ecosystem is consistent within itself; its numerous components are compatible with each other and with the whole. Such a harmonious structure is the outcome of a long period of trial and error: 5 billion years of biological evolution. The biological sector of the ecosphere, the biosphere, is composed of living organisms that have survived this test through finely tuned adaptations to their particular ecological niche. Left to their own devices, ecosystems are conservative; the rate of evolution is very slow, and temporary changes such as the overpopulation of rabbits are quickly readjusted by the wolves.

However, most revealing is the nexus of the ecosphere and technosphere to debt. Commoner urges us to compare the ecosphere and the technosphere with respect to the consequences of failure. In the ecosphere, "there is no such thing as a free lunch." Any distortion of an ecological cycle or the intrusion of an incompatible component such as a toxic chemical leads unavoidably to harmful effects.

At first glance, the technosphere seems to be extraordinarily free of mistakes, that is, a technological process or product that failed not because of some unanticipated incident but because it was unable to do what it was designed to do. Yet nearly every modern technology has grave faults, which appear not as failures to accomplish their designed purposes but as a serious impact on the environment.

A free lunch is debt. In the technosphere, a debt is an acknowledged but unmet cost, the mortgage on a factory building. Such debt is tolerable because the technosphere is a system of production; if it functions properly, the system generates goods that represent wealth potentially capable of repaying the debt. In the technosphere, debts are repaid from within and at least in theory, are always capable of being paid off or in some cases, canceled. In contrast, when the debts represented by environmental pollution are created by the technosphere and transferred to the ecosphere, they are never canceled; damage is unavoidable.

People are caught in the clash between the ecosphere and the technosphere. What we call the "environmental crisis" is an array of critical unsolved problems ranging from local toxic dumps to the disruption of the global climate. This crisis is a product of the drastic mismatch between the cyclical, conservative, and consistent processes of the ecosphere and the linear and innovative but ecologically disharmonious processes of the technosphere.[16]

Since the environmental crisis has been generated by the war between the two worlds that human society occupies, it can be properly understood only in terms of their interplay. Of course, as in conventional war, the issues can be simplified by taking sides, ignoring the interests of one combatant or another. But this is done only at the cost of understanding. If the ecosphere is ignored, it is possible to define the environmental crisis solely in terms of the factors that govern the technosphere: production, prices, and profits, and the economic processes that mediate their interaction. For example, factories are allotted the right to emit pollutants and even buy and sell these rights. But unlike the conventional marketplace that deals in useful goods, this scheme creates a marketplace for negative externalities meaning pollution. This creates debt.[17]

If the technosphere is ignored, the environmental crisis can be defined in purely ecological terms. Human beings are then seen as a peculiar species, unique among living things that are doomed to destroy their own habitat. Thus simplified, the issue attracts simplistic solutions: reduce the number of people, limit the share of nature's resources, protect all other species from the human marauder by endowing them with rights. However, the technosphere is a critical and permanent component of modern society.[18]

The gap of complex solutions was critical during the Great Flood and remains an urgent issue today. However, outstanding questions remain.

According to Ostrom, best environmental management practices are possible in closely defined areas. However, regulating an entire river is more problematic, and an even larger body of water is more so.[19] By this, Ostrom leans toward collective action principles. This approach is premised upon a function of cooperative federalism whereby the federal government divulges its great regulatory powers to promote the common good.

This is not necessarily a top-down approach, but significant national mandates or guidelines are necessary, which was nearly absent during the Great Flood of 1927. This approach also requires actors at the state and local levels as well as input from private citizens and local relief agencies. Today, more actors are being included in all phases of the policy process including formulation, implementation, monitoring, and compliance.

Still, the term *governance* at the national level warrants further assessment. National governments retain ultimate power but must mobilize numerous actors at the federal, state, and local levels. States are not unitary players, either, and must work with federal and local entities. This remains an outstanding concern with recent hurricane management strategies.[20]

Ostrom supports Common Property Resources Management Theory (CPRMT), which evaluates institutional impact on behaviors and outcomes in the area of natural resources. CPRMT is based on the premise that people have coequal rights, specifically rights that exclude the use of these resources by other people. The purpose of CPRMT is to conceptualize how individuals and groups can organize themselves to govern and manage common property resources. This approach is based on the philosophy of self-organization and self-governance.[21]

These interpretive perspectives offer clues into why the shift from a levees-only approach was necessary. Water, like any resource, can be protected or wasted, depending upon the level of decision making. Yet, water is power. Water gains power as a policy instrument in terms of locality because it is not distributed evenly.[22] Water is also an independent force. State claims over water sources reflect resource-based conflicts. And finally, water is part of economic and urban growth. There are countless stories about water management. What remains is that w*ater politics rests in the complex intersection of institutional, economic, and ideological conditions at the national, state, and local levels* that have actually made the flow of water possible.[23]

According to Smith, politics is the practical process of working and compromising across competing and antagonistic positions. He argues that politics is about "Who does what to whom for whose benefit?" Politics is always about people making decisions that affect other people. Political institutions favor those with greater lobbying capacity.[24] To think political outcomes will be equal is naïve.[25]

Collective action is a steep challenge for water management. Water cooperation is a simple, rational choice problem that could be resolved by competitive pricing. Privatization reduces access to those who cannot pay the price. "The Tragedy of the Commons" suggests limited sanctions applied by some external power will suffice. Yet Ostrom notes real social cooperation and successful management depend on communication, trust, and reputation. Rather than seeing this behavioral nexus as a single set of institutional arrangements, Ostrom looks to a range of institutional possibilities that include ordinary citizens. This means rules and regulations must be provided if any policy is expected to prevail. This does not mean propinquity, but clear communication is essential.[26] This background allows us to now shift focus toward understanding the role of federalism and presidential disaster declaration responses.

NOTES

1. Adam Trexler, *Anthropocene Fictions: The Novel in a Time of Climate Change* (University of Virginia Press, 2015).

2. Robert Kerr, *Land, Wood, & Water* (New York: Fleet, 1960), 21.

3. Lynn Willoughby, *Flowing through Time: A History of the Lower Chattahoochee River* (Tuscaloosa: University of Alabama Press, 1999), 1–3.

4. John Barry, *Rising Tide: The Great Mississippi Flood of 1927 and How It Changed America* (New York: Simon and Schuster, 1997), 371–381.

5. Marc Reisner, *Cadillac Desert: The American West and Its Disappearing Water* (New York: Penguin Press, 1986), 15–31.

6. Eric Rauchway, *Winter War: Hoover, Roosevelt, and the First Clash Over the New Deal* (New York: Basic Books, 2018), 75–105.

7. Kenneth Whyte, *Hoover: An Extraordinary Life in Extraordinary Times* (New York: Vintage Books, 2017), 3–15.

8. George H. Nash, *The Life of Herbert Hoover Master of Emergencies, 1917-1918* (New York: Norton, 1996), 6–13.

9. Harris Gaylord Warren, *Herbert Hoover and the Great Depression* (New York: Norton, 1959), 3–51.

10. Robyn Spencer, "Contested Terrain: The Mississippi Flood of 1927 and the Struggle to Control Black Labor," *The Journal of Negro History* 79, no. 2 (1994): 170–181, https://doi.org/10.2307/2717627.

11. Richard M. Mizelle, "Black Levee Camp Workers, the NAACP, and the Mississippi Flood Control Project, 1927-1933," *Journal of African American History* 98, no. 4 (2013): 511–530, https://doi.org/10.5323/jafriamerhist.98.4.0511.

12. Richard M. Mizeller Jr., *Backwater Blues: The Mississippi Flood of 1927 in the African American Imagination* (Minneapolis, MN: University of Minnesota Press, 2014), 1–5.

13. Susan Scott Parrish, *The Flood Year 1927: A Cultural History* (Princeton, NJ: Princeton University Press, 2017), 8–29.

14. George H. Nash, *Herbert Hoover versus the Great Depression* (Hoover Digest, 2016), 181.

15. Barry Commoner, *Making Peace with the Planet* (New York: The New Press, 1992), 5–15.

16. Commoner, *Making Peace*, 5–15.

17. Ibid.

18. Ibid.

19. Elinor Ostrom, "Institutional Rational Choice: An Assessment of the Institutional Analysis and Development Framework," in *Theories of the Policy Process*, ed. Paul Sabatier (Boulder, CO: Westview Press, 2007), 2–21.

20. Ostrom, "Institutional Rational Choice," 2–21.

21. Ibid.

22. Ibid.

23. John Agnew, "Water Power: Politics and the Geography of Water Provision," *Annals of the Association of American Geographers* 101, no. 3 (May 2011): 463–476, http://dx.doi.org/10.1080/00045608.2011.560053.

24. Agnew, "Water Power," 463–476.

25. Zachary Smith, *The Environmental Policy Paradox* (Pearson, Prentice Hall, 2005), 35–40.

26. Smith, *The Environmental Policy*, 35–40.

Chapter 3

Disaster Management, Federalism, and the Presidency

The nexus between the presidency and disaster management has changed over the past century from disengagement to direct intervention. According to figure 3.1, presidents have issued increasingly more disaster declarations. In essence, a disaster declaration is when the governor of a state lacks the capacity to address a major cataclysmic event. These types of events are often associated with natural disasters but can also include acts of terror, economic crises, and pandemics. As figure 3.1 indicates, presidents have increasingly issued disaster declarations. This is a very good function of cooperative federalism in that there is effective communication and policy development between national, state and local governing levels. According to figure 3.1, presidents have issued 64 disaster declarations on average per year. However, that trend features a marked upswing in the twenty-first century. As of June 2020, President Trump has issued an average of 135.75 disaster declarations per year. Of his prior two predecessors, President Obama issued 117 and President Bush issued 128. This is in stark contrast to the 1950s, when presidential disaster declarations were rarely issued. The discrepancy may be a time and space concern. Cooperative federalism was still developing, and the president was overtly involved in managing and bringing World War II to a close. However, such management initiatives did not immediately follow force majeure cataclysmic events. Today, expectations have changed considerably. But this was clearly not always the case.

A short glance back to the late nineteenth century tells a different story. In 1889, President Harrison had no statutory authority to assist local communities during the Johnstown Flood, and he directed the U.S. Army Corps of Engineers to rebuild.[1] Instead, greater emphasis was placed on volunteerism. Harrison convened a meeting with key officials and implored them to make monetary and material contributions to the amount of $10,000.[2] There were

Year	Number	President
2020	181	Trump
2019	101	Trump
2018	124	Trump
2017	137	Trump
Average	135.75	
2016	103	Obama
2015	80	Obama
2014	84	Obama
2013	95	Obama
2012	112	Obama
2011	242	Obama
2010	108	Obama
Average	117.7143	
2009	115	Bush
2008	143	Bush
2007	136	Bush
2006	143	Bush
2005	155	Bush
2004	118	Bush
2003	123	Bush
2002	119	Bush
2001	100	Bush
Average	128	
2000	114	Clinton
1999	110	Clinton
1998	128	Clinton
1997	47	Clinton
1996	158	Clinton
1995	38	Clinton
1994	57	Clinton
1993	58	Clinton
1992	53	Clinton
Average	84.77778	
1991	45	H.W. Bush
1990	43	H.W. Bush
1989	32	H.W. Bush
Average	40	
1988	16	Reagan
1987	31	Reagan
1986	29	Reagan
1985	36	Reagan

Year	Number	President
1984	42	Reagan
1983	24	Reagan
1982	27	Reagan
1981	18	Reagan
Average	27.875	
1980	31	Carter
1979	59	Carter
1978	41	Carter
1977	61	Carter
Average	48	
1976	45	Ford
1975	45	Ford
Average	45	
1974	53	Nixon
1973	55	Nixon
1972	48	Nixon
1971	20	Nixon
1970	19	Nixon
1969	29	Nixon
1968	19	Nixon
Average	34.71429	
1967	11	Johnson
1966	11	Johnson
1965	25	Johnson
1964	25	Johnson
Average	18	
1963	20	Kennedy
1962	22	Kennedy
1961	12	Kennedy
Average	18	
1960	12	Eisenhower
1959	7	Eisenhower
1958	7	Eisenhower
1957	16	Eisenhower
1956	16	Eisenhower
1955	18	Eisenhower
1954	17	Eisenhower
1953	13	Eisenhower
Average	13.25	
Composite Average	64.30166[i]	

Figure 3.1   1953–2016 Presidential Disaster Declarations. *Source:* Data from https://www.fema.gov/disasters/year.

no federal relief disbursements. The president communicated with the Pennsylvania governor and the Johnstown mayor but only offered pro forma statements of condolence. There is no indication that President Harrison took any further action.[3]

One hundred and twenty years later, another disaster transpired in the United States. In 2010, the BP Deepwater Horizon oil drilling platform became the scene of a gas blowback and subsequent explosion that killed eleven people. Kapucu explains that faulty safety mechanisms on the sea floor produced a sea floor breach that leaked massive amounts of oil into the Gulf of Mexico for nearly three months. These seemingly dissimilar events, which are distanced by more than a century, both reflect common elements: negligence and irresponsible risk taking. Yet there is one categorical difference. By 2010, the public expected the president to be officially, comprehensively, and protractedly involved. The presidential role in emergency management did not occur suddenly, but as Birkland explains, it evolved over time through a series of distinct eras.[4]

Kapucu states that there are four discernible eras to classify change in presidential disaster management authority. The first era (approximately 1889–1926) saw greater public awareness. This was due to better communications and mass transportation. The invention and dissemination of the telegraph and telephone helped reporters disseminate news stories quickly. The 1889 Johnstown Flood, the Galveston Hurricane of 1900, and the Great Miami Hurricane of 1926 were covered nationally and internationally. These disasters revealed glaring deficiencies in the preparedness and response of state and local governments. The shortcomings of charities and social institutions were also exposed. People recognized their vulnerability and purchased insurance against potential disaster losses. Disasters and emergencies had clearly become part of risk management for both corporations and households.[5]

The second era (1927–1949) began with the Great Mississippi Flood of 1927, generally considered to be the most extensive flood in American history. This era extends through the 1940s. Before he assumed the presidency, Herbert Hoover was perceived by the public as a capable manager, as a result of his World War I food crisis management in Western Europe. Coolidge tasked Hoover with the job of central coordinator, linking the federal government, the American Red Cross, and volunteer efforts. Hoover's initial efforts were for the most part perceived favorably by both the general public and the national media. Both factors aided his path toward the 1928 presidency. Yet his relief efforts were not as calibrated as one might think. A significant portion of relief came from private foundations, even though his authority far exceeded his position as secretary of commerce.[6]

In the third era (1950–1978), the federal government developed a more coherent approach. The Federal Disaster Relief Act of 1950 empowered presidents to issue disaster declarations to states. This new executive feature greatly expanded the president's role in disaster management. A system slowly emerged where governors who were facing major crises could ask the president to issue them a disaster declaration. And by 1974, presidents had complete discretion. Despite increasing executive-legislative tension, Congress trusted the president to make sound determinations.

The final era (1979–present) demonstrates increased formalization of emergency management as exemplified by the creation of the U.S. Federal Emergency Management Agency (FEMA) IN 1979. The public demanded swift and authoritative responses to major disasters. Presidents assumed the title of manager, and emergency management had a formal presence in the executive branch.[7]

FEMA focused on professionalized emergency management, aiding states and local governments to develop their own systems of emergency management. However, FEMA struggled in its role, and sharp criticism emerged that the new agency was incompetent, slow, and disorganized in hurricane management. Intense news coverage worked against both the agency and the president. The managerial reputation of President George H.W. Bush (1989–1993) was adversely affected and was a factor in his failure to win reelection.[8]

Two epic events during the administration of President George W. Bush reshaped the contours of federal emergency response. The September 11th terror attacks compelled the president to make dramatic changes in emergency management. First, emergency management, law enforcement, and counterterrorism merged. This meant consolidation. Efforts were sought to integrate, coordinate, and standardize the disaster response of local, state, and federal levels as well as to redefine the roles of non-profits and volunteers. The Homeland Security Act of 2002 brought about the largest federal reorganization since the creation of the Department of Defense in 1947. This act culminated in the creation of the U.S. Department of Homeland Security (DHS). Federal emergency management and homeland security officials then moved to restructure the National Incident Management System (NMS) and the National Response Plan (NRP).[9]

The second event was Hurricane Katrina, which struck the U.S. Gulf Coast in 2005. This catastrophe demonstrated that despite extensive changes, grant funding infusions, and a new focus on terror among DHS, FEMA, the states, and even the president, they were not prepared for such a destructive event. Katrina proved that regardless of increased resources and training, disaster management could fail. Specifically, Katrina spotlighted imprudent mitigation strategies, ineffective inter and intragovernmental collaboration, inexperience, and major failures in leadership. President G.W. Bush offered the nation a personalized public apology from the government on television. In early 2008, federal authorities formally replaced the NRP with the National Response Framework (NRF). The NRF incorporated

NIMS and reflected improvements prompted by problems discovered after Hurricane Katrina.[10]

Some presidential administrations have been blessed with few or no catastrophes, though no administration escapes them all. History shows that from 1950 to 2000, presidents received an average of about two disaster declarations per month, though this average has risen considerably from 1989 to present. Some presidents, including Johnson, Carter, Reagan, Clinton, and G.W. Bush, attained executive experience in emergency management while serving as governors.[11]

Emergency management is intertwined with national security. In the Eisenhower and Kennedy years (and arguably through the terms of Nixon, Ford, Carter, and Reagan), federal emergency management was predicated largely on preparing the nation for a Soviet attack with nuclear weapons; non-war disaster management was often a secondary concern. The USSR detonated its first atomic bomb in 1949. The Cold War involved a weapons rivalry during which both the United States and the Soviet Union possessed thermonuclear bombs. Intercontinental ballistic missiles in 1957, the nuclear weapons embargo standoff with Cuba in 1963 (Kennedy), and later the 9/11 attacks convinced several presidents that civil and homeland defense should be the centerpiece of federal emergency management. Johnson, Nixon, Carter, and Clinton saw federal emergency management as less civil of homeland defense and more as management of nonwar disasters and calamities.[12]

Some presidents take a keen interest in emergency management, appointing capable leaders to top emergency management posts and pressing for adequate federal disaster management budget authority. Others intentionally or unintentionally neglect these needs. For some presidents, the level of commitment depends on whether states and localities suffer catastrophes. Major disasters and catastrophes tend to change presidents and their policies; rarely do presidents alter their disaster management behaviors and policies "pro-actively."[13]

According to Kapucu, proactiveness is related to the four phases of emergency management—prevention, mitigation, response, and recovery. The response and early recovery phases are critical because they shape the public's perception of a president's leadership skills. According to Pfiffner,[14] there is both continuity and volatility in presidential rankings. Professional historians and popular sentiments do not always concur. The general public tends to rank Kennedy and Reagan higher than historians. In turn, historians tend to rank Johnson higher than the public. There is no clear consensus about how to evaluate and rank presidents based on their disaster management performance.[15]

Some think that superior disaster management performance is linked to those who have been able to distinguish between national security and natural disasters. There is also the assumption that natural or human-caused tragedies—like industrial accidents and biological disasters—are not made secondary to civil or homeland security concerns. Many emergency managers possess professional knowledge, skills, and abilities. However, rigid hierarchy limits effective decision making. For instance, top federal emergency managers need access to the president at certain points. Some presidents have made access easy (Carter and Clinton) and others have made it challenging (G.H.W. Bush and G.W. Bush).[16]

By the 1970s, emergency management stature continued to grow in the executive office. President Carter helped consolidate a bevy of disparate agencies into FEMA. Carter ensured that the head of FEMA would report directly to the president. By the mid-1990s, President Clinton elevated the director of FEMA to cabinet status, signifying his concern about emergency management and his desire for FEMA-led interdepartmental coordination in times of disaster.[17]

Second, presidents enhance their records when they select and appoint experienced, competent emergency management directors who have the ability to communicate well with both the president and the public. The reverse is true when presidential political appointees who lack knowledge or experience in emergency management win political appointment. While highly capable but inexperienced individuals often succeed in appointed posts, this is much less common in emergency management. The work often requires performing in compressed time frames. There is little or no time to "learn the job" or "exchange business cards."[18]

The number of disaster declarations issued by a president is useful in determining a president's engagement and support. While some presidents encounter more catastrophes than others, governors sometimes request disaster declarations from the president to exploit political advantage. Presidents who rarely turn down governor requests (Clinton, G.W. Bush, and Obama) may tempt governors to frequently seek help for events that are only marginally definable as disaster. Conversely, presidents who are documentation of need, and who relatively high turn-down rates (Carter and Reagan) may discourage governors from requesting declarations.[19]

Presidential-congressional relations are part of the nexus of emergency management as well. Presidents with poor congressional relations may be challenged by the Congress. Political opponents or dissatisfied allies may make the administration's efforts seem uncoordinated. Regular communications between a governor and president may expedite federal relief. This could translate into federal aid and loan programs. In some rare but publicized instances of emergency management failure, problems arose when a president and respective governor of different political parties engaged in political feuding.[20]

Effective communications means engaging the public and skillfully applying political persuasion. Too much or too little could impact reelection efforts or in the long run, impact a president's legacy. The media counts too, and in an age of advanced social media, even more so. The media offers onsite views of disaster regions. This can elicit numerous responses ranging from compassion to indignation. The media also channels symbolic management or at least offers the president the chance to demonstrate concern and engagement. However, in the end, presidential approval of governors' disaster relief requests provides an opportunity for political credit.[21] Each president has been faced with disaster response situations. The following reflects a composite list from President Truman to President Trump on the number of disaster declarations issued:

PRESIDENT TRUMAN (1945–1953)

Harry S. Truman served several months as President Franklin D. Roosevelt's last vice president. Before that, he had served in Congress. Truman's executive experience prior to his election to Congress consisted of his roles as chief county administrator in Missouri and in 1922, as judge, primarily an administrative position, for the Jackson County Court. He is most remembered for his decision to drop atomic bombs on Hiroshima and Nagasaki in an effort to force the surrender of Japan in World War II. Later, Truman confronted Soviet communist expansion into Eastern Europe. In 1950, he faced a North Korean invasion of South Korea, and with UN support, entered U.S. troops in a three-year war concluded by his successor through an armistice.[22]

Truman's term coincided with the Texas City ship explosion in 1947, on which 2,000 tons of ammonium nitrate blew up. Still considered to be the deadliest industrial disaster in U.S. history, the detonation killed 581 and injured an estimated 3,500. Truman ordered in the National Guard but had no authority to provide financial assistance. Ultimately, a long legal battle by Galveston citizens for relief under the Federal Tort Claims Act was denied by a Supreme Court decision in 1953 in the famous *Elizabeth Dalehite, et. al. v. United States* case. Afterwards, in 1955, Congress finally passed a private bill to provide relief.[23]

Truman signed both the Disaster Relief Act of 1950 and the Civil Defense Act of 1950 (CDA). He also proposed flood insurance programs in 1951 and 1952 due to the Great Flood of 1951 in the central Midwest; however, Congress did not endorse these proposals. Truman also signed the Small

Business Act of 1953, which expanded federal involvement in disaster relief into the private sector. He issued twenty major disaster declarations.[24]

It is fair to say that Truman's role in helping the nation cope with two wars, his backing of the Marshall Plan to rebuild and finance postwar Europe, his approval of the Berlin airlift (1948–1949), and his handling of domestic emergencies provided him substantial experience in international and domestic disaster management. The early 1950s started a new era in emergency management which was reflective of cooperative federalism. Disaster management was coordinated at all three levels of government.[25]

PRESIDENT EISENHOWER (1953–1961)

A West Point Military Academy graduate, Dwight D. Eisenhower extended a successful military career into a political career. He is highly rated as a capable president by both public opinion and professional historian surveys. In World War II, Eisenhower ascended the ranks until he commanded the Allied Forces in North Africa in November 1942 and then the Supreme Allied Expeditionary Force on D-Day, 1944. After the War, in 1951, Eisenhower assumed supreme command of the new NATO forces.[26]

Three great tornado clusters, each killing more than 100 people, occurred during his presidency. These included the May 1953 "Waco" Tornado sequence, the June 1953 tornado sequence from the Midwest to New England, which killed 247, and the 1955 Great Plains Tornado Outbreak of forty-six tornadoes, two of which were F5s. Eisenhower signed more than 100 presidential disaster declarations, conveying more than 65 million dollars in 2003 constant dollars. However, Eisenhower did not see a relationship between the role of disaster declarations and the health emergency posed by the 1957 Asian flu epidemic. The disease took the lives of 70,000 Americans. He took a relatively passive role in the rapidly occurring health event rather than taking a more active leadership role for the government, allowing the free market to regulate inoculations as it had done successfully with the polio vaccine.[27]

In civil defense, Eisenhower advanced a mass evacuation policy and shelter defense program. The Soviet launch of the world's first intercontinental ballistic missile in 1957, followed by Sputnik, the first earth orbiting satellite, increased pressure for corresponding technological successes by the United States. The Eisenhower administration reacted in part by launching a federal reorganization: The Federal Civil Defense Administration and the Office of Defense Mobilization were merged, forming the Office of Civil and Defense Mobilization under the leadership of Leo Hoegh, former governor of Iowa. The primary result was a renewed emphasis on civil defense at the expense of the federal government's natural disaster management efforts.[28]

PRESIDENT KENNEDY (1961–1963)

Although narrowly elected, he became a popular president due to his personal qualities and his hard-line stance against the Soviet Union. His public appeal has remained extremely high over time, though less so with professional historians. Kennedy signed more than fifty presidential disaster declarations, the most prominent of which was for Hurricane Carla in 1961. Later, not long before his assassination in November 1963, Hurricanes Donna and Ethel occurred. Because of the Cuban Missile Crisis (1962–1963) and heightened tensions in the Cold War, Kennedy's focus was clearly on the side of civil defense. Kennedy "emphasized the importance of home, school, or workplace fallout shelters as a means to save lives."[29] He separated civil defense from disaster management in 1961 by transferring most civil defense functions to the U.S. Department of Defense. With Kennedy's approval, the U.S. Department of Defense created the Office of Civil Defense (OCD) to manage civil defense functions. Kennedy's reorganization efforts gifted emergency management a strong civilian identity but did little to emphasize emergency preparedness and response related to other types of disasters.[30]

PRESIDENT JOHNSON (1963–1969)

President Lyndon B. Johnson was known for promoting the Great Society program. This initiative included aid to education, civil rights, attack on disease, Medicare, urban renewal, conservation, development of depressed regions, a wide-scale fight against poverty, control and prevention of crime and delinquency, and removal of discriminatory obstacles blocking the right to vote. Although generally appreciated by professional historians for his administrative agenda, Johnson holds poorer public ranking due to overreach in foreign and domestic policy.[31]

The Johnson presidency downplayed civil defense on account of several enormous natural disasters: Hurricane Hilda (1964), the Great Alaskan Earthquake (1964), Hurricane Betsy (1965), and the Palm Sunday Tornado (1965). The Great Alaskan Earthquake alone took 141 lives, left thousands homeless, and disrupted the economy of the state. In 1965, Hurricane Betsy devastated portions of the southeast, resulting in seventy-six deaths and an estimated $1 billion in losses.[32] Hurricane Betsy mobilized a tremendous response from federal and American Red Cross representatives, who worked with state and local civil defense agencies. President Johnson monitored the actions of federal agencies and ordered federal personnel to remain in the affected areas. Kapucu et al write, "President Johnson modeled a new role for the president as an active and engaged emergency manager." Further, he signed the 1966 Disaster Relief Act and the National Flood Insurance Act of 1968.[33]

PRESIDENT NIXON (1969–1974)

President Nixon gained administrative experience as vice president under the Eisenhower administration. He ultimately suffered greatly due to political scandals. However, he had a relatively strong legislative and administrative record. Nixon signed 196 presidential disaster declarations. This total exceeded that of all previous presidents and was only topped by the Clinton (380) and G.W. Bush (est. 457) administrations years later. Nixon awarded the declarations for the Rapid City, SD Flood, for Hurricane Agnes in 1972, and for the 1974 tornado outbreak, with a count of 148. Nixon charted a new course for federal emergency management, especially after a poor federal response with Hurricane Camille in 1969.[34]

He first introduced National Security Decision Memorandum (NSDM) 184, which recommended a dual-use approach to federal citizen preparedness programs. He then replaced the OCD with the Defense Civil Preparedness Agency (DCPA) and placed it under the auspices of the Department of Defense. The Nixon administration also established significant federal disaster management reorganization plans in 1970 and 1973. However, this led to confusion because several different agencies were created throughout the executive branch. In effect, Nixon created some 100 different disaster-related federal agencies, which satisfied a wide array of Congressional interests without impacting his cabinet.[35]

The Nixon administration is credited with moving the federal government away from preoccupation with structural hazard mitigation (building dams, levees, and other flood works) to greater emphasis on the use of nonstructural mitigation efforts (use of wetlands to buffer against flooding and regulating better land use). These reforms and increasing expectation of federal responsiveness to natural disasters encouraged Nixon to support the Disaster Relief Act of 1974. This first-time measure provided direct assistance to families after disasters, rather than distributing the funds to state and local jurisdictions. Nixon increased federal disaster funding levels and authorized a 1974 law to issue emergency declarations and subsidized state and local funding.[36]

PRESIDENT FORD (1974–1977)

President Gerald R. Ford served as vice president assumed by appointment rather than election. He was elevated to the presidency after Nixon's resignation in 1974. Ford eventually issued Nixon a presidential pardon, which probably tarnished his political reputation. He signed seventy-six presidential disaster declarations in his single term and produced some $800 million in current dollar spending. There were no exceptional natural disasters during his presidency, and he discouraged dual use (civilian and national security) activity that worked to the benefit of civilian emergency management.[37]

PRESIDENT CARTER (1977–1981)

President James E. Carter defeated President Ford in the 1976 general election, serving from 1977 to 1981. Carter had administrative experience as governor of Georgia, where he emphasized ecology, efficiency in government, and the removal of racial barriers. His general reputation is mixed. Carter "knew natural disasters well, and he was anxious to respond to the call of other governors and the National Governor's Association for improvements in the organization of federal disaster management."[38] In 1977, Carter directed a study on federal preparedness and response to natural, accidental, and wartime emergencies, which had been plagued with problems in defining responsibility and accountability stemming back to the 1950s. In response to these problems, Carter created the Federal Emergency Management Agency (FEMA) in 1979. FEMA had numerous responsibilities and was comprised of certain offices from the Department of Housing and Urban Development, the Federal Insurance Administration, the National Fire Prevention and Control Administration, the National Weather Service Community Preparedness Program, the Federal Preparedness Agency of the General Services Administration, and the Federal Disaster Assistance Administration. FEMA provided the president significant power in addressing disasters in a more focused way. Few presidents have had as much positive influence on federal emergency management efforts.[39]

Carter issued 112 major disaster declarations and 59 declarations of emergency. This was an extraordinarily high level of declaration issuance for a four-year interval. Perhaps even more remarkable was that Carter turned down ninety-one major declaration requests and thirty-seven emergency requests, a record unmatched by any president. Carter faced some relatively unique incidents, such as the Three Mile Island nuclear power plant emergency in Pennsylvania in March 1979 and the eruption of Mount St. Helens in southern Washington State in 1980. The nuclear accident at Three Mile Island proved to be both a corporate and governmental fiasco, with conflated responsibilities and bungled communication to the public. Nonetheless, the failures of the U.S. Nuclear Regulatory Commission gave Carter grounds to furnish FEMA authority to review and then approve or deny off-plant site emergency plans of commercial nuclear power generating stations, an authority shared with the NRC.[40] The volcanic eruption at Mount St. Helens was predicted by the U.S. Geological Survey, but nonetheless, fifty-seven people were killed, most of who disregarded evacuation warnings. The federal response through FEMA, the Small Business Administration, and the Army Corps of Engineers amounted to nearly $1 billion in supplemental funding to help those suffering losses in the downwind multistate recovery area. Carter paid close attention to these events, personally visiting Mount St. Helens and its environs.[41]

PRESIDENT REAGAN (1981–1989)

President Reagan's administrative experience started in 1966, when he was elected Governor of California. He served two terms as president. At the end of his presidency, "the Reagan Revolution . . . aimed to reinvigorate the American people and reduce their reliance upon Government. For much of his administration, Reagan was very popular, though he has been held in less esteem by professional historians.[42]

President Reagan issued 184 major disaster declarations, though his tenure as president was surprisingly free of catastrophic disasters. Reagan, like Eisenhower, Johnson, Nixon, and Carter, had a high rate (34 percent) of turn down for major disaster declaration requests from governors. Reagan turned down 64 percent of emergency declaration requests he received—a rejection rate unmatched by any other president. Emergency declaration requests were made without having to justify need in terms of damage assessment. President Reagan obviously looked at most of these requests with disfavor. This may also in part be attributed to Reagan's federalism approach. He advocated less federal involvement in state and local affairs and greater decentralization or delegation of federal powers to the states. Consequently, this policy may have discouraged governors from automatically requesting help from the federal government, encouraging states and localities to assume more disaster management responsibilities independent from the federal government. Reagan intermittently used FEMA's sheltering and public evacuation functions as a tool of his aggressive anti-Soviet foreign policy.[43]

In 1988, he signed the Robert T. Stafford Act, named for its chief Senate architect. This law was a major overhaul of the Federal Disaster Relief Act of 1974 and previous federal disaster-related statutes. The Stafford Act increased the president's role in national disaster-related management and promoted disaster mitigation and prevention in a variety of ways. The Stafford Act "authorizes the president to issue major disaster or emergency declarations, sets broad eligibility criteria, and specifies the type of assistance the president may authorize."[44] While Congress deserves much credit for its careful deliberation in crafting the Stafford Act, one of those rare instances when disaster legislation was crafted in an environment largely free of immediate disaster demands, President Reagan deserves credit as well for signing this measure into law.[45]

PRESIDENT G. H. W. BUSH (1989–1993)

President George H. W. Bush was inaugurated on January 20, 1989. His overall record is generally ranked in the middle of modern presidents. He served as vice president for two terms, ambassador to the United Nations and China, and director of the CIA. Though tremendously experienced in foreign and domestic affairs, his perceived administrative competence while in office was poor. In the G. H. W. Bush years, civil defense issues moved to a lower priority as Soviet communism collapse improved relations with the Soviets.[46]

President Bush issued more major disaster declarations on average (158 for four years) than did President Reagan (184 for eight years, an average of 92 per term). Like Reagan, G.H.W. Bush turned down a high percentage of emergency requests (60 percent), but unlike Reagan, he turned down only one in five requests for major disaster declarations. Bush had to deal with several large-scale events. The October 1989 Loma Prieta earthquake caused widespread damage (estimated more than $8 billion) and resulted in more than $1 billion in FEMA spending, reminding the nation of the costliness of natural disasters. Two additional enormous disasters occurred during his presidency: Hurricane Hugo in 1989 and Hurricane Andrew in 1992 (nearly coincident with Hurricane Iniki, which heavily damaged areas of the Hawaiian Islands). Hurricane Hugo left thousands of people homeless, forcing Bush to dispatch military police to restore public order and resulting in $2 billion in damage. Hurricane Andrew killed twenty-three people and caused more than $26 billion in damage, mostly in South Florida.[47]

Bush passed over his FEMA director and instead appointed Andrew Card, secretary of transportation, to lead the federal response to Hurricane Andrew. This is considered a low point in the history of federal emergency management, and Bush was criticized for poor responsiveness. Most importantly, the Director of Emergency Response for Dade County, Kate Hale, exclaimed in a news conference three days after Hurricane Andrew: "Where the hell is the cavalry on this one? They keep saying we're going to get supplies. For God's sake, where are they?" Critics blamed many pre- and post-Hurricane Andrew problems on state and federal administrative and political deficiencies. South Carolina Senator Ernest Hollings lambasted FEMA'S Hugo response in these

words: "FEMA is widely viewed as a political dumping ground, a turkey
farm, if you will, where large numbers of positions exist that can be conve-
niently and quietly filled by political appointment."[48]

PRESIDENT CLINTON (1993–2001)

Clinton is lauded among professionals of emergency management for appointing James Lee Witt to head FEMA for all eight years of his presidency. Witt,
who compiled considerable experience in emergency management as a
county official in Arkansas, improved FEMA's morale and deftly interacted
with Congress and the public in times of disaster. President Clinton extended
Witt ex officio cabinet member status in 1996. Rubin writes, "Indeed, with
this positive publicity and concomitant presidential promotion, foreign leaders sought advice from FEMA administration about how other nations could
form or improve their emergency management agencies."[49]

In the summer of 1993, widespread and continuous rainfall across the
central Midwest saturated the soil and resulted in prolonged and extensive
flooding. Eventually dubbed the Great Midwest Flood, this was the first major
emergency management challenge for Clinton. Witt sent out regional staff
before the flooding became serious to help states apply for disaster assistance,
and they prepared preliminary damage assessments before Clinton's formal
declaration was issued. "Witt directed FEMA workers to respond immediately to any state requests and he anticipated requests rather than waiting for
state officials to tell FEMA, what they needed."[50] In 1994, southern California
experienced the Northridge Earthquake; the event totaled $6.97 billion and
became one of the most expensive pre-9/11 disasters dealt to FEMA. In
1999, Hurricane Floyd lashed fourteen mid-Atlantic and northeastern states.
Again, the Clinton-Witt FEMA responded capably, evacuating 2.6 million
people, the largest peacetime evacuation in U.S. history winning congressional praise.[51]

Near the start of Clinton's first term, a new era of terrorism began. The
1993 World Trade Center bomb attack and the 1995 truck bombing of the
Murray Federal Building in Oklahoma City impelled the Clinton administration to adapt emergency management policy for terrorist attacks in the
United States by adding a terrorism annex to the Federal Response Plan in
1998. According to Kapucu et al., "The Oklahoma City bombing was the first
disaster in which FEMA officials had to work closely with FBI officials."[52]

Clinton, at the behest of Witt, advanced many reforms in emergency management. One made the process of governor declaration requests more expe-
ditious by dispatching federal damage assessment teams without waiting for a
formal state request for these teams; another helped reduce the administrative

burden of paperwork by FEMA for federally assisted state programs and officials. Clinton issued 380 major disaster declarations and 68 declarations of emergency during his presidency and helped increase the level of federal aid significantly. Clinton and H.W. Bush have identical turn down rates for major disaster requests (21 percent), but Clinton turned down only 16 percent of emergency requests he received. His receptivity to governor requests for both major disasters and emergencies was significantly greater than all predecessors extending back to Truman. Clinton's supporters view his prodigious issuance of major disaster and emergency declarations as evidence of both his interest in disaster management and his desire to express compassion to disaster victims. Clinton's critics tend to judge him as having used disaster declarations for his political gain and as an instrument of presidential distributive politics. They also allege that his frequent trips to damage zones were mostly for reasons of favorable public opinion. Regardless, the Clinton-Witt era is sometimes referred to the golden age of emergency management.[53]

PRESIDENT G. W. BUSH (2001–2009)

The September 11 terrorist attacks inspired the G. W. Bush administration to make massive changes in emergency management policy. President Bush signed a rare Declaration of National Emergency soon after the attack. Congress quickly approved a $40 billion emergency supplemental appropriation for disaster relief for both antiterrorism and counterterrorism actions. Though initially reluctant, President Bush proposed the formation of the Department of Homeland Security (DHS), "a super department with 180,000 employees." G. W. Bush made counterterrorism the top priority of his administration; and helped create the Homeland Security Act of 2002. DHS represented the largest federal reorganization since Truman's Department of Defense reorganization in 1947. As a result, FEMA lost its independent agency authority and was folded into DHS.[54]

President G. W. Bush was criticized for political cronyism; in his first term and in part of his second, his FEMA directors of administrator nominations lacked emergency management experience. However, FEMA director Michael Brown, with no emergency management experience before his appointment, had argued against the absorption of FEMA into DHS. He sent a long memorandum arguing that the new plan would "fundamentally sever FEMA from its core functions," "shatter agency morale," and "break longstanding, effective and tested relationships with states and first responder stakeholders."[55]

President G. W. Bush issued a record breaking 457 major disaster declarations and about 139 declarations of emergency over his total eight years in office. These totals exceed those by any other president, including Clinton. Bush dispensed emergency declarations to all states that incurred expenses for hosting Katrina evacuees, thus driving up his emergency declaration totals. The Bush turndown rates for governor major disaster and emergency requests paralleled those of Clinton. The Bush administration's declaration totals generally escalated annually. Moreover, the Bush administration experienced many multistate disaster incidents, which tend to multiply declaration numbers.[56]

Yet the Bush presidency stumbled just as Brown had predicted when Hurricanes Dennis, Katrina, Rita, and Wilma struck the United States consecutively in 2005. FEMA's response was highly criticized. However, Hurricane Katrina alone constituted a true catastrophe for the Gulf Coast, and most particularly, for New Orleans and surrounding areas. The Hurricane Katrina Emergency Reform Act of 2006, signed into law by President Bush, reinvigorated FEMA organizationally and ensured that future FEMA administrators would have access to the president in times of disaster or emergency. The measure, as well as hard-earned lessons of the Bush administration, ensured that future FEMA administrators would be vetted for their emergency management expertise prior to their confirmations. FEMA Administrator David Paulson, Michael Brown's successor, helped G. W. Bush's administration improve its federal emergency management legacy as it ended.[57]

PRESIDENT OBAMA (2009–2016)

President Barack Obama established his own record in disaster management. He was quick to issue disaster declarations for states hit hard by blizzards in the winter of 2009. He appointed an experienced and respected FEMA administrator named Craig Fugate. Presidents Clinton and G. W. Bush both dramatically increased the number and frequency of disaster declaration issuance, but it was President Obama who broke the record for the largest number of presidential disaster declarations issued in a single calendar year (2010). However, a deep and persistent recession may have tempted him to generously encourage governor requests of federal disaster relief as a form of targeted economic recovery.

The Obama administration issued 227 major disaster declarations and 41 declarations of emergency. He approved fifty-four majors in 2009, eighty-one in 2010, and eighty-two in 2011. The 2010 and 2011 totals stand as annual high records unmatched by any previous president. Obama turn down totals are difficult to obtain, though it is fair to say the administration had a relatively low rate of federal assistance rejections.[58]

Despite this success in emergency management, the Obama White House suffered a setback in April 2010 when the BP Deepwater Horizon oil platform disaster occurred. Investigations revealed the deficient offshore drilling regulations of the scandal-ridden Minerals Management Service, which is now reformed and renamed Bureau of Ocean Energy Management and Enforcement. Like President G. H. W. Bush in the case of the 1989 Exxon Valdez oil tanker spill, President Obama chose not to use FEMA and the Stafford Act to manage the federal response and recovery. Obama told the public that he would assume responsibility for managing the spill and its effects. The U.S. Coast Guard was given lead agency authority. Management of the spill was conducted with conformity to the National Response Framework and the National Incident Management System.[59]

PRESIDENT TRUMP 2016–2020

President Trump's disaster declarations may be the epitome of the changing executive role. First, President Trump has faced several if not the most daunting societal concerns. President Trump absorbed criticism for federal intervention regarding Hurricane Irma (2017), which battered Puerto Rico and Hurricane Harvey (2017), which deluged portions of Houston. That being said, his greatest challenge and highest inducement of disaster declarations has been COVID-19. This could further explain additional increases in annual disaster declarations and why he has issued more declarations than any other president. More importantly, Trump's numbers imply that federal involvement transverses party ideology and that the relationship between the executive office and disaster management is increasingly changing. Yet how this relationship impacts a campaign is quite complex. Federalism had enabled presidents to become more involved in state and local disasters. Looking forward, we must ask this: Are such decisions campaign-related or simply about the general good? The next section explores these questions and addresses presidential campaign strategy.

NOTES

1. Naim Kapucu et al., "U.S. Presidents and Their Role in Emergency Management and Disaster Policy: 1950-2009," *Risk, Hazards & Crisis in Public Policy* 2, no. 3 (2011): 1–34, https://doi.org/10.2202/1944-4079.1065.
2. Kapacu et al., "U.S. Presidents," 1–34.
3. Ibid.
4. Ibid.

5. Ibid.

6. Ibid.

7. Ibid.

8. Ibid.

9. Ibid.

10. Ibid.

11. Thomas Birkland, *Lesson of Disaster* (Washington, DC: Georgetown University Press, 2006).

12. Birkland, *Lesson of Disaster*, 2006.

13. Richard Sylves and Zoltan I. Buzas, "Presidential Disaster Declaration Decisions. 1953-2003: What Influences Odds of Approval," *State and Local Government Review* 39, no. 1 (2007): 3–15, https://doi.org/10.1177/0160323X070 3900102.

14. James P. Pfiffner, "Ranking the President: Continuity and Volatility," *White House Studies* 3, no. 1 (2003): 23–34, http://mason.gmu.edu/~pubp502/Pres.rating .mss.pdf.

15. Pfiffner, "Ranking," 23–34, p. 45.

16. Pfiffner, "Ranking," 23–34.

17. Brian J. Gerber and David B. Cohen, "Katrina and Her Waves: Presidential Leadership and Disaster Management in an Intergovernmental Context," in *Disaster Management Handbook*, ed. Jack Pinkowski (New York: CRC Press, 2008).

18. Kapacu et al., "U.S. Presidents," 1–34.

19. Ibid.

20. Ibid.

21. Richard Neustadt, *Presidential Power: The Politics of Leadership* (New York: John Wiley and Sons, 1960).

22. David M. Oshinsky, "Harry Truman," in *The American Presidency*, eds. Alan Brinkley and David Dyer (Boston, MA: Houghton Mifflin, 2004).

23. Melvin Belli, *Ready for the Plaintiff* (New York: Bobbs-Merrill, 1963).

24. FEMA, "A Chronology of Major Events Affecting the National Flood Insurance Program," *American Institutes for Research* (Washington, DC: under contract 282-98-0029 to the Federal Emergency Management Association, 2002), https ://www.fema.gov/media-library-data/20130726-1602-20490-7283/nfip_eval_chron ology.pdf.

25. Kapacu et al., "U.S. Presidents," 1–34.

26. Ibid.

27. Sylves and Buzas, "Presidential Disaster," 3–15.

28. Ibid.

29. Ibid.

30. Ibid.

31. Vision Critical, 2011 Angus Reid Public Opinion, http://www.visioncriti-cal.com.

32. Vision Critical, 2011 Angus Reid Public Opinion, http://www.visioncriti-cal.com.

33. Kapacu et al., "U.S. Presidents," 1–34.

34. Ibid.

35. Richard Sylves, *Disaster Policy and Politics: Emergency Management and Homeland Security* (Washington, DC: CQ Press, 2008).

36. Sylves, *Disaster Policy.*

37. Ibid.

38. Ibid.

39. Vision Critical. 2011 Angus Reid Public Opinion, http://www.visioncritical.com.

40. James Miskel, *Disaster Response and Homeland Security: What Works and What Doesn't* (Palo Alto, CA: Stanford University Press, 2008).

41. Miskel, *Disaster Response.*

42. Ibid.

43. Sylves, *Disaster Policy.*

44. Ibid.

45. Ibid.

46. Kapacu et al., "U.S. Presidents," 1–34.

47. Ibid.

48. Bill Gertz, "Mikulski Faults FEMA Officials, Calls for Probe," *Washington Times,* September 4, 1992.

49. Claire B. Rubin, ed. *Emergency Management: The American Experience 1900-2005.* VA: PERI, 2007.

50. Claire B. Rubin, ed. *Emergency Management: The American Experience 1900-2005.* VA: PERI, 2007.

51. Congressional Record – Senate 2000. *Amendment No. 342 July 14, 2000. P. 10649.*

52. Kapacu et al., "U.S. Presidents," 1–34.

53. Ibid.

54. Jane A. Bullock et al., *Introduction to Homeland Security* (Burlington, VT: Elsevier, 2006).

55. Bullock et al., *Introduction.*

56. Ibid.

57. Sylves, *Disaster Policy.*

58. Kapacu et al., "U.S. Presidents," 1–34.

59. Ibid.

Chapter 4

Presidential Campaign Strategies and Farley's Law

Andrew Jackson pioneered a "new" understanding of the presidency and the public. While his predecessors saw the executive role as mainly representing the government, Jackson refocused the executive office by claiming to speak for the people and fight powerful interests such as the national bank. He derived legitimacy from the public and asserted that the presidency was a policymaking institution. Yet it was Lincoln who stated, "With public sentiment, nothing can fail. Without it, nothing can succeed."[1]

Presidential scholars disagree regarding Lincoln's observations. Today, presidential decision making is influenced by public opinion polling, a concept that did not develop until the second FDR administration. Presidents believe public approbation is a key component of political success. In some ways, public approval contributes to their legacy.[2]

According to Ponder, presidential approval conveys part of the story. He wonders why, if presidents are popular when government itself is held in high esteem, should high approval lead to an increased likelihood of success? He suggests that observing a president when political trust is low may be more beneficial. If they are popular when trust is low, presidents can legitimately use their standing, which offers better insight into effective leadership during difficult times.[3]

There are a number of theorists who plumb presidential decision making. Easton formulated a policy pathway to uncover the concept of political leverage. He posited that specific and diffuse supports are vital to the long-term survival of political regimes and presidential administrations.[4] Easton defined support for governmental leaders as reactionary to political outputs. Easton also seeks redress by focusing on leaders demonstrating the action-reaction syndrome. For example, a citizen evaluates a leader on outputs such as the state of the economy or even political partisanship. This is followed

71

by a reaction where support increases, decreases, or stays the same. Easton explains, "Specific support flows from the favorable attitudes and predisposition stimulated by outputs that are perceived by members of the society to meet their demands as they arise or in anticipation."[5] Clarifying this concept a decade later, Easton wrote that specific support is "closely related to what the political authorities do and how they do it."[6]

National tragedies and war generally increase the presidential support, otherwise known as the rally-around-the-flag phenomenon. Other influencing factors are economic conditions, policy orientations, peace, prosperity, and competence. As long as presidents are perceived to deliver on their promises, approval can grow. Various approval levels hint that the time is right to move on policy, maintain the status quo, or change the governing strategies.[7]

According to Lowi, the presidential campaign is a continuation of the personal relationship between the candidates and their popular base. However, it is exemplified by organizational strategies and party nomination. The campaign is the true nature of the "plebiscitary presidency-scale," proceeding in the following manner: campaign organization, primary participation, and the relationship between the president and the people. These factors all come together during the campaign to offer insight into how presidents react to public opinion and make policy decisions.[8]

The presidential campaign is an extension of the primary season. The national committee becomes the property of the nominee and serves as a functional titular head of the party. Candidates must maintain distance from the national committee as well as with the most recent president of their party. Most candidates want independents and opposite party affiliates to split their tickets. This requires tact and careful word management. At the same time, a presidential candidate must rise above the party or in the language of theater, be a "single."[9]

Being "single" limits personal appearances. Richard Nixon made a terrible mistake in 1960, vowing to make an appearance in every state of the Union. No one is likely to follow that, but all candidates mirrored Nixon in another way, which was to speak "over the heads" of the press by using television, and today, Twitter, Facebook, and a plethora of other social media techniques. At least half of all presidential campaign budgets are directed toward mass communications. Grassroots political campaigning such as knocking on doors and passing out bumper stickers and buttons has declined.[10]

Presidential candidates have achieved political presence before nomination. Most have usually had extensive political careers serving as senators, governors, or other high-level positions. Many candidates announce their candidacy fifteen months before an election. It may surprise the public, but many candidates have prepared for the long political journey. How the public interprets that is another matter. The 1976 election offers clues. Carter's initial approach was modest but in a short time made significant stylistic campaign changes.

Carter's initial persona revealed self-deprecating humor: a modest guest carrying a garment bag over his shoulder, antagonism to Washington politics, and hesitancy to make campaign promises. However, once the possibility of actually winning the Democratic presidential nomination became a reality, he began to exhibit a presidential aura. Carter adapted to the political circumstances and couched his campaign promises in political rhetoric. One study identified 111 promises Carter made during the primaries and election campaign. As Theodore White put it, these promises "were fair and decent promises, they embodied every hope of every group and institution that goodwill people had created in leaving the old system."[11]

Although Carter was not the first candidate to use high language, he was distinctly modern in making it personal. Nothing prepared him for an inflated and arrogant view of himself. Nothing had prepared him to state that the income tax was "a disgrace to the human race," or that he would put all agencies on a "zero-base budget." Nothing had prepared him to say that he would reorganize welfare, reach all the poor and mistreated, clean up the environment, and balance the budget within three years. The job and the process were forcing these changes upon him. This happened before the inauguration. With his cardigan sweater and the silencing of the band playing "Hail to the Chief," Carter tried to maintain the aura of modesty after he took office. But there was a new factor, and that was personality. This is something he shared with his predecessors as well as his successor.[12]

Schmertz, in his great *Oxford History of the American People*, cites historian Samuel Eliot Morison, who demonstrates another aspect of presidential strategy. Schmertz notes that "everything that [President] Washington said was repeated, everything he did was watched. No other subsequent President of the United States lived in such a glare of publicity. Morison wrote this passage in 1964, after the death of President John. F Kennedy for whom some called the first television President. Presidents and challengers are under intense scrutiny. At the dawn of the nation beginning, news travelled slowly and could take days if not weeks. Today political news is instantaneous and for some merciless."[13]

Media influence is so intense that sometimes it is impossible to distinguish the Oval Office from its institutional role. Schmertz labels media examination of the Oval Office as cynosure—meaning stage like, with settings surrounded by lights, microphones, photographers, and sleepless watchers. It is far from what the Founding Fathers may have imagined; the White House is no longer a home or a retreat—never quiet, still, or relaxing. The press is an eternal and vigilant presence.[14]

There is no period of presidential history devoid of media influence. Early critics viewed the presidency with a sense of disdain and intimidation.

There were no newspapers in Washington's day, and there was considerable fear that the presidency could morph into a kingship. Andrew Jackson was dubbed King Andrew I by the Whig Press. Sometimes the relationship was reciprocal. Whether muckraking journalists of the Progressive Period used Theodore Roosevelt, or whether T.R. used them is unclear. President Theodore Roosevelt was able to manipulate the media to advance his policies. Roosevelt established the first permanent White House press, the first daily interviews with reporters, the press secretary, and the first uniform management of White House news, meaning there was a strategy to choosing best news days. This is in stark contrast to earlier times. A legend persists from the Cleveland administration. One reporter won a five-dollar bet by calling the president on the newly installed telephone and asking whether there was any news. The president answered the telephone himself and told the reporter that there was no news, and therefore, the reporter could safely go to bed.[15]

Woodrow Wilson was the first president to schedule biweekly news conferences. Franklin Delano Roosevelt held over 900 press conferences during his thirteen -year presidential tenure. Yet in Roosevelt's case, he refused to be quoted directly and chided reporters who offered meritless questions. Roosevelt's "Fireside Chats" was an early but ingenious use of the new radio technology to advance his presidential goals. Eisenhower used television to garner support for his programs. However, it was Kennedy whose four televised debates with Nixon were crucial to his election success. Some would even say he made electronic media an art.[16]

In some ways, presidential personality has become more important than achievement. A president who charms and fascinates could be viewed as more important than one who advances the nation's goals. Evaluating presidential habits and tendencies is far easier than judging their public policy impact. This is a trap with hard-to-resist pressure from the media. Images supplant the need for detailed solutions. The media is also pressured to seek the largest audience for a given story. Whether about mass shootings, immigration, or impeachment proceedings, sensationalist news runs contrary to electoral diversity and pluralism. The United States is a large country, yet news is simplified.[17]

The danger is that the White House may become ineffective in addressing ambiguous and complex issues. Simplistic messages are easy for the press to understand and reconvey to the American public. However, this does not guarantee that the proposed solutions will be vetted in a democratic and ethical manner. Presidents and challengers must be tempered to offer valid perspectives. The caveat is that an unchecked White House could develop a distorted view of power.[18]

According to Saldin, the rise of the "rhetorical presidency" in the early 1900s was seen as a pivotal development. Early presidential theory posits that Theodore Roosevelt and Woodrow Wilson changed the executive policy landscape by diverging from the traditional restrained mode of presidential leadership to a more visible, popular direction rooted in public speaking. Yet their public speaking was more than rhetoric; it was dialogue that advanced nationalist causes at home and abroad.[19]

Developed in the late 1980s, the rhetorical presidency scholarship is central to the study of America's executive branch. Tulis distinguishes between the "old way" and the new way of presidential speech. "Since the presidencies of Theodore Roosevelt and Woodrow Wilson," Tulis asserts, "popular or mass rhetoric has become a principle tool of presidential governance." The "new way" presidents engage in practices that were once taboo: speaking directly to the people instead of Congress, giving more speeches and fewer written messages, addressing public policy issues, and routinely engaging in partisan politics, such as campaigning. This shift poses a dilemma for constitutional governance. Public appeals run the risk of undercutting the constitutionality of government, particularly Congress, and allowing public opinion to become the source of presidential authority.[20]

This model runs counter to the Founders' intentions. The Articles of Confederation demonstrate the need for executive power, even with inherent dangers. Alexander Hamilton's inaugural essay in the *Federalist* highlighted the concern. The Founders were wary of leadership based on public opinion and thought that excessive passionate appeals to the American people would result in overreliance on the mob's fickle and often ill-informed views. In the words of Hamilton, "The voice of the people has been said to be the voice of God, and however generally this maxim has been quoted and believed, it is not true in fact. The people are turbulent and changing; they seldom judge or determine right. Rhetoric tailored to the public risks mob rule and threatens the president's ability to deliberate.[21]

To counter demagoguery, the Founders sought important statesman qualities. Most notably, presidents must avoid becoming demagogues and speaking directly to the people about policy matters. Washington codified this norm by refusing to propose legislation for Congress, going no further than the generic support of a Bill of Rights. Therefore, Tulis argues, presidential rhetoric was restrained in the nineteenth century. Presidents rarely addressed policy matters, and when they did, their statements were conveyed directly to Congress often in writing.[22] Rhetoric delivered to the public focused on broad constitutional principles, lacking policy specificity.[23]

It was important to control and thereby preserve the office's unique independent position or what Jefferson called a "view of the whole ground." Several presidents valued independence. Presidents eager for a second term and those desperate to win the office operated from a distance and demonstrated disinterest in personal political advancement. Reelection speeches were awkward. As Tulis notes, "By feigning disinterest, candidates exemplified a thought that political campaigns were beneath their dignity. Presidential behavior emphasized the need for deliberation without emotion."[24]

According to Tulis, Andrew Johnson was the only exception to the "old way orthodoxy." Johnson went on a three-week speaking tour to promote his Reconstruction plan and directly appealed for public support while simultaneously attacking Congress. The tour and the president's belligerent approach backfired, leading to his impeachment and near removal from office. Johnson's debacle only solidified rhetorical norms for his immediate successors, who were firmly rooted in the "old way."[25]

Tulis argues that presidential rhetoric changed under Roosevelt and Wilson. Roosevelt's "middle way" was characterized by paying lip service to the Founders' provincial sentiments while ignoring the established behavioral norms they inculcated. Most unseemly were Roosevelt's overt "swings around the circle," in which he openly went "over the heads" of Congress to campaign for passage of the Hepburn Act, a key pillar of his Square Deal. Notably, though, Roosevelt ceased his advocacy once Congress began deliberating on the bill.[26]

Under the "new way," presidential-led energy and action in government outweighed the risks associated with popular leadership and demagoguery. Presidential speeches were directed toward the public rather than Congress, and presidents were expected to establish their own political agendas. Anything less could be construed as leadership failure. In the era of the rhetorical presidency, the ability to communicate effectively with the citizenry was critical. Many of Tulis's assertions have been challenged by other rhetorical presidency scholars. Critics argue that Tulis inaccurately characterized several nineteenth-century presidents. Richard Ellis's work, for instance, demonstrates that presidents including James Monroe (32–39), Martin Van Buren (65–69), and Zachary Taylor (74–82) exhibited "new way" behavior at times.[27]

According to Simon and Ostrom, the politics of prestige is comprised of six basic characteristics: Characteristic 1: While proscribed by the Framers of the Constitution, cultivating public support has become an inescapable necessity for the modern president; Characteristic 2: Presidential power and the president's standing in the opinion polls are inexorably intertwined; Characteristic 3: Public support is well-behaved so that its pattern over time is both understandable and predictable; Characteristic 4: Public support is a valuable predictable resource; Characteristic 5: Public support influences presidential behavior; and Characteristic 6: Public support influences both the process and product of national policymaking.[28]

The politics of prestige is an integral part of the presidency. The Constitution was based, in part, on the fear of public opinion and the power a leader might derive from the ability to arouse the public. For the framers, a government too dependent upon public opinion would invite tyranny and mob rule. Leadership strategies based upon public appeals would produce poorly qualified presidents and possibly open the door to "demagoguery and regime instability." Accordingly, the drafters sought to "establish institutions which could operate effectively without the immediate support of transient opinion." To this end, the president was insulated from public opinion. The Electoral College was designed to reduce the centrality of the public in the selection of presidents. The authority of the office would flow from the Constitution, and executive authority would be limited and checked by a diverse legislative branch.[29]

Several presidents were adamant in their unwillingness to accept the restrictions on popular leadership. This can be evidenced with Jefferson's use of the political party and the press to fashion a mass-based party. Theodore Roosevelt's use of "the bully pulpit" and Woodrow Wilson's "rhetorical presidency" held similar motivation strategies, part of the historical movement toward an increasingly broader idea of presidential constituency. According to Lowi, this movement culminated in Franklin Roosevelt's efforts to bypass traditional party organizations and establish a "direct, unmediated relationship between the president and the people." In a sense, each of these presidents believed that insulation from the public deprived them of their most potent political weapon.[30]

Second, the modern doctrine of presidential power provided an intellectual rationale for rejecting the insulation of the president. The major force of this doctrine was Woodrow Wilson, who argued that the separation of powers was a major defect that limited the government's capacity to solve problems. He regarded insulation of the president and parochialism of Congress as impediments to effective government. For Wilson, the vitality of government depended upon a president who actively engaged in popular leadership. The tasks of the Wilsonian president would be to articulate public concerns, shape opinion, and use it to overcome constraints.[31]

Jefferson, Jackson, Theodore Roosevelt, Wilson, and Franklin Roosevelt pursued ambitious policy agendas. Each cultivated public support and developed particular strategies. The rise of the "modern presidency" altered this approach. The presidency became institutionalized, meaning it was subject to legal requirements and regulations. This created the expectation that the president was obliged to present a policy agenda. Prior presidents had greater discretion whether or not to present an agenda.[32]

In the post-FDR period, presidential literature not only acknowledged the necessity of popular leadership but also developed presidential theories that identified public support. The writings that appeared between 1960 and 1980 decidedly describe these efforts during volatile times. This is noted with

Rossiter's "magnificent lion," Burns' Hamiltonian President," and Neustadt's power maximizing chief executive.[33]

Public support is closely related to presidential power and carefully evaluates presidential image, credibility, and competence. The public view of the president helps define the political arena where decisions are made. As Neustadt observes, "The prevalent impression of a president's public standing tends to set a tone and to define the limits of what Washingtonians do for him, or do to him."[34]

Washington politics is a formal decision-making authority fragmented among "multiple pockets of power"—the president, the Cabinet, congressional committees and subcommittees, executive bureaus and agencies—each pursuing their own objectives, each responsive to different constituencies, and each exercising checks upon the authority of others. In this setting, shared partisanship and formal lines of organizational authority offer little guarantee of cooperation in the formulation, passage, or implementation of policies. Different initiatives require different supporting coalitions, and success on one policy front neither ensures future successes nor extensions to other areas. Policy coalitions are thus fragile and transient. The ability to construct and maintain such alliances is a critical test of leadership.[35]

In *Presidential Power*, Neustadt suggests the power of the president is largely determined by the president's ability to persuade. Persuasion is the ability to elicit cooperation or acquiescence from rival decision makers. As Dahl notes, "The closest equivalent to the power relation is the causal relation." Presidential persuasion causes potential adversaries to act as allies. Viewed in this light, power is not automatically conferred upon the occupant of the White House. It is not constant during the tenure of a single president or across different presidents.[36] Power is ephemeral. It is also subjective. The effectiveness of presidential persuasion rests largely upon the perception of those who are potential targets of the president's efforts.[37]

Certain vantage points are associated with executive unilateral action. They provide the president with the authority to command (for instance, to remove Cabinet officers); in other instances, they give the president the advantage of the first move (for instance, submitting an annual budget to Congress). Neustadt's analysis clearly demonstrates that the use of prerogatives, while important, is limited. Seldom will the conditions necessary for the execution of command be met. Moreover, the use of prerogatives is often a last resort (like the veto) and signifies a failure to persuade (e.g., Truman's seizure of the steel mills).[38]

Reputation pertains to the judgments of other decision makers, the evaluation of the "Washington elite" based upon a presidential predisposition to play the "insider" game, protect himself, win allies, and maximize the political discomfort of adversaries. Prestige refers to the president's standing outside the Washington community, primarily his standing with the American public. Herein lies the importance of the opinion polls. The president's approval score is a vital piece of information that shapes the perception of Washington decision makers. As Neustadt argues, "Most members of the Washington community depend upon outsiders for support. In turn, public support serves as an integral component of power because it provides a president with leverage over other decision makers."[39]

The measurements of public support provide justification for a variety of judgments about an administration. The approval rating is often accompanied by a host of commentaries that attempt to decipher the "meaning" within the latest reading of public sentiment. Ratings have been employed to compare a president to his predecessors, to assess the image and credibility of the incumbent, and to judge the electoral prospects of the president and his party.

No poll question, however, has proven more interesting or important than the general performance item first introduced by the Gallup organization in 1938. With a frequency that is unmatched in political discourse, the Gallup Poll has posed the following question to cross- sections of the American Public: "Do you approve or disapprove of the way (name of incumbent) is handling his job as president?" This simply elicits a general evaluation of the president's conduct of office: approve, disapprove, or no opinion. The proportion of respondents who select the approve option is typically used as a measure of public support, prestige, or popularity of the president, and thus serves as general summary of the relationship between the president and the public.[40]

Presidential approval is responsive to environmental conditions and events. This *environmental connection* is comprised of three general types of factors. The first consists of outcomes from both the domestic and international arenas. These outcomes include the rates of inflation and unemployment, battle deaths during times of war, the level of international tension, and the legislative activity and success of the president.[41] The second factor pertains to salience. Prior research has demonstrated that public support is dependent on public support of outcomes. For example, the erosion of public support produced by a rising unemployment rate will depend upon the degree to which public concern is concentrated on the economy.[42]

The third type of influence on public support consists of presidentially relevant events. These consist of episodes that are (1) specific, dramatic, and sharply focused; (2) connect to the president; and (3) the object of extensive media coverage. The attention and effort devoted to the study of presidentially relevant events originate in the work of Mueller, who demonstrated that such episodes can trigger a "rally round the flag" effect that will produce a short-term burst of public support for the president.[43] Since Mueller's initial analysis, the rationale and range of episodes have expanded to include other approval-enhancing events as well as approval-diminishing events. Examples of the former include diplomatic initiatives (like Nixon's 1972 trip to the People's Republic of China) and even events, relating to the personal health and wellbeing of the president (like the attempted assassination of President Reagan). Instances of the latter include domestic unrest (like the urban violence in the summer of 1966), economic disruption (like the oil embargo of 1973), and scandals within an administration (like Watergate).[44]

Despite this, the connection between public support and presidential performance evaluations remain subject to debate. There are factors such as the president's public standing that exerts a marginal impact on presidential power. Roll and Cantril have argued that "popularity ratings represent little more than an artifact of the polling technique created in response to journalistic interest, and they certainly are not meaningful for guidance. Such observations assert that such have little political consequence."[45] Public support is tied to political outcomes and behaviors. If public support is unimportant in explaining outcomes, then, as Roll and Cantril suggest, presidents could be advised to ignore the polls and scholars encouraged to direct their attention elsewhere.[46]

Considerable evidence suggests that popular support impacts presidential outcomes. Simon and Ostrom evaluate presidential contests between 1952 and 1984. They demonstrate how the electoral fortunes of the president are tied to performance. Both Truman and Johnson suffered from low support and withdrew from their respective presidential races in the face of strong primary challenges. Ford and Carter secured their party's nomination only after lengthy and divisive primary battles.[47]

Electoral fortunes of the president and party are inextricably linked to retrospective voting, or how the president did over the past four years. Simon and Ostrom show that public support is matched by predictive capability. Public support levels correlate with presidential electoral success. This suggests public support will influence presidential behavior. As Neustadt observes,

> the weaker his apparent popular support, the more his cause in Congress may depend on the negatives at his disposal like the veto or 'impounding'. He may not be left helpless, but his options are reduced, his opportunities diminished, his freedom for maneuver checked in the degree that Washington conceives him unimpressive to the public. Variations in presidential support may not only expand or contract the set of feasible alternatives in a given situation, but also enhance or reduce the value of those actions.

For these reasons, public support can be expected to influence presidential decisions about agendas, strategies, and use of prerogatives.[48]

The president's capacity to guide and influence the policy-making process in an innovative, comprehensive way varies with public support. High-level public support provides the president with discretion to accept the risk and the credibility to direct public pressure toward Congress. But as support declines, the president will become less risk acceptant. The boldness of initiatives will be reduced, and policy making will assume an incremental character with conflict centering on the adjustment of "fine tuning" existing programs. When support declines well below 50 percent, the president is in danger of becoming politically impotent. He will be viewed as an electoral liability by members of his party and will lack credibility with the public. In turn, this will fragment the legislative process, and the end result will be poorly coordinated, particularistic policy making dominated by subgovernments.[49]

Public support reveals that presidents have an incentive to manage, manipulate, or otherwise control how they are evaluated. Maintaining public support has become a key instrumental goal of the modern president. This incentive becomes even more compelling in light of two factors. First, some presidential resources have declined in value. The importance of the political party, both as an organization useful to the president and as a "tie that binds" decision makers to presidential goals, has eroded. The role of reputation, another factor in Neustadt's "power equation," is also subject to question. Because the public has grown increasingly distrustful of politicians, political experience appears to have become a less valued asset in recent presidential contests.[50]

Recent research addresses the question of whether and how presidents influence. There are three distinct schools of thought. The first focuses on the economic determinants of popular support and includes studies of the political business cycle and economic management. The objective is to ascertain the sensitivity of public support to economic outcomes and investigate the policy instruments that can be employed to regulate or manipulate these outcomes. A second branch concentrates on the more "event-based" influences. These include general studies of popular leadership along with research investigating alternative strategies for triggering the "rally effect." The third school of thought challenges the efficacy of any strategy and asserts that public support is inherently unmanageable. The most prominent example of this argument is presented by Lowi in *The Personal President*. Lowi's "second law" asserts that insofar as pleasing a mass constituency is concerned, "the probability of failure is always tending toward 100 percent."[51]

According to Powell, the national party conventions attract a considerable amount of attention. For example, Republicans are often credited with substantially aiding their victory in 1980 by selecting Detroit as their convention site. Conventional wisdom holds that Ronald Reagan used the Detroit convention as a way to reach out to Midwestern, working-class whites who had traditionally voted Democratic.[52] Similar stories exist about other party conventions. In their discussion of the site-selection process, Nelson Polsby and Aaron Wildavsky explain, "Political considerations are often important: San Francisco was chosen by Democrats in 1984 partly because the party was having trouble in the West . . . In 1988 both parties wanted to bolster their strength in the South. . . . so the Democrats selected Atlanta and the Republicans, New Orleans."[53] Cities in large states, especially those expected to be competitive in the fall are logical choices. According to Stephen Wayne, these same factors weighed heavily in the Democrats' choice of Los Angeles for their 2,000 convention and the Republicans' choice of Philadelphia. Both cities were located in states and regions critical to that party's success.[54]

The second factor that should be examined is the home states and regions of presidential and vice presidential candidates. A number of anecdotal stories indicate that elections can be won or lost depending on whether parties achieve proper geographic balance on their tickets. Perhaps the most notable example of this is the 1960 election. According to political lore, John F. Kennedy would not have won the presidency if not for his shrewd choice of Lyndon Johnson as a running mate. Johnson is said to have delivered eighty-two Southern electoral votes to the Democrats that could not have been won otherwise, because white Southerners had suspicions about Kennedy's presumed liberalism on racial issues. In the words of Polsby and Wildavsky, John F. Kennedy chose Lyndon Johnson to help gather Southern votes, especially in Texas; Republicans chose Henry Cabot Lodge of Massachusetts in 1960 to offset the Democratic Party advantage in the Northeast. Such accounts are common for just about every campaign over the past century. According to William Mayer, there has only been a handful of major party tickets formed without some regard for geographic consideration.[55]

The electoral success of candidates in their home states and regions has received some attention in the literature, but not within a systematic framework that controls for other state indicators. Prior studies have generated mixed feelings about the effects of localism and regionalism, because they have examined different time periods and used models with very different specifications. In general, candidates have been found to enjoy a modest electoral boost in their home states but with some variation depending upon partisanship, region, state size, and whether the candidate was running for president or vice president.[56]

Accordingly, the contrast between the predictability of presidential elections and the variability of early polls is viewed as evidence that campaigns provide crucial information to voters. This information enables voters to select the candidate that best corresponds with their "fundamentals." Further, "the function of the campaign is to inform voters about the fundamental variables and their appropriate weights. This means voters gather and use increasing amounts of information over the course of a campaign, with the largest increase occurring just before election day." This theory of campaign enlightenment accounts for the variability of early polls as well as the predictability of election outcomes. Campaign learning suggests that many Americans are politically uninformed.[57]

Scholars have identified several additional mechanisms by which campaigns may help voters vote based on fundamentals such as party identification. Campaigns reduce uncertainty if knowledge is transparent. For instance, voters want to know the candidate's characteristics and where they stand on issues. Voters are then better able to identify the candidate with their preferences. Another perspective suggests that campaigns influence voters through priming by emphasizing some considerations and ignoring others.[58]

Lenz offers a contrasting perspective, arguing that voters are merely updating their issue preferences to match their preferred candidate's. Although Lenz's argument reverses the causal arrow, campaign information still serves to increase the relationship between the fundamentals and voter choice. Despite these differences, each perspective focuses on information provided by the campaign. As Peterson explains, "Each theory shares the same basic function of the campaign. It provides information to the electorate, which leads voters to change how they weigh determinants of vote choice."[59]

Doubts about the effects of presidential campaigns on presidential elections arise from several sources. One notable principle is "Farley's Law," an observation attributed to Franklin Roosevelt's campaign manager James A. Farley by historian Gil Troy. Farley's Law held that "most elections were decided before the campaign began."[60] Some of the earliest scientific voting raised questions about the impact of presidential campaigns. These studies found that the net change in vote intentions during the campaign was small and that most voters made their voting decisions early in the election year. Later research emphasized that most voters enter the campaign with strong partisan attachments that usually guide their vote decisions.

Accompanying this research was a theoretical explanation for why campaigns should have minimal effects on voters. Other research placed greater emphasis on issue voting by focusing on voters' retrospective evaluations of the previous administration. Such research suggests that campaigns play only a minor role in voter decisions. Most recently, doubts about the overall impact of campaigns have been fueled by the success of presidential election forecasting models that have accurately predicted election results before the start of the campaign.[61]

According to Campbell, early studies of presidential voting suggest that campaigns marginally affect the vote. The first was a landmark sociological exploration of voting called *The People's Choice* first published in 1944, and was a study based on a panel survey in Erie County, Ohio, during the

1940 presidential campaign between Democrat president Franklin Roosevelt
and his Republican opponent, Wendell Willkie. The main panel of survey
respondents was questioned at seven points over the course of the election
year, monthly from May to November.[62]

The People's Choice found that the principal effect of the campaign was
to reinforce or stabilize preferences, rather than change them. Most vote
intentions of individual survey respondents in November were the same or
about the same as they had been six months earlier in May. About half of
those surveyed (49 percent) did not change their vote intention in any way
between May and election day. Of the remaining respondents who changed
their preferences did so only marginally. Only 8 percent definitively changed
their minds. These "party changers" initially indicated a vote intention for
one party's presidential candidate and later favored the opposing candidate.[63]

Although about half of the electorate changed their vote intentions in some
way between May and November (using a seemingly generous definition of
"change"), this overstates the origins of significant preference during the general election campaign. Both *The People's Choice* as well as the follow-up
study *Voting*, which examined the 1948 election, found that nearly four out of
five voters say they made up their minds by August of the election year, after
the second nominating convention and just before the traditional kickoff of
the general election campaign.[64] A study called *The American Voter*, examined the 1952 and 1956 elections, and found that a majority of voters claimed
to have reached an early decision. Subsequent studies have confirmed the
prevalence of early vote decisions.[65]

Doubts about campaign effects on election results were highlighted by
The American Voter's findings of the pervasiveness, stability, and impact of
party identification on partisan attitudes and vote choices. An electorate that
is highly partisan, that holds firmly to its party identifications through many
presidential campaigns, and that views and evaluates political events, policy
issues, and political candidates in partisan terms does not leave much room
for the effects of a particular campaign. The fundamental stability of partisanship is at odds with the mercurial nature of a campaign.

The path-breaking collection of studies in *Elections and the Political
Order* provided additional grounds for skepticism about campaign effects.
Philip Converse's concept of normal vote, an aggregate baseline measure of
partisanship's effect on the national vote, suggested a stability in political
judgements that minimized the likely impact of short-term campaign effects.[66]

Complementing the evidence of long-term partisan effects on the vote
was evidence that short-term forces in elections made only marginal effects.
Angus Campbell laid out the conceptual framework by using the normal vote
to classify elections. Donald Stokes examined the variation in the national
vote around the normal vote to determine the likelihood of a deviating

presidential election. His analysis determined that the minority party had only about one chance in four (27 %) of winning a two-party popular vote majority. Moreover, since pre-campaign factors, such as an initial assessment of the presidential candidates or economic circumstances before the campaign season, probably contributed to the chances of a deviating election, the likelihood of the campaign itself swaying voters from their partisan predisposition seemed rather remote.[67]

Another study in *Elections and the Political Order* provided an individual theory of political information processing that supplied yet additional reasons why campaigns have minimal effects. Philip Converse developed a theory to explain why partisan attitudes remained stable despite the heavy flow of political information during campaigns, much of which is intended to disturb or change preexisting attitudes and vote intentions.[68]

The theory of minimal effects is built on four interrelated and eminently reasonable premises. The first two involve the effects of an individual's interest in politics. The first premise it that a person's political involvement or innate interest in politics positively affects how much he or she knows about politics. People naturally tend to know more about what they find interesting. Second, a person's level of interest in politics positively affects how much new politically relevant information is absorbed. People naturally follow more closely subjects in which they are interested, allowing them to acquire and understand more new information about those subjects.[69]

The third and fourth premises of the minimal effects theory address the likelihood of changing opinions. On the one hand, if a person knows a great deal about something, the position is likely to be more definite. On the other hand, views that are not anchored may be more easily changed. The final premise of the minimal effects theory is that acquiring new information increases the likelihood of attitude change. New information is more likely to challenge preexisting views. Conversely, if a person learns nothing new about a subject, there is no reason to change opinions.[70]

There is substantial research indicating that that many voters decide over issue preference. If a voter favors more government spending on education, for instance, then he or she would most likely vote for the candidate believed to also hold that policy view, all things being equal. Issue voting suggests that campaigns make a great deal of difference. After all, much of the candidates' campaigns are devoted to the discussion of issues. Even the much-maligned negative campaigning involves issue content, which portrays the opposition in an unfavorable manner.[71]

According to Campbell, campaign effects are not only limited but predictable in advance of the campaign. Although there are outlier events, most campaign effects are systematic and anticipatory.[72]

Another fundamental aspect is the economy. The public is likely to keep the president's party in office during periods of prosperity but may be reluctant if the economy has been weak. The voters' evaluations of how an administration has affected their economic wellbeing undoubtedly affects vote decision making during the campaign, but economic conditions may have broader implications as well. Good economic times allow voters to believe the best about the in-party candidate on noneconomic matters as well as on strictly economic issues. In contrast, a weak economy may sour the public on the president's party. Voters may not only hold the in-party responsible for the nation's economic woes but may also be inclined to believe the incumbent party has underperformed.[73]

In essence, presidential campaigns are predictable. A large number of voters have made up their minds before the campaign begins. Nothing in the campaign, barring perhaps cataclysmic events, can change vote intentions. Some voters may waver over the course of a campaign, but their votes are all but cast before the campaign gets underway. In any election year, a substantial number of voters are already committed to vote for a particular presidential candidate before the campaign begins. The campaign can only realistically hope to change the preferences of a subset of voters who lack a pre-campaign commitment or whose commitment is so tenuous that they might be persuaded to change.[74]

While long-term partisan commitments secure voters prior to the campaign, others may reach a pre-campaign vote decision based on the evaluations of preceding presidential administrations. Independent voter and some politically disenfranchised groups may be swayed by reactions to a particular. The experience of these voters with the in-party's administration is a tangible basis for reaching a verdict of whether to keep that party in office or turn it out.[75]

Information introduced during the campaign stands little chance of reversing preexisting views, especially those grounded in personal experience. Voters lived through an administration and may have felt policy directly or indirectly. They may feel that the campaign offers little that they do not already know or that the campaign would only distort what they already know. Hard information and information learned through direct observation are more convincing than the relatively soft information of charges, countercharges, claims, and promises.[76]

Voters should be skeptical of campaign promises and charges. Candidates make many promises, which are often hard to fulfill. Voters may dismiss campaign promises and charges that conflict with what they already know from experience. If voters think that a candidate acted dishonestly, then it is unlikely for the candidate to recover. Past performance establishes campaign credibility, and voters know much of this prior to the start of the campaign season.[77]

Incumbency is advantageous and is linked to the party or office in power. In short, incumbency provides opportunities and resources not normally afforded to other candidates. They can be used effectively to garner votes or they can be squandered. Presidents who avoid major policy failures or are fortunate to hold office during peace and prosperity will be rewarded by voters. Some of these voters will decide early whether or not to renew the president's contract. Others may be ambivalent of incumbency and may still be hesitant to support a specific candidate.[78] It is also tied to early voters and undecideds.

There are several reasons why campaigns favor incumbent presidents. According to incumbency theory, presidential advantages include (1) the trappings of the office and the role of the president as national leader; (2) inertia among otherwise undecided voters; (3) the particular advantage that first-term presidential incumbents have in communicating a strong campaign message to voters; and (4) the easier road that incumbent presidents often travel to receive their presidential nomination.[79]

The primary advantage of incumbency is that, as the leaders of the nation, the incumbent's stature in the eyes of many voters is higher than that of a mere politician. Patriotic feelings become intertwined with their impressions of the president as candidate. It is difficult, if not impossible, to separate feelings about the office from feelings about the current occupant.[80]

This creates an unusual phenomenon. From the candidate's perspective, all of the pomp and pageantry of the office can be used while at the same time preserving the appearance of rising above politics by not campaigning—the familiar Rose Garden strategy. This means a president acts natural and still appears presidential. Presidents can claim credit for specific accomplishments and government largess, whether delivering disaster relief to flood victims or appearing with mayors who have been awarded additional federal funds to increase the size of their police force in a war against crime.[81]

Voter inertia also works to the advantage of incumbent presidents. If voters are in doubt about which candidate to support, they may give the benefit of the doubt to the incumbent candidate. The burden of proof rests with the challenger, who has to make a convincing case for reversing the voting pattern. Moreover, given the general psychological positivity bias (most people prefer to focus on the good rather than the bad), the challenger has a particularly difficult job devising a convincing campaign message to displace an incumbent president.[82]

A third major advantage is limited to incumbents whose party has been in the White House for only a single term. There are two great themes in presidential elections. The first is the stability theme (stay the course or don't change horse in the middle of the stream). The stability theme's message is that the administration should have more time to enact and implement its program. The change theme, the second theme, suggests that one party has held power too long; we've tried it their way and there are still problems, so let's try something new. These are, respectively, the insider and outsider arguments for power.[83]

Presidents in campaigns routinely employ the "Rose Garden Strategy." In essence, the incumbent president campaigns for election by simply appearing presidential, or campaigning without overtly campaigning. The intent is to have the media and the public witness the president doing the job. The president is to be seen by voters as not merely another candidate but a national and world leader. Photo ops of the president meeting with other national and international leaders at the White House are staged to pick up political advantage. A suitable spin of every official presidential act is passed along to the press for public consumption.[84] Being seen simply doing the job, the president can campaign while appearing above politics and at the same time, can deny the opponent the national stage as an equal contender for the office.[85]

While the Rose Garden strategy suggests a non-campaign approach, the essence of the strategy is much broader: to connect the candidate with the office in a more casual manner. Presidential image is critical and the Rose Garden strategy is a way to achieve positive public approval.[86]

Wolak shifts the debate to regionalism and the Electoral College. She states that due to the Electoral College, presidential candidates have incentives to concentrate their energies and resources in strategic geographic areas. There are numerous influences. One is media driven. In the battleground areas, thousands of presidential ads are aired, while the least competitive region can pass the campaign season without a single ad.[87]

A second source of influence is the allocation of presidential time, as battlegrounds are more likely to be visited by the presidential and vice presidential candidates. While Florida saw over eighty-five campaign appearances from the presidential and vice presidential candidates in 2000, thirteen other states were not visited at all by presidential candidates during the general electoral season. The distinctiveness of battlegrounds is also a product of partisan divisions that draw candidates to these regions. Battleground states are characterized by partisan diversity—a close division between Democrats and Republicans, as well as a base of voters interested in but uncommitted to a particular candidate. This party competitiveness translates into more active party support systems and greater chances of citizens confronting challenges in social networks.[88]

Wolak's findings offer important insight about battleground states. She states that in considering the pathways of campaign influence, the expectation is that exposure to candidate messages prompts interest, which is then channeled into information gains and political action. However, she explains that the standard expectations are not compelling. Citizens are cognizant of the changes that campaigns bring to their information environment; residents of battleground states report greater exposure to campaign ads on television and more frequent campaign contact from political parties and other groups.[89]

These results highlight the limits of battleground influence. While media accounts suggest that Electoral College strategies produce dramatic differences in citizen reaction to presidential races, it is often presumed that campaigns have influence by catching the interest of voters and motivating them to pursue greater engagement. These results suggest that information gains arguably reflect passive learning from campaign advertising, and thus, campaign strategies must follow other routes. Yet mobilization to action seems less driven by specific campaign events than levels of state mobilization and outreach.[90] The differences between battleground and non-battleground states reflect not only allocation of resources but also the underlying partisan nature of the state. In all, the story of battleground influence is a nuanced one, conditioned on a kind of presidential contest, the nature of each state's context, and the individual habits and predispositions of the voters.[91]

McClurg and Holbrook find that voters behave in a more predictable fashion in intense campaign states than in low intensity states. A key difference is how states structure voting. McClurg and Holbrook also found that presidential campaigns enhance the effects of retrospective presidential evaluations and partisanship on the eventual vote choice in 1992 and on race and ideology in 1988. Also of interest is that interpretation of the cross-election differences suggests a link between the choice of message used in campaigns and the types of fundamentals significant for voting in battleground states.[92]

Language intensity is most commonly defined as "the quality of language which indicates the degree to which the speaker's attitude toward a concept deviates from neutrality."[93] For example, when Herbert Hoover called the New Deal "Fascism," "despotism," and "the poisoning of Americanism,"[94] he was using high-intensity language on the presidential campaign trail. Language intensity deviates from neutrality in two linguistic ways: (1) directness toward the audience and (2) emotionalism of word choice.[95] Clementson et al. write, "Most researchers have manipulated language intensity as a combination of language specificity and non-obscene emotional intensity." High-intensity, direct language includes personalized, specific, assertive messages explicitly directed at an audience. Low-intensity, indirect messages are ambiguous, unclear, and imprecise. Nonobscene, emotional intensity involves extremity in word choice through exaggeration or inflated adjectives. For example, in a high-intensity language discourse, a politician might say, "This election is the most important election of your life." And as an example of a low-intensity message of indirect, unemotional language, a politician might say, "This election presents a choice between two contrasting visions for our country."[96]

Despite a relative dearth of research in the literature, that the persuasiveness of language intensity would depend on the circumstances of the communicative transaction seems intuitive. Conjectures about an interaction between situations and language can be traced back to the Palo Alto group, which noted that "certain situations" call for varying directness and intensity in messages. More specifically relevant to political communication, a theory of presidential influence posits that the U.S. president succeeds rhetorically through persuasive language employed in concert with the situation.[97]

In another vein, Holbrook offers interesting insight about campaigns. The campaign is able to influence public opinion by performing its primary function, disseminating information. The campaign events do not influence public opinion simply because they occur. Instead, they derive their influence from the amount and type of influence they generate. In addition to media coverage of specific events, information is also provided through campaign advertisements. One way contemporary campaigns differ from forty years ago is that television advertisements now represent the biggest expenditure of most campaigns. Campaign information can be obtained much easier today. Since 1960, Electoral College change is more likely linked to voter conversion than mass mobilization.[98]

As Popkin states, campaigns make a difference because voters have limited information about government and uncertainty about the consequences of policies. If voters had full information and no uncertainty, they would not be open to influence from others, and hence, there would be no campaigns. In reality, they do not know very much about what government is doing or is capable of doing. Thus, voters are open to influence by campaigners who offer more information or better explanations of the ways in which government activities affect them.[99]

Popkin is not alone in his argument about the importance of campaigns as agents of information. Salmore and Salmore posit that one of the results of the decline of partisanship is that parties are used increasingly less as a source of information about candidates. Instead, campaigns are replacing parties as a source of information about candidates. This theme is echoed in Wattenberg's thesis about the rise of candidate-centered campaigns. One cynical view holds that the information generated by campaigns is so important that campaign consultants have the ability to easily manipulate candidate image and public opinion toward candidates.[100]

Gelman and King assign importance to information. They note that voters learn about the campaign through the media, which report on campaign events, and then adjust their preferences accordingly. Through the information generated by campaigns and provided by the media, voters are able to form enlightened preferences.[101] Although Gelman and King make a strong case for the importance of information, they also find that information only supports the candidate voters would have chosen based on their political predispositions. This occurs because of the balanced nature of campaign information; if all candidates are waging serious campaigns, the information generated is likely to have a canceling-out effect. If Gelman and King are correct, then campaigns are most likely to have a real effect on election outcomes when there exists an *information asymmetry* between the two campaigns, either because of biased reporting or because one campaign was run better than the other.[102]

Accurately depicting the role of the campaign is difficult. Clearly, partisan predispositions and retrospective evaluations appear to dominate the individual voting decision, and aggregate outcomes appear to be driven by evaluations of the incumbent party's performance. Part of the problem with addressing the issue of whether campaigns matter lies in defining what it means to "matter." All too often, it is assumed that for campaigns to be relevant, they have to determine the election outcome. If what we mean by "matter" is more broadly construed, however, it is easier to find evidence of significant campaign effects. The panel studies of Lazarsfeld et al. and Finkel found that a small percentage of the population (8 percent in 1940 and 4.8 percent in 1980) actually change their mind during a campaign. These "converted" voters may represent a small percentage of the voting public, but they also represent an artifact of the campaign. According to Lazarsfeld et al. and Finkel, the more likely effect of the campaign is to reinforce or activate latent partisan dispositions. Typically, the small rates of conversion and the reinforcement and activation functions of the campaign are used to illustrate the inefficacy of presidential campaigns. One could argue, however, that activation and reinforcement are important parts of the voting decision and that even small rates of conversion can be important.[103]

Holbrook states that candidates can expect a bump in public support following their party's nominating convention. The origin of this bump lies in the ability of the campaign to dominate the media and to receive generally positive coverage during the campaign period. Holbrook found that press coverage does take on a net positive tone for the convening party. By providing the party with a relatively uncontested stage on which to present their candidate, the conventions provide a rare opportunity for the campaigns to reach voters. In most cases, this opportunity translates into positive movement in the polls.[104]

But some conventions clearly generate more movement than others; some bumps are substantial, whereas others are modest. In particular, the party holding the first convention traditionally experiences a larger postconvention surge than the party holding the second convention. Part of the explanation is that the information provided by the first convention is of more value to voters, because political information is scarcer earlier in the process and most voters have relatively little information about the nominee from the challenging party. The message conveyed by the convention can also affect the popular response of the convention.[105]

Holbrook finds real limits to the potential effects of conventions on public opinion. On the one hand, the effects of conventions are limited by the potential for improvement in the polls, referred to here as equilibrium balance. If a candidate is doing better than expected in the preconvention polls, there is little room for improvement and the convention bump is likely to be modest. On the other hand, if a candidate is doing substantially worse than expected in the preconvention polls, there is a larger reservoir of untapped support waiting to be activated and the convention bump is likely to be of a larger magnitude. The second limitation on convention effects has less to do with the magnitude of the bump and more to do with the potential for influencing the election outcome. Large convention bumps in some years are not necessarily more important to the eventual outcome than smaller bumps in other years.[106]

One must also consider momentum. Momentum effects, also known as *bandwagon* effects, occur when increases or decreases in a candidate's poll standing, perhaps as a result of a campaign event, generate more or less support for the candidate. In short, success generates more success. Not much is known about momentum in general election contests. Most of the existing research on momentum is based on small-sample experimented studies and has produced mixed results. Most of what we know about momentum in real-world contests is based on presidential primary election research. Momentum is a key variable in explaining success in the primary election process. In primary elections, momentum translates into viability, which translates into increased media attention, and ultimately, increased fundraising ability. General elections, however, are different from primary elections. First, in primary elections, momentum is gained by winning early primaries and generating attention and support for later primaries. In general elections, momentum is gained not from early election victories but from doing well, or at least better than expected. Another difference between primaries and general elections is that primaries involve several candidates, many of who are relatively unknown to voters. Most general election campaigns, however, involve two major party candidates about whom voters usually have more information. Because information about candidates is scarcer in primary elections, it is reasonable to assume that information generated by increased media coverage is more important to primary voters than to general election voters.[107]

Another possible explanation for the momentum effect considers not the value voters place on supporting a winner but the way political and media elites react to poll numbers. First, potential campaign contributors may feel more comfortable betting on a perceived winner, making them more forthcoming with contributions that might strengthen the campaign. Perhaps more important, however, is the way the media respond to poll results. There is some tendency for the media to treat candidates differently depending on their standing in the polls.[108]

Good poll numbers may influence voters directly or indirectly. Whatever the mechanism, momentum plays a role in the dynamics of general election campaigns. According to Holbrook, both consumer sentiment and presidential popularity serve as good measures of the political and economic climate of the country during and across election campaigns. Yet in addition to the state of the economy and presidential popularity, events occurring in the national or international political arena might spill over into the presidential campaign. In other words, events occurring outside the campaign might have an influence on the standing of the candidates. For example, if some type of international incident or crisis involving the United States occurs, voters might rally around the president, benefiting the incumbent party presidential candidate. On the other hand, a scandal involving members of the administration could hurt the incumbent party candidate in the court of public opinion.[109]

In the end, political campaigns are wrought by opportunity and obstacles. The above section offers a modern interpretation of these challenges. Next, the abovementioned theoretical framework will be applied to the Hoover case study and the 1928 and 1932 elections. The elements evaluated will include (1) media, (2) campaign strategies, (3) political trust, (4) momentum, (5) bandwagon effect, (6) incumbency, (7) Rose Garden strategy, and (8) retrospective voting. Additionally, Farley's Law and the theory of minimal change will be integrated into the analysis to offer insight into the challenges Herbert Hoover faced before and after the Great Mississippi Flood of 1927. This will also help explain the presidential outcomes of 1928 and 1932.

NOTES

1. Daniel E. Ponder, *Studies In The Modern Presidency: Presidential Leverage, Presidents Approval, and the American State* (Stanford University Press, 2018).
2. Ponder, *Studies.*
3. Ibid.
4. Ibid.
5. Ibid.
6. Ibid.
7. Paul J. Quirk, "Politicians Do Pander: Mass Opinion, Polarization, and Lawmaking," *The Forum* 7, no. 4 (1994): Article 10, https://doi.org/10.2202/1540 -8884.1343.
8. Theodore Lowi, "The State in Political Science. How We Become What We Study," *American Political Science Review* 86, no. 1 (1992): 1–7, https://doi.org/10 .2307/1964011.

9. Ponder, *Studies*.

10. Ibid.

11. Ibid.

12. Ibid.

13. Hebert Schmertz, "The Media and the Presidency," *Presidential Studies Quarterly* 16, no. 1 (1986): 11–21, https://www.jstor.org/stable/27550307.

14. Schmertz, "The Media," 11–21.

15. Ibid.

16. Ibid.

17. Ibid.

18. Ibid.

19. Robert Saldin, "William McKinley and the Rhetorical Presidency," *Presidential Studies Quarterly* 41, no. 1 (2011): 119–34, https://doi.org/10.1111/j .1741-5705.2010.03833.x.

20. Jeffrey K. Tulis, *The Rhetorical Presidency* (Princeton, NJ: Princeton University Press, 1987).

21. Tulis, *The Rhetorical Presidency*.

22. Ibid.

23. Ibid.

24. Ibid.

25. Ponder, *Studies*.

26. Ibid.

27. Richard J. Ellis, *The Development of the American Presidency*, 2nd edition (New York: Routledge, 2012).

28. Dennis M. Simon and Charles W. Ostrom, Jr., "The Politics of Prestige: Popular Support and the Modern Presidency," *Presidential Studies Quarterly* 18, no. 4 (1988): 741–59, https://www.jstor.org/stable/40574727.

29. Simon and Ostrom, "The Politics," 741–759.

30. Ibid.

31. Ibid.

32. Ibid.

33. Ibid.

34. Ponder, *Studies*.

35. Ibid.

36. Robert A. Dahl. *Preface to Democratic Theory* (Chicago, IL: University of Chicago Press, 1956).

37. Richard Neustadt, *Presidential Power* (New York: Wiley, 1960).

38. Simon and Ostrom, "The Politics," 741–759.

39. Ibid.

40. Ibid.

41. Ibid.

42. Ibid.

43. Ibid.

44. Ponder, *Studies*, 1–32.

45. Ibid.

46. Roll and Cantrill, *Polls: Their Use and Misuse in Politics* (New York: Basic Books, 1972).

47. Simon and Ostrom, "The Politics," 741–759.

48. Ibid.

49. Ibid.

50. Ibid.

51. Theodore Lowi, *The Personal President: Power Invested, Promise Unfulfilled* (Cornell University Press, 1986).

52. Lowi, *The Personal.*

53. Ibid.

54. Ibid.

55. Ibid.

56. Ibid.

57. Peter K. Enns and Brian Richman, "Presidential Campaigns and Fundamentals Reconsidered," *Journal of Politics* 75, no. 3 (2013): 803–20, https://doi.org/10.1017/S0022381613000522.

58. Andrew Gelman and Gary King, "Why Are American Presidential Election Campaign Polls so Variable When the Votes Are so Predictable?" *British Journal of Political Science* 23, no. 4 (1993): 409–51, https://doi.org/10.1017/S0007123400 006682.

59. Gabriel S. Lenz, "Learning and Opinion Change, Not Priming: Reconsidering the Priming Hypothesis," *American Journal of Political Science* 53, no. 4 (2009): 821–37, https://doi.org/10.1111/j.1540-5907.2009.00403.x.

60. Gil Troy, *See How They Ran: The Changing Role of the Presidential Candidate*, revised and expanded edition (Cambridge, MA: Harvard University Press, 1996).

61. Troy, *See How They Ran.*

62. James Campbell, *The American Campaign: U.S. Presidential Campaigns and the National Vote* (Texas A & M College Station, 2000).

63. Campbell, *The American Campaign.*

64. Bernard B. Berelson, Paul Lazarsfeld, and William N. McPhee, *Voting* (Chicago: University of Chicago Press, 1954).

65. Angus Campbell et al., *The American Voter* (New York: Wiley, 1960).

66. Campbell, *The American Campaign.*

67. Donald E. Stokes, "Some Dynamic Elements of Contests for the Presidency," *American Political Science Review* 60 (1966): 19–28, https://doi.org/10.2307/195380.

68. Campbell, *The American Campaign.*

69. Ibid.

70. Ibid.

71. Ibid.

72. Ibid.

73. Ibid.

74. Ibid.

75. Ibid.

76. Ibid.

77. Ibid.

78. Ibid.

79. Ibid.

80. Ibid.

81. Ibid.

82. Ibid.

83. Ibid.

84. Ibid.

85. Theodore White, *The Making of the President* (New York: Athenum, 1961).

86. Campbell, *The American Campaign*.

87. Jennifer Wolak, "The Consequences of Presidential Battleground Strategies for Citizen Engagement," *Political Science Quarterly* 59, no. 3 (2006): 353–61, https ://doi.org/10.1177/106591290605900303.

88. Wolak, "The Consequences," 353–61.

89. Ibid.

90. Ibid.

91. Ibid.

92. Scott D. McClurg and Thomas M. Holbrook, "Living in a Battleground; Presidential Campaigns and Fundamental Predictors of Vote Choice," *Political Research Quarterly* 62, no. 3 (2009): 495–06, https://doi.org/10.1177/10659129083 19575.

93. John Waite Bowers, "Language Intensity, Social Introversion, and Attitude Change," *Speech Monographs* 30 (1963): 345–52, https://doi.org/10.1080/036377 563093753380.

94. James L. Sundquist, *Dynamics of the Party System: Alignment and Realignment of Political Parties in the United States*, revised edition (Washington, DC: Brookings Institution, 1983).

95. James Bradac, John W. Bowers, and John A. Courtright, "Three Language Variables in Communication Research: Intensity, Immediacy, and Diversity," *Human Communication Research* 5 (1979): 257–69, doi:10.1111/j.1468-2958.1979. tb00639.x.

96. David E. Clementson, Paola Pascual-Ferra, and Michael J. Beatty, "When Does a Presidential Campaign Seem Presidential and Trustworthy? Campaign Messages Through the Lens of Language Expectancy Theory," *Presidential Studies Quarterly* 46, no. 3 (2016): 592–617, https://doi.org/10.1111/psq.12299.

97. Clementson, Pascual-Ferra, and Beatty, "When Does," 592–617.

98. Thomas Holbrook, *Do Campaigns Matter?* (Sage, 1996).

99. Samuel Popkin, *The Reasoning Voter: Communication and Persuasion in Presidential Campaigns* (Chicago, IL: University of Chicago Press, 1994).

100. Barbara Salmore and Stephen Salmore, *Candidates, Parties and Campaigns*, 2nd ed (Washington, DC: CQ Press, 1989).

101. Gelman and King, "Why Are American," 409–51.

102. Clementson, Pascual-Ferra, and Beatty, "When Does," 592–617.

103. Paul Lazarsfeld, Bernard Berelson, and Helen Gaudet. *The People's Choice.* (New York: Duell, Sloane & Pearce, 1944).

104. Holbrook, *Do Campaigns.*

105. Ibid.

106. Ibid.

107. Campbell, *The American Campaign.*

108. Thomas E. Patterson, *The Press and Its Missed Assignment in the Election of 1988*, ed. Michael Nelson (Washington, DC: CQ Press, 1989).

109. Holbrook, *Do Campaigns.*

Chapter 5

Herbert Hoover (World War I, the Great Flood, and the 1928 and 1932 Elections)

In order to understand the political linkages between Herbert Hoover and the Great Mississippi Flood, gauging his prior humanitarian relief experience is important. The evaluation of Herbert Hoover will be conducted in three parts. The first section will review his work as the Great Humanitarian or Food Czar during World War I. The second portion will evaluate his performance during and after the Great Mississippi Flood of 1927. The final part will offer evidence about the 1928 and 1932 elections, making the causal link between flood management and election outcomes. Numerous variables and interpretive measures impacted these elections. However, Hoover's overreliance on volunteerism, principle of association, and rigid adherence to a "levees only policy" cast a regressive political path.

This analysis is not dichotomous. Hoover missed a step, but a compilation of numerous factors influenced 1928 and 1932 elections. Looking forward to today, elections are fraught with controversy and intense competition. The Hoover case reveals not only new insights in explaining an electoral outcome but also uncovers deep policy gaps within federalism. Federalism has changed significantly over time but remains the cornerstone in addressing pertinent public policy concerns. In Hoover's time, federalism's modern concept was in its infancy, with limited federal intervention. Today, due to the development of shared or cooperative federalism, governmental intervention in force majeure events is not only expected but also required. And this is where the policy fallacy lies. Federalism was ineffective in Hoover's time because it was immature. Today's federalism is mature but still circumscribed in addressing policy conundrums. Who is primarily responsible for emergency management? Who should be first responders? Should the president assume responsibility even if he is not near the point of impact? Further, what exploratory measures could be achieved? Managing disasters is hard. This thus creates a paradox leading to the "damming of the presidency." The president is the commander in chief. However, due to shared federalism, numerous other stakeholders are integral in addressing great floods and hurricanes. What can be achieved is a slippery slope. The case of Herbert Hoover offers important insight not only to explain the "damming of the presidency" from a past time but also how and to what extent a president should be at the helm in managing macro-environmental events.

HOOVER AS THE GREAT HUMANITARIAN

In 1917, Herbert Hoover was the food administrator for the Wilson administration. The word "Hooverize" meant to conserve food for the war effort. In 1932, when Hoover was president, the word "Hooverville" meant a squalid collection of shacks in which the poor and underemployed tried to manage survival.[1] The political characterization of one political figure is staggering. What happened? And how could a political figure be so successful in one instance and fail in another?

George Nash is a good starting point. He provides a plethora of research to understand Herbert Hoover from several lenses: humanitarian, statesman, and president. He details the food crisis in Western Europe during World War I in which Hoover painted a somber picture in England, France, and Italy. In 1917–1918, a combined population of approximately 120,000,000 faced severe food shortage. The existing food supply was supposed to last only eight to ten weeks. The matter was further exacerbated because prewar food suppliers like Russia and Romania were cut off by enemy lines. This was a global crisis. Argentina had suffered a crop failure and declared an embargo. Australia had food to export but was prohibitively distant; the Allies could not afford to tie up scarce tonnage on voyages that took three times as long as those from the east coast of North America. In France, a severe frost destroyed at least half of the winter wheat harvest. On the home fronts, women cultivating the fields had been "unable to make up for the depletion of the men," while soldiers in the trenches and workers in the munitions industries were necessarily consuming more food than ever before.[2]

As a result, Hoover estimated the Allies would need to import at least 800,000,000 bushels of grain. The main sources would be Canada and the United States.[3] Hoover met the challenges administratively, carving out a position in the newly founded Food Administration to secure "volunteer food donations" from the public. In this position, he gained valuable executive management experience and assumed the title of "Great Humanitarian," which set the template for his future flood management responsibilities a decade later.[4]

Hoover proposed that the U.S. government establish fixed prices on crops like wheat. This methodical process was applied in the following manner: The government would determine a wheat price based on the prewar average. It would then request grain elevators (which handled over 90 percent of the nation's grain) to pay wheat farmers. The elevator operators would then resell it at a higher, fixed price to the millers, who in turn would sell their flour at another predetermined price to their customers. In effect, the elevator owners and millers would become "agents of the Government working on a commission from the Government." According to Hoover, a "fixed price of bread" would eliminate any component of pernicious speculation. If at the end of a crop year, the elevator men had been unable to sell all the wheat, the government would buy from them.[5]

Hoover required discretion in order to manage a broad food relief effort. He disdained the Department of Agriculture and advocated for a new independent governmental agency, of which he would become the food czar. He believed this new and separate agency would better administer his pricing mechanism. And he was opportune, since Europe was in crisis. Hoover believed that effective public administration principles could stabilize food prices, though not all intentions were altruistic. He claimed that Europe found it necessary to separate administrative bodies of equal importance for the sake of "prestige" in dealing with commercial interests and foreign governments and for creating "in the minds of people a certain imaginative alarm" resulting in food conservation.[6]

Hoover did not rest his case exclusively on the subtleties of "prestige." He declared that the task ahead was a "commercial job," requiring initiative and willingness to assume responsibility. He stated that redistribution must be managed by commercial men rather than by minds "instinctively of Government character."[7] Hoover was skeptical of government efforts; as he stated, in "the soul of a bureaucracy, there is an instinctive avoidance of responsibility or initiative; to avoid error is the essence of successful promotion."[8] These were not the traits required for successful food control. Without being too explicit or offensive, Hoover intimated that his "organism" would perform far more effectively if it were not an adjunct of a stodgy government department like the Department of Agriculture.[9]

Hoover entered the political arena with caution. He was a power seeker and believed that a total war effort required top-down vertical management. Yet philosophically, he remained an individualist concerned that wartime restraints and regulations might eclipse individual initiative. He told the House committee that a separate and temporary agency could best avert the collectivist danger, stating, "My feeling is that the whole basis of democracy lies in the free and rightful play of individual effort, and here (food regulation) is the most tremendous restraint which can put upon the free play of individualism in the country, and it is a most serious restraint to undertake."[10] "The restraint is only justified by a very great emergency, and it should carry within itself the seeds of its own destruction. To set it up as part of the existing organism of the government means its continuance after the war, but if it is set up boldly and frankly as an emergency measure, dying absolutely with the coming of peace, you will save the possibility of facing an enormous difficulty in the end." Here, Hoover saw that a temporary agency would have a short mandate, which would then be "dismantled upon conclusion of the war."[11]

Hoover believed in staffing his agency with business people because such people would not be entrenched in government bureaucracy, and thus more amenable with the food agency's dismantlement after the war. Hoover explained his scheme for emphasizing the price of wheat and then determining the allowable margins for stabilizing prices. He carefully avoided any reference for maximum and minimum prices, but supported the fixed-price program as the only practical solution.[12]

While Hoover expected the vast majority of grain elevators and other wheat distributors to cooperate voluntarily, he was naïve to expect universal assent. He contended that the government must have power to coerce compliance from any opposition who might "destroy the equity of the whole arrangement." At the same time, he shied away from the even more coercive idea of food rationing. He believed that for his scheme to work, it would require at least 1,750,000 bushels of wheat.[13]

Hoover's management style seems contradictory. He distrusted government but at the same time believed government was integral to the European relief effort. Hoover relied upon "engines of indirection," including propaganda for decreased food consumption. War has "very few even partial compensations," but one of them was stirring up in the heart of the people the spirit of self-sacrifice.[14] Propaganda for food conservation would be "absolutely necessary." One target would be the American home. By a "sufficiently intensive organization of women throughout the country," said Hoover, "we might introduce into every household a feeling of sacrifice in the interests of this war." We "ought to be able to teach the women of this country the rudiments of dietetics. This kind of activity, the 'voluntary side' could have the most lasting importance, long after the instruments of coercion have been abolished."[15]

Hoover felt that in order to "compel the imagination of this country as to the possibilities of saving and self-denial," to "command prestige" among the nation's "large commercial bodies," and to "erect a temporary organism here which will appeal to the people as a temporary organism," the new food control agency must be endowed the rank and power of a Cabinet department. "To set it up as a bureau in the Department of Agriculture," he explained, "is hopeless."[16]

However, there was conflict with this proposition. According to Hoover, the president was reluctant to establish a single-headed agency with comprehensive authority over food. Wilson was concerned about building "dictatorial powers" through presidential aggrandizement. Wilson was also fearful of conflict with the Department of Agriculture. Instead, he created a temporary food commission and appointed Hoover as its chairman. The body would include representatives from the departments of agriculture, industry, and labor.[17]

Hoover accepted Wilson's invitation and was under the general assumption that Congress would grant the president "broad powers" to establish a "competent" food administration. The Food Commission would be governed by five principles. First, the food problem was one of "wise administration," expressed not by "dictators" or "controllers" but by a food administrator. Second, this administration would largely operate through existing channels of production and distribution. Third, communities should be organized for voluntary conservation of food. Fourth, "all important positions" should be staffed by volunteers. Fifth, the food administration would not only be independent and accountable directly to the president but would also cooperate with the Department of Agriculture and other relevant agencies. Hence, an early tenet of Hoover's management style was volunteer based.[18]

Nash asks a critical question to this study and beyond: Why had Hoover prevailed? Nash hones in on the role of the president, stating that Hoover's conception of proper management appealed to the one man who had authority to confer power: Woodrow Wilson. Wilson shared Hoover's aversion to bureaucracy and statism. Yet like Hoover, Wilson believed that success in the war required an unprecedented state-directed mobilization of the American economy. Hoover persuaded Wilson by suggesting that effective policy would be exercised by "administrators," not "dictators."[19] Absolute power was important but need not be practiced if the people could be awakened, exhorted, and mustered into action without coercion. And here we have evidence of Hoover's management style. He valued both absolute and temporary power in that somehow both approaches safeguarded him from abuse. Volunteerism was the linchpin, the path to "planning without bureaucracy," the way to mediate successfully between a libertarian political system and the collectivist demands of a world war. Hoover had directed the Belgian relief for two-and-a-half years without accepting a salary or expenses, articulating the code of volunteerism masterfully. The president of the United States was convinced.[20]

Hoover was also aided by David Houston, secretary of agriculture. Nash states Houston lacked "the energy and driving force" of Hoover, which in essence was an overall Wilsonian appointee strategy: the new men were able, energetic, and ambitious in creating novel, ad hoc agencies and shunting traditional government departments aside. But above all, Hoover was viewed as a great humanitarian. Hoover succeeded because of his reputation as the man who had "held dying Belgium in his arm." The *New York Times* stated that Hoover enjoyed the confidence of his compatriots on food issues, and no one else had his "prestige." No man anywhere, said the *New Republic*, equaled him in "experience in international food administration." Further, they stated Hoover was "Enwrapped in two and a half years of international approbation, he could not but be, for the American public, a satisfactory choice." One newspaper even made the appellation, "Hoover of Belgium" is a title as significant of a great work well done as "Kitchener of Khartoum."[21]

In the end, the Food Administration's Grain Corporation purchased 17,358,832 bushels of Canadian wheat during the 1917–1918 crop year, a figure that apparently included the 430,000 tons (or nearly 16,000,000 bushels). If so, the total was far from the 19,000,000 or so additional bushels that Hoover had initially requested. According to one of Hoover's associates, "the major portion" of the Grain Corporation's Canadian purchases "was returned to the Allies in the form of flour."[22]

In the United States, similar patterns evolved. For example, in Arkansas, families returned more than 2,500,000 pounds of flour in excess of their "private portion." In Texas, flour shipments were turned back. There were also reports that Indiana and Montana even adopted a totally wheat-less diet. Three-quarters of the householders in New York had pledged to abstain from wheat products until summer. Some of these reports were exaggerated. Still, there was no gainsaying the considerable grassroots popularity of Hoover's campaign, particularly in the South and West.[23]

And the Food Commission worked. For twelve months, the United States exported more than $1.4 billion worth of food to Europe for the use of the Allies, the American military, the Belgian relief, and the Red Cross. Most of this had been purchased "through or with the collaboration of the Food Administration." The shipments included more than 3,000,000,000 pounds of meat and fats as well as 340,800,000 bushels of cereals. These aggregate figures constituted an enormous increase over the year before.[24]

Hoover informed the president that he exceeded the Allies' request for wheat (by ten million bushels), equaling 85,000,000. Hoover attributed success to the American people, and this was despite a poor wheat crop in 1917. Yet the American people managed to adjust. However, there may have been some misinterpretation of figures. In 1917–1918, the United States exported 132,578,633 bushels of wheat, a decrease of more than one-third from the 203,573,928 bushels sent abroad the prior year. The percentage of wheat exported also decreased from 32 percent to just 20.8 percent. In reality, the United States helped Allies less in Hoover's first year as food administrator than it had in the year before it entered the war. Yet this statistic bore little relevance to Hoover's claims. In 1917–1918, he could only administer what he had: a national supply of wheat nearly 100,000,000 bushels below that of the previous crop year. While the 1917 crop itself was no smaller than that of the year before, the carryover was substantially less, giving Hoover much less room to maneuver.[25]

Still, a pressing question remains: How large was the American wheat surplus prior to his conservation crusade? Hoover lacked reliable data. His estimates varied considerably. In August 1917, he put the exportable surplus from the new wheat crop at 80,000,000 bushels. By December 1, his agency had reduced its estimate of the exportable surplus to 70,000,000 bushels. Hoover's correspondence with the president on November 15, 1917, implied that the surplus was under 30,000,000 bushels. Yet on January 25, 1918, the Food Administration stated that the normal surplus from the last harvest was 60,000,000 bushels. Two months later, Hoover told the White House that he had no export surplus. If there was any surplus, it was simply a measure of Americans' self-denial.[26]

By mid-November 1917, Hoover informed the president that the "average yearly domestic wheat consumption in the United States for the past three years had been about 615,000,000 bushels." A few months later, his own statisticians estimated that it had been nearly 87,500,000 bushels less for the three years. Such discrepancies raise the possibility that Hoover deliberately understated America's wheat reserves and overstated domestic wheat requirements in order to provide himself a cushion against disaster. These discrepancies underscore the excruciating perplexities that Hoover faced as a policy maker and the difficulty of determining his success. The United States exported about 132,000,000 bushels of wheat to the Allies in the crop year 1917–1918. Yet it is unclear how much was generated by Hoover's food-saving campaign, a statistical puzzle that probably cannot be solved.[27]

What is clear is that by January 1918, Hoover's conservative drive accelerated. Over the next six months, the United States exported more than 70,000,000 additional bushels of wheat. If the bulk of this reflected reduced American consumption, was the reduction ascribable to Hoover's efforts? Or did he, in taking credit for it, commit the fallacy of *post hoc, ergo propter hoc*, meaning correlation does not mean causation?[28]

In the winter of 1917–1918 (and for several months beforehand), American consumption of wheat initially rose in defiance of Hoover's propaganda. Adherence to the Food Administration's rules varied widely among social and ethnic strata. Middle- and upper-class Americans were much more observant of "meatless" and "wheat-less" practices than working class and foreign-born individuals. Secondly, as economists subsequently pointed out, Hoover's wheat policy was somewhat self-contradictory. While he feverishly implored Americans to consume less, his price policy simultaneously encouraged more consumption. Price ceilings actually made wheat, flour, and bread more attractive to consumers. His stabilization measures were an incentive to eat more wheat rather than less.[29]

Wheat prices fell in the final months of the 1917–1918. Hoover publicized the claim that Americans normally consumed 40,000,000 or more bushels of wheat per month. Since the United States obviously lacked the reserves to permit the continued use of wheat at this level, the Food Administration sought to cut their consumption by at least 50 percent. However, this was deceiving. It was not true that America's "normal consumption" of wheat was 40,000,000 bushels every month. American wheat consumption traditionally declined substantially in the months of March, April, May, and June. From 1914 to 1917, in fact, national wheat consumption during these months averaged only about 26,500,000 bushels, barely half the other eight months of the year. With the advent of spring, many Americans customarily switched to newly available fruits and vegetables. Thus, when Hoover made his national request, he asked the public to do what had always been done and without instruction. In fairness, millions of Americans obeyed Hoover's injunctions during the winter and spring of 1918.[30]

Hoover's July 11, 1918, letter to the president asserted that food sacrifices had been voluntary. This was effective propaganda for a nation in the midst of a war. It was morale boosting and good advertising for Hoover. But just a few weeks later, in another, unpublicized report to President Wilson, Hoover submitted data indicating that nearly all of the wheat savings resulted from *compulsory* measures, notably the 50–50 rule and the enforced commercial baking of Victory Bread.[31]

In short, Hoover derived less from voluntary self-restraint than from coercion. The popular response to his campaign was selective, but it cannot be inferred that his approach lacked volunteerism. Much had to do with the time period. In 1917–1918, the United States was far less accustomed than its European allies and enemies to expect governmental interventionism and even more so during war time. Hoover's policies never won universal acceptance. However, he was effective in communicating with the American public that wheat consumption practices had to change.[32]

Hoover was proud of his contribution to the war effort. A few weeks before the conflict ended, he sent the president a set of price indices showing that since the Food Administration had been created, the price of food had stabilized, farmer prices had increased, and profits of middlemen had declined. Even as inflation had come under control, food consumption had declined by 7 percent, while food production was showing a "nutritional increase." All this, he stated, refuted "theoretical economists," who had been warned that interference with supply and demand endangered production and that consumption reduction could only be obtained by higher prices.[33]

The essential feature of the Food Administration's plan was that individual conscience should rule under the guidance of local leadership. This meant volunteerism. Hoover ascribed America's comparative price stability and enormous food surpluses not to domestic price controls and selective price incentives but rather to a pervasive spirit of volunteerism in 20 million American households.[34]

Hoover continued his public service efforts after the war. In 1920, he led the American Child Health Association, which carried on an extensive program until 1935. Hoover's interest in housing led to efforts by the government to promote better homes. This campaign embraced a study of all major housing problems, from building codes to finance.[35] Hoover's progressive federalism may have been ahead of his time. He favored collective bargaining but opposed closed shops. He supported private unemployment insurance, favored a child labor amendment, and sparked such a skillful publicity campaign against "barbaric hours in the steel industry" which led to Judge Elbert H. Gary abolishing the twelve-hour day. Hoover clashed with banker-managers when he tried to settle the railway laborers strike in 1922, but later helped in the development of the Railway Labor Mediation Board, created by Congress in 1926.[36]

Hoover created the Aviation Division within the Commerce to address the fledgling aviation industry. He also applied regulatory powers to radio broadcasting.[37] He supported business but recognized potential abuse. In earnest, he wanted business to police itself. Yet he was vigilant with antitrust legislation. Hoover recommended ways for cooperation within the law, preparing codes of business practice and ethics. He did not believe in the elimination of competition, but he refused to publicize wrongdoings. The *New Republic* offered an editorial about Hoover when he was secretary of commerce labeling him a "big five-footer." Forced to subordinate ideas to loyalties in a feeble administration, Hoover was judged to be "but a shadow of his old figure."[38]

HOOVER'S PHILOSOPHY

Hoover's management style can be linked to his college years at Stanford, where he enrolled in 1891. This was a time of rising nationalism. Henry George, champion of social justice, was nearing the end of his long crusade to reform the economic order. Lester Frank Ward, first of American sociologists, was preaching democratic socialism. Edward Bellamy's *Looking Backward* had been a best seller for three years, and scores of nationalist clubs were seeking to promote the brotherhood of man. William Graham Sumner, the prodigious intellect and champion of laissez faire, taught self-reliance and warned against the welfare state. Sumner's teachings at Yale had a national audience and were echoed, consciously or unconsciously, in Hoover's writings and in his many speeches.[39]

Hoover's political and social philosophy was not complicated. He adhered to a few major premises but did not permit questions about his philosophy. Hoover wrote *American Individualism* in 1922. According to Hoover, individualism made America great by remedying social order inequities.[40]

Individualism would lead to a better quality of life, whether political, social, or economic. The government's role would be to protect this opportunity. This meant that each person was treated equally. However, this created a paradox. On the one hand, this promoted individualism but on the other hand, supported limited social and economic mobility. While Hoover supported both social responsibility and equality of opportunity, he believed society must afford full expression of self-interest and reward individual enterprise. And it was the individual who would protect the common good and demonstrate responsibility. His self-reliance protocol would apply to industry and maximum distribution of wealth. In simple terms, Hoover believed the community must work as a unit to preserve the democratic ideal of equality and self-reliance. In essence, Hoover championed limited regulation supported by both individualism and governmental stewardship. "Government must stay out of business and must not compete with its own citizens. Hoover believed that government must cure abuses, as well as develop institutions. These institutions over time will mature to develop a 'sense of trusteeship of public interest.'"[41]

Hoover favored government regulation to preserve competition, conserve natural resources, prevent abuses, and protect individual liberties. However, according to Hoover, government should regulate only when necessary to achieve these objectives, and federal regulation should apply only when state and local governments were unable to protect equality of opportunity and the public interest.

Hoover supported tariffs to protect labor, industry, agriculture, and the economy. Farmers' cooperatives should be organized with federal aid then sent on their way to promote the welfare of their members. Government must help industry approach full employment, "to provide a job for all who have the will to work." "Government must not deprive labor of equal opportunity by unfair use of the injunction; and unions must not deprive the worker of the right to a job by insisting on the closed shop."[42]

Hoover's system did not preclude government business enterprise. He supported local government enterprise, yet as a general rule, government could not operate a business. Public funds could be used in scientific research, building highways, and other general public improvements. Yet more complex enterprises were circumscribed to the private sector, such as the sale of electrical energy to consumers or the operation of transportation systems. He would approve the use of federal funds to subsidize private enterprise but would oppose direct government subsidized service as socialistic. These governmental standards followed logically from Hoover's philosophy of individualism. Extension of government would undermine rugged individualism, the development of the individual according to his ability, and equality of opportunity. Hoover once stated, "You cannot extend the mastery of government over the daily working life of a people without at the same time making it the master of the people's soul and thoughts."[43]

Hoover was an idealist and thought that all groups could benefit from

a land where men and women may walk in ordered freedom in the independent conduct of their occupations; where they may enjoy the advantages of wealth, not concentrated in the hands of a few but spread through the lives of all; where vantages and opportunities of American life; where every man shall be respected in the faith that his conscience and his hear direct him to follow; where a contented and happy people, secure in their liberties, free from poverty and fear, shall have the leisure and impulse to seek a fuller life.[44]

Hoover has his critics. Some find no human insight in Hoover's humanitarianism. Warren states that Hoover's philosophy was hostile to everything in democracy except its catch words. Oswald Garrison Villard, editor of the *Nation,* could not forgive Hoover for his silence during the Harding scandals, for accepting reactionary attitudes toward domestic and foreign problems, for having "forgotten all the stuff he was talking, when he came back from Europe, about a new deal and a better political life in America."[45]

Calling him a peoples' choice, *Time*'s political analyst wrote with rare foresight:

The central fact militating against Candidate Hoover is that many people cannot understand what he represents. He is no forthright protagonist of an ideal or program. He puts forth no clear-cut political or social theory except a quiet "individualism," which leaves most individuals groping. Material well-being, comfort, order, efficiency in government and economy-these he stands for, but they are conditions not ends. A technologist, he does not discuss ultimate purposes. In a society of temperate, industrious, unspeculative beavers, such a beaver-man would make an ideal King-beaver. But humans are different. People want Herbert Hoover to tell where, with his extraordinary abilities, he would lead them. He needs it would seem, to undergo a spiritual crisis before he will satisfy as a popular leader.[46]

UNDERSTANDING THE GREAT MISSISSIPPI RIVER

Mark Twain called it one of nature's most powerful wonders. Proverbially known as the Father of Rivers, the Mississippi River stretches close to 2,500 miles from its origin in northern Minnesota's Lake Itasca to the Gulf of Mexico and has a drainage basin encompassing 1.2 million square miles; only South America's Amazon River and the Congo River in West Central Africa surpass it. The Mississippi River and tributaries move like a pulsating bloodline through thirty-one U.S. states and two Canadian provinces. By the turn of the twentieth century, it provided not only life-sustaining water and rich alluvial soil but also a transportation network of goods and commerce vital to the entire country's prosperity. This vast network of tributaries and distributaries, which includes the Missouri River; Illinois River; Ohio River; Tennessee River; St. Francis and White Rivers in Arkansas; Arkansas River; Yazoo River in Mississippi; and Ouachita, Red, Atchafalaya, Old Morgnanza, and Bonnet Carre Rivers in Louisiana, connect the main stem of the Mississippi River to roughly 40 percent of the coterminous or boundaries of the United States.[47]

Human interactions with the Mississippi River have traditionally been more combative than benign. When Charles Dickens saw what he called the "great father of rivers" in the early nineteenth century, he noted its width, numerous obstructions to traffic, and "strong and frothy current," concluding that the river had "nothing pleasant in its aspect but the harmless lightening which flicker every night upon the dark horizon." During the massive floods of 1927, the river was so intimidating that New Orleans dynamited the levees protecting downstream residents in order to avoid possible flooding in their own areas. Many in the Corps of Engineers have traditionally battled the river, citing a Mark Twain passage wherein the most famous riverman admits to being impressed that "the military engineers have taken upon their shoulders the job of making the Mississippi over again."[48]

In the late nineteenth century, Congress told the Corps to facilitate navigability on the Mississippi. In the twentieth century, the federal mandate grew to include flood control. Specifically after the 1927 flooding, Congress passed legislation making the federal government fully responsible for maintaining the Mississippi. The prescribed solution for both maintaining navigation and controlling flooding was the same, although early debates between scientists and engineers, notably James Eads and Andrew Humphrey, over how best to control flooding and enhance navigation on the river were long and intense. The final prescription from the Mississippi River Commission and later the Corps involved the intense use of artificial structure.[49]

Engineers conducted a massive effort that lasted throughout much of the twentieth century. Historically, the river meandered, cutting new channels and side channels as it turned. The Corps stabilized riverbanks, dredged sediment, removed snags, and built navigation structures such as locks and dams to channel and straighten the river. The logic was that a narrower channel would occur and thus deepen the river, facilitating barge traffic and constricting the river from flooding. Engineers attempted to close off many of the side channels. The Corps also attempted to smooth out the curves and vigorously pursued a nine-foot deep channel for the length of the river with levees, dams, and even cutoffs that shorten the total length by more than 150 miles. On the lower Mississippi, the structure most relied on was the levee. Levees in this river are massive earthworks, often 30 feet high and nearly 200 feet wide with a flat, 8-foot-wide crown. The levees are separated from the river by a strip of land and a moat, usually 300 feet wide, from whence came the dirt for the structure. By 1996, more than 1,600 miles of levees lined the river.[50]

The changes to the river accomplished several goals. In part, the Corps was able to restore some of the historical dimensions of the river. Claude Strauser, chief hydrologist for the St. Louis district of the Corps, calls this "one of the greatest environmental achievements in history." Domestic traffic on the river has been and continues to be intense. In 1999, barges carried 329 million tons of cargo on the river, more than any other inland waterway in the United States. The port of South Louisiana is the busiest in the nation (by tonnage), and the state of Louisiana is first in commercial traffic (by tonnage). Channelization has also enabled considerable development in the floodplains along the river, as attested by the millions of residents who are threatened whenever the river floods.[51]

Structuring the river also had other consequences. The system of levees and other flood control measures created a false sense of security among residents of what had been flood plains. Thus, the Great Flood of 1927 washed out entire towns and even regions. Further, structural engineering has narrowed the channel to the point that severe floods are now more likely. A river flow of a certain discharge today will produce higher levels of water than did the same flow thirty years ago. Nor is the problem alleviated by the fact that the water is moving more swiftly at any one point. In view of this situation, the Great Flood of 1993 does not seem surprising. This flood killed fifty people, damaged more than 50,000 structures, inundated millions of acres of farmland, and ultimately caused at least $19 billion in losses.[52]

Butler states the Mississippi was managed by a levees-only policy for nearly 200 years. It was a central management process but limited, as it did not factor into overall environmental and social implications. Either way, Mississippi residents were involved in flood control since 1726, when New Orleans built levees to protect the city from flooding. Federal governmental involvement dates back to 1824, when the U.S. Supreme Court ruled in *Gibbons v. Ogden* that it was constitutional for the federal government to

finance and construct river improvements. Congress responded by appro-
priating funds and authorizing the U.S. Army Corps of Engineers (USACE)
to remove navigation obstructions from the Ohio and Mississippi Rivers.[53]
The USACE increased its federal role through the mid to latter part of the
nineteenth century. The Swamp Land Acts of 1849 and 1850 reflected the
levees-only policy. It transferred "swamp and overflow land" along the lower
Mississippi River from federal ownership to state governments on the condition that the states use revenue from the sale of the lands to build levees
and drainage channels. In 1850, Congress commissioned two surveys of the
Mississippi River delta to determine "the most predictable plan for securing
it from inundation." These surveys ultimately led to the federal levees-only
policy.[54]

The Mississippi River Commission was created in 1878 to regulate private and local entities who were trying to control the river. According to the
Association of State Flood Plain Managers (ASFPM), 1879 marked a turning
point for flood control, and Congress gradually increased federal government
flood control responsibility. By 1890, the entire lower Mississippi Valley
from St. Louis to the Gulf of Mexico had been divided into state and local
levee districts. In 1926, just a year before the Great Flood, USACE publicly
declared that the levee system would prevent future floods in the Mississippi
River basin.[55]

In another approach, Progressive Era debates about levees devolved into
dialogue about what to do with the overabundance of water in the Yazoo
Mississippi Delta region. This was consistent with conservation policy of the
time in how to make water and land productive for human use. Consumption
was a fundamental tenet of early-twentieth-century conservation theory. In
his epic work, *Conservation and the Gospel of Efficiency*, Samuel P. Hays
describes the movement:

> Conservation, above all, was a scientific movement, and its role in history arises
> from the implications of science and technology in modern society. It was
> rational planning to promote efficient development and use of natural resources.
> Conservation leaders believed not only that science and new forms of technol-
> ogy made the rational planning an endless possibility but also that proper deci-
> sions over land use should be left to the most qualified.[56]

In other words, the rational and efficient use of landscapes was a scientific
and technical enterprise best performed by those trained to make technical
assessments of resources. Hays explained, "Foresters should determine the
desirable annual timber cut; hydraulic engineers should establish the feasible
extent of multiple purpose river development and the specific location of reservoirs; agronomists should decide which forage areas could remain open for

grazing without undue damage to water supplies." In terms of flood control and the "levees-only" policy, the United States Army Corps would supersede all others in terms of river design and levee construction. The "levees-only" policy was never absolute, and the corps' authority over the matter was tenuous at best during the early 1930s. Civilian engineers suggested the corps plan was untenable because it confined the Mississippi River from spreading over its natural watershed and taxed the system's artificial levees to a unsustainable degree. Corps engineers refuted those claims by relying on a conservationist and progressive faith in science and making the case that confining the Mississippi River within its natural floodplain with artificial levees would only cause the river to deepen its river bed naturally over time without major environmental damage.[57]

Nonetheless, by the second decade of the twentieth century, the "levees-only" policy had firmly taken shape and was increasingly blamed for record-breaking floods in the Yazoo Mississippi Delta. One chief officer of the corps, writing internally after the disastrous 1912 and 1913 Mississippi and Ohio floods, reaffirmed the case. He wrote, "There is only one way to protect the Mississippi Valley from floods, and that is by an adequate system of well-defined levees," It would take a disaster the caliber of the 1927 flood to shake the stubborn "levees only" and dissuade engineers from their conviction that levees alone could protect the region.[58]

In 1926, the Mississippi drainage basin, which includes tributaries in thirty-one states and southern Canada, received unprecedented precipitation. Heavy rains culminated the prior summer and continued through winter of 1927. On April 16, 1927, a 1,200-foot section of the levee collapsed thirty miles south of the confluence of the Ohio and Mississippi Rivers, flooding 175,000 acres. Soon after, much of the levee system along the lower Mississippi failed, affecting areas in Arkansas, Illinois, Kentucky, Louisiana, Mississippi, Missouri, and Tennessee. By May 1927, the flood stretched sixty miles south of Memphis. It was an unprecedented presidential and federal challenge.[59]

The Great Mississippi Flood was unique due to the large swathe of destruction that lasted over four months. The Mississippi Flood was the first great disaster to capture headlines using radio, moving pictures, and aviation. This impact made the suffering more vivid and reached Americans living thousands of miles from impact, placing new pressure on politicians to respond to emergencies, even in the conservative political culture of Coolidge's America.[60]

Politicians from the Mississippi Valley region urged Coolidge to visit the disaster scene and implored him to make radio broadcasts, as well as summon a special session in Congress. This was a time of limited federal intervention, which meant that most responsibility remained with the state and local levels. The concept of collective action was stunted due to a modest administrative state, even smaller when Congress was out of session. Serendipitously, many of the Mississippi River's deadly spring rises during the previous half century had occurred in even numbered years. This was when Congress was in session, and legislators had been able to give the Army and the Army Corps of Engineers the authority and necessary funds to address wide range flooding. But in this case, lame-duck 69th Congress had recently ended, and the new 70th Congress was not due to convene for another nine months.[61]

Action was needed. Newspaper reporters flew directly over disaster scenes and provided dramatic flood footage. Newspapers reproduced photographs, and popular entertainers such as Will Rogers broadcast pleas for voluntary donations. The overall presidency was increasing in power. Recent presidencies of Theodore Roosevelt and Woodrow Wilson had established precedents for aggressive executive leadership. However, Coolidge moved slowly in addressing the situation.

Coolidge looked to his commerce secretary, Herbert Hoover, for disaster management strategy in mitigating the 1927 flood. This was tactical for two reasons. First, Hoover had an unparalleled reputation for handling humanitarian emergencies (Belgian food aid during World War I, the famine relief in Russia in 1919, and dealing with the postwar spike in U.S. unemployment). Second, Hoover was connected to the American Red Cross. The selection of Hoover satisfied the need for volunteerism and charitable giving. In other words, the federal government was not required to increase its level of internal commitment. And at some level, it worked. The Red Cross provided a massive evacuation and relief effort with limited federal involvement.[62]

Over time, federal intervention would change during the Hoover and Franklin Roosevelt presidencies. Much of this had to do with the overall changing role of the federal government and the Great Depression. There were other surrounding natural disasters as well. The Appalachian droughts of 1930 and 1931, the Category 5 hurricane in the Florida Keys in 1935, the New England and Ohio River floods in 1936, and the Mississippi River Valley flood in 1937. The New Deal was the fulcrum policy point in creating the political aperture for the federal government to morph into a significant disaster relief role. People expected more from the federal government. Congress remained in session longer and a panoply of new federal agencies was created to meet this demand. When disaster struck, Washington could make a more substantial contribution than before.[63]

But 1927 was different. Hoover referred to the flood as the greatest peacetime disaster in U.S. history. The 1927 floods caused major economic loss and suffering. Over 16 million acres in seven states were inundated, and property loss estimates varied from $236 to $363 million. Nearly 700 people are known to have died. Another 637,000 were left homeless. The American Red Cross, responsible for most of the relief work, provided food and shelter for more than 300,000 people in refugee camps. But relief efforts were not distributed evenly. Black refugees were particularly harmed. Imprisoned in refugee camps, they were coerced to perform manual labor and prevented from fleeing the Delta because planters were afraid of losing their workforce.[64]

The Great Mississippi Flood revealed numerous policy inconsistencies. Mizelle offers insight, explaining that the sheer breadth of the Mississippi River Flood of 1927 was unique and continues to challenge scholars. While other disasters such as the Galveston Hurricane, the 1906 San Francisco earthquake, and the more modern Hurricane Katrina have resulted in more physical damage and loss of life, the 1927 flood stands alone in its impact on the environment and culture. No other single environmental catastrophe affected so many states and encompassed such a wide area of devastation. Hurricane Katrina, considered the worst environmental disaster in American history, destroyed property and claimed lives in the Gulf Coast states of Louisiana, Mississippi, and Alabama. The 1927 flood affected seven states, resulting in a logistical nightmare for the federal government and the American people in how best to respond to citizens in need. Scholarship on the 1927 flood is similarly uneven, with a heavy focus on Mississippi, Louisiana, and to a lesser degree, Arkansas. Little is known about how the 1927 flood played out locally in Illinois, Kentucky, Missouri, or Tennessee, and only a little about how it played out in Arkansas.[65]

The Mississippi Yazoo Delta is a distinct region politically, socially, and culturally. As historian James Cobb argues, the Mississippi Delta is distinctively more Southern than any part of the South. Eight years after the 1927 flood, sociologist Rupert Vance described the relations between blacks and whites and the region's political and economic culture as still reminiscent of slavery. Nowhere but in the delta "are antebellum conditions so nearly preserved."[66]

There were numerous political entities ranging from the Mississippi River Commission, farmers, sharecroppers, riverboat operators, and business people. Under this milieu, Hoover assumed the title of "relief manager." Hoover remained unpopular among African Americans due to indifference and political miscalculations. When the stock market crashed in 1929, Hoover's popularity plummeted with most Americans, setting the stage for Franklin Delano Roosevelt of New York to assume the presidency in 1932. Roosevelt had the difficult task of bringing the country out of the depression and making a "New Deal" for America. Still, some historians have long inferred that the New Deal was more like a "raw deal" or "no deal" for African Americans, especially during the First Hundred Days. Yet the NAACP did not champion black causes and expose the Mississippi Flood Control Project (MFCP) debt peonage scheme until late 1932, at a time when Hoover's presidency was clearly vulnerable and months before the New Deal was put onto place.

When the federal government began putting mechanisms of the New Deal into place, the NAACP was already positioned to demand changes on behalf of black levee workers.[67]

The Great Flood offers insight into the ways the NAACP demanded that the federal government protect African Americans. As word of mistreatment in Red Cross relief camps spread, the NAACP lobbied Hoover and Coolidge to assume leadership roles and provide protection for displaced black flood survivors. However, this was not well received by Hoover. He was broadly designated as a national relief manager and did not want any unwelcome negative publicity. Hoover viewed such potential complaints as nuisance, whether from the NAACP or black newspapers. However, Hoover eventually bowed to pressure and reluctantly agreed to authorize a special civilian commission in late May 1927 to address allegations of mistreatment and peonage inside Red Cross relief camps.[68]

Yet problems continued. The NAACP questioned the appointment of a civilian rather than federal committee since the appointees did not represent the NAACP. Questions arose: Who would head the civilian committee and constitute its members? Would they have the necessary protection to conduct the investigation and be unyielding in vocalizing what they found? What authority would a civilian committee have to bring significant changes if not backed by the threat of federal legislation or power? The NAACP presented these questions to Hebert Hoover, and their fears were realized when Hoover announced the appointment of Robert Russa Moton to lead the "Colored Advisory Commission." Moton was a protégé of Booker T. Washington. He became head of the Tuskegee Institute after Washington's death in 1913. Hoover was familiar with Moton and the Tuskegee Institute through past endowment work. Moton's conservative approach to race relations made him less threatening to the general white community. Moton was given authority to select a sixteen-member commission including the following: J. S. Clark, president of Southern University in Louisiana, Claude Barnett of the Associated Negro Press, L. M. McCoy, president of Rust College in Mississippi, Eugene Kinckle Jones of the National Urban League, the YMCA's Eva Bowles, Albon Holsey, National Business League secretary, and three members of Moton's staff at Tuskegee. Moton did not choose a single committee member with ties to the NAACP. This infuriated W. E. B. Dubois and other prominent black leaders.[69]

The Colored Advisory Commission released two reports on peonage conditions inside Red Cross relief camps. The first report was submitted to Herbert Hoover and James Fieser of the Red Cross on June 14, 1927. The sixteen commission members visited Red Cross camps for ten days, mostly in the Yazoo Delta. The investigation was difficult because committee members were rarely allowed to talk to black refugees without local white supervision.

This called into question the truthfulness of the refugees' testimonies about white violence. Although commission findings suggested that many camps were public health threats and African Americans were subjugated to daily forms of brutality, including forced labor, restriction of movement, and rape of black women by National Guardsmen, the first submitted report provided little criticism of Herbert Hoover or the Red Cross. As expected by the NAACP, the first report brought about little in the form of change.[70]

Yet a July 1927 report was more direct about unsanitary conditions, detailing National Guardsman brutality and slavery-like conditions. However, the Red Cross dismissed many of these complaints. The report revealed that given options, some black flood refugees preferred residing in swamps, woods, abandoned buildings, and neighbors' homes than subjecting themselves to Red Cross relief camps.[71]

Parrish yields a wealth of information about the black predicament, linked centrally to cash crops. She states that for many powerful Delta interests, the flood was about property and crop values. This was not merely a physical crisis. Poor whites, Acadians, and blacks could threaten their livelihoods. The concept of refugee status only exacerbated socio-political conditions. It was particularly acute for African Americans. An April 19 editorial in the Memphis *Commercial Appeal* opined that "when some great crisis looms and threatens the people of an entire community or section, men forget to hate each other . . . and instead join forces. The spirit of brotherhood of man well strong within and their better selves come to surface."[72] Representative William Nelson, a Democrat from Missouri, professed on April 28 that "in the saving of human life, in great humanitarian undertakings, we know no color line." What all the Race Men and Women and their supporters who looked into the social conditions in the flood zone agreed upon was that such statements were patently false.[73]

Further, the *Chicago Defender* stated, "Now while the whole Southland is under the greatest devastating flood in its history, the color line is given its most rigid enforcement. An editorial in the *Pittsburgh Courier* urged, "In time of stress, people reveal their souls. The flood has brought home to Negroes the fact that the white South is still adamant in its attitude toward the Negro. This spirit withstands floods, fires, and hurricanes. Physically it may be a new south, socially and psychologically it is the same old South."[74]

This meant that a black-white split still pervaded the Deep South, and newspapers offered assessments that mirrored antebellum days. At some level, black refugee suffering reflected a neo-slavery construct that extended long after 1863. Free movement and right to gainful employment were at stake. Black refugee camps became associated with "concentration camps." Both black and white reporters detailed injustices of local black sharecroppers. There were white reporters who wrote for the black press and black authors who wrote for white-owned papers. Both detailed somber living conditions under Jim Crow policy.[75]

The 1927 flood affected areas all along the Mississippi River and its tributaries from Illinois down to Louisiana. Water covered 27,000 square miles, an area the size of Massachusetts, Connecticut, Vermont, and New Hampshire combined. Rescuers in boats saved more than 300,000 people from rooftops. African Americans were hit particularly hard. Slavery had ended decades before but racism lurked in the hearts of many white Southerners. These hateful feelings, like the waters of the Mississippi, overflowed in the crisis of the flood.[76]

In wealthy cotton-growing communities, white plantation owners forced their African American workers, often at gunpoint, to build up the levees. White policemen rounded up African American men and marched them to work. When the levees failed, tens of thousands of African Americans were stranded with no food or water. In some areas they were denied help, even after the Red Cross arrived to set up tent cities for evacuees. Hundreds died. Reports of these abuses outraged people around the country. Many criticized President Calvin Coolidge for not acting quickly enough to help some of the country's most-powerless citizens.[77]

Mizelle argues that the colossal failure of levees during the 1927 flood led directly to public demands for a national flood control policy in the Mississippi Valley, as well as plans for rearranging the flow of the Mississippi River. After just a few months of hearings, Congress created the 1928 Flood Control Act. At the time of its passage, some called it the "greatest piece of legislation ever enacted by Congress," with a price tag of $325 million. Barry notes that it set the precedent for the New Deal by requiring the federal government to actively intervene in local and regional economic development. NAACP leaders would refer to it as the Mississippi Flood Control Project (MFCP) and voiced opposition towards black refugee management.[78]

In the years following the 1927 flood, the condition of Southern black laborers deteriorated. Depressed cotton prices and debt peonage kept large numbers of blacks in abject poverty. As the 1920s turned into the Depression era, the National Urban League's T. Arnold Hill commented that at no time in the seventy years since the end of slavery had the "economic and social outlook seemed so discouraging . . . for African Americans." By 1927, levee camps had developed well-deserved reputations for violence and exploitation of black labor. William Hemphill, a Southern born white levee inspector working in an isolated camp near Friars Point, Mississippi, occasionally published on life inside a Yazoo Delta levee camp and reported about the frequent violence directed at black laborers in the Jim Crow South.[79]

Work conditions were exhausting. Levee camp workers rose early in the morning for work around 3 a.m. to prepare for the day's hard labor. Some might immediately harness and feed the mules that would work alongside them, while others repaired broken wheelbarrows and carts used to carry materials. Most worked from the dark of morning until the dark of night in twelve-hour shifts with few breaks. By 1933, the Mississippi Flood Control Project maintained a workforce of between 25,000 and 30,000 men in the Yazoo Delta, and the overwhelming majority were African Americans.[80]

The machinery used in levee construction, which included caterpillar tractors, scrapers, and stump pullers, were dangerous, and accidents likely occurred at a much higher rate than the remaining records reveal. There are only a few references in the historical documentation of camp workers suffering injury from stump pullers or other machinery. While workplace accidents and injuries have historically led to changes in law and increased public awareness, levee workers had no way of making claims for injuries. Racism largely excluded African American workers from the more skilled jobs such as operating tractors, thus trapping them into the drudge work of levee building. African American workers might spend upwards of twelve hours bending over and shoveling soil, placing such strain on their back that by the end of a shift many could barely stand up straight.[81]

Soon criticism extended to the Colored Advisory Commission. The NAACP described the appointment of Moton as an effort of appeasement and there was little expectation of tangible improvements. In the November 1927 issue of the *Crisis*, W. E. B. Dubois observed,

> We have grave suspicions that the colored committee recently appointed by Mr. Hoover to investigate flood conditions and peonage in the Mississippi Valley will be sorely tempted to whitewash the whole situation, to pat Mr. Hoover loudly on the back, and to make no real effort to investigate the desperate and evil conditions of that section of our country. Slavery still exists in the Mississippi Valley and the Committee knows it.[82]

When the floodwaters finally receded, approximately 1,000 people were dead. Tens of thousands of buildings were destroyed. Fifty percent of all animals in the area—horses, cows, mules, chickens, and hogs—had drowned. Whole tows were wiped out. Residents spent months cleaning up mountains of foul-smelling mud and debris. But people vowed to rebuild. "We shall stay here and see it through," promised one Mississippi business leader. Slowly, communities began to recover. Thousands of African Americans were determined to rebuild their lives up North where they hoped to find equality and opportunities. This eventually led to the Great Migration north. The events of the flood made it impossible for them to return to their old lives under the power of their white bosses. Within a year, half of the African Americans from the Mississippi Delta area had left for Northern cities.[83]

As for the river itself, by late that summer, it had returned to its normal state—slow and lazy in many places. The decades passed, and most signs of the flood disappeared. The government rebuilt the flood controls along the river, adding features early engineers had called for. They claimed that those levees would withstand a flood far stronger than the one of 1927.[84]

In his memoirs, Hoover reveals flood challenges but avoids political accountability. He states that the cause of the "unprecedented flood" on the lower Mississippi River in 1927 was the coincidence of the floods on the Ohio, the Missouri, and the upper Mississippi, which brought down more water than the lower Mississippi could carry tranquilly to the sea between the thousand miles of levees. The levees broke in scores of places, as much as 150 miles wide, stretched down the river 1,000 miles from Cairo to the Gulf.[85]

Governors of six endangered states asked for federal cooperation and suggested that Hoover be placed in charge of the emergency. Hoover had strong institutional support from President Coolidge. He traveled to Memphis and mobilized the state and local authorities and their militias, the Army Engineers, the Coast Guard, a naval air contingent, the Weather Bureau, and the Red Cross. This early advent of appearing to be in charge generated a lot of public support for Hoover.[86]

It took approximately two months for the flood waters to crest through 1,000 miles of levee systems. Hoover and the government were able to control flooding but not manage the refugees. As many as 1,500,000 people were driven from their homes, some 2,000,000 acres of crops and thousands of animals were lost, and hundreds of millions of dollars in property was destroyed. There were, of course, countless fatalities.[87]

Hoover states, "We took over some forty river steamers and attached to each of them a flotilla of small boats under the direction of the Coast Guardsmen. As the motorboats, we could assemble proved insufficient." Yet he was able to get the local sawmills to produce 1,000 boats in ten days. There seems to be some confusion over the role of these quick construction boats. Hoover states that he rented 1,000 outboard motors, but was only able to return 120 of them. Hoover felt that a key to this tragedy was movability and that scores of fishermen attached motors to their boats. The end result was that tent cities were created on high grounds. Here, one can discern Hoover's engineering ability; he states that he helped create wooden platforms for the tents, laid sewers, put in electric lights, and installed huge kitchens and feeding halls. It was impressive. Each tent-town had a hospital, and as the flood receded, people were even rehabilitated on their own farms and in homes. People were provided tents, building materials, tools, seed, animals, and furniture, among other sundries. Sanitary measures were in place to combat malaria, typhoid, pellagra, and contagious disease.[88] Yet Hoover seems focused on the descriptive rather than incorporating Southern political issues germane to the situation, such as segregation and Jim Crow policies, which impacted the recovery and relief effort.

What is clear is that the Great Mississippi Flood occurred at a different time in American history. The federal government's intervention was limited in directing state practices. It was also assumed at the time that individualism, including volunteerism, was the cornerstone of personal improvement. Hoover believed in self-help and looked at private and nonprofit relief for flood support. He helped establish a Red Cross drive from the flood area by radio, which raised $4,150,000. He writes that he secured $1,000,000 from the Rockefeller Foundation to finance the after-flood campaign of sanitation, to be matched with equal contributions from the counties. He helped organize a nonprofit organization through the U.S. Chamber of Commerce to provide $10,000,000 of loans at low rates for rehabilitation, all of which were eventually paid back. His emphasis on self-help is clearly evident in his words: "Those were days when citizens expected to take of one another in time of disaster and it has not occurred to them that the Federal Government should do it."[89]

Further, the Rockefeller Foundation gift helped establish a health unit for each of the flooded counties. Each unit comprised a physician, a trained nurse, and a sanitary engineer, the counties funding half the cost. It was they who stamped out malaria, pellagra, and typhoid. They improved health and raised money and gave the afflicted hope. The end result was that these health units showed a significant reduction in diseases, even below preflood averages.[90]

Yet force majeure events are complex. The flood was described as the "greatest peace-time calamity in the history of the country." It deluged thousands of square miles in the Lower Valley. It destroyed more than a million farms animals, caused losses amounting to hundreds of millions of dollars, and drowned more than 250 people. It also swept away the levees put in place by the Mississippi River Commissions (MRC). This in turn forced a thorough reevaluation of the federal program of flood control for the Lower Valley. Yet there were other forms of political friction that in part contributed to further Southern alienation from the Democratic Party.

ALIENATING THE SOUTH

Initial critical leadership on flood control came from Illinois rather than Louisiana or more generally, from the Upper Mississippi Valley rather than the Lower. President Calvin Coolidge involved himself in a limited way in the legislative process. His conservative influence precipitated a crisis within the GOP, pitching the Republican chair of the House Flood Control Committee, Frank R. Reid of Illinois, and his comprehensive visions for the

Lower Valley against the administration and tight fiscal policy. The Chief of the Army Corps of Engineers Major General Edgar Jadwin joined Coolidge in his efforts at cost control and tailored the Army's engineering plan to the fiscal conservatism of the administration, assuring that the reassessment of flood control policy would be politically rather than technologically driven.[91]

The stubbornness with which Coolidge refused to work with the Mississippi Lower Valley did not portend well for the region in its push for federal flood control. By all early indications, the president was not friendly to its needs and increasingly the people of the Delta sensed that. A late-August 1927 dispatch from New Orleans reported Louisiana's growing anxiety: "Reviewing the record of the Federal Administration during the flood, many people of [Louisiana] were apprehensive." The concern was that President Coolidge and his advisors would fail to advocate adequate action. These concerns were realized. Throughout the flood crisis, the president pursued a policy of restricting appropriations for flood control. A central reason was that he did not want to "throw his budget out of line." Coolidge's level of influence would shape the national legislative process but leave a dire impact on Louisiana and the rest of the Lower Mississippi Valley.[92]

In the past, Louisiana had piloted the struggle in Congress for federal flood control on the Mississippi River. New Orleans was the nation's second leading port city and the Mississippi River its lifeblood. Improving and later controlling the great river had been the first order of business for Louisiana legislators for more than a hundred years, but progress had been incremental. Until the mid-nineteenth century, riparian landowners assumed sole responsibility for the construction and maintenance of levees. In 1849, Louisiana led a Congressional fight to secure the transfer of swamp and overflowed lands to the states of the Mississippi Valley, culminating in the Swamp Land Grants of 1849 and 1859. "Revenue raised from the sale of lands paid for further levee improvements and encouraged the organization of levee districts throughout the Lower Valley."[93]

Beginning with the establishment of the MRC in 1879, the districts formed a close working relationship with the federal government, which included federal funds for levee building. The commission also adopted a "levees-only" policy for flood control and over the next forty years stood by the Lower Valley in its opposition to a more comprehensive and diverse approach flood control management that would include outlets, reservoirs, reforestation, and levees. The ongoing struggle came to a head in 1917, when Senator Joseph E. Ransdell of Louisiana overcame the antagonism of leading waterways advocate Senator Francis G. Newlands of Nevada to secure passage of the Ransdell-Humphrey's Flood Control Act, considered a great victory for levees-only. The 1917 act authorized the federal government to assume for the first time primary responsibility for flood control, with local interests paying just one-third of the cost and furnishing all rights of way. By 1927, Louisiana had spent its considerable political capital on the realization of levees-only, but it had backed a loser. The great flood of that year devastated the Lower Valley and discredited the levees-only policy. Louisiana was slow to recover, both economically and politically.[94]

With much of Louisiana still under water in the spring of 1927, Illinois seized the initiative in the struggle for federal flood control and kept it, their motives clear. Positioned at the confluences of the Wabash, Ohio, Missouri, and Mississippi Rivers, Illinois had serious flood control problems of its own. In 1927, the first of the mainline Mississippi levee breaks occurred in Illinois, followed a week later by four additional breaks; the resulting floods covered 220,000 acres of some of the most productive agricultural land in the state. Damages throughout Illinois approached $20 million. Even before the great flood, interest in the Mississippi River had reached unprecedented levels, particularly in Chicago. In January 1927, Congress authorized the construction of a deep waterway from the "Second City" to New Orleans that promised increased trade for both cities. The realization of the Lakes-to-the Gulf scheme fed Chicago's growing aspirations and fueled its interest in Mississippi River improvements.[95]

Illinois also had the charismatic "Big Bill" Thompson, the three-time mayor of Chicago. Among America's most notorious urban demagogues and a supposed personal friend of Al Capone, Thompson was a new convert to the cause of the Mississippi River development. After witnessing firsthand the overwhelming devastation visited upon the Lower Valley, he told a gathering of Louisiana business interests that "Chicago is ready to join hands with New Orleans to secure adequate flood control for the Mississippi River, entirely at federal expense." He also called for a united demand to convince Washington.[96]

The Chicago Flood Control Conference opened on June 2, 1927. Thompson held center stage, presiding over the three-day conference. The conference focused on the Valley's flood devastation and led to the creation of a new lobby in the form of a permanent executive committee. This increased the already mounting pressure on Congress to facilitate adequate and comprehensive flood control legislation and assured that Chicago rather than New Orleans would direct the struggle.[97]

Bill Thompson was a pivotal figure. According to Congressman Frank Reid, "No man has done more for the cause of flood control than William Hale Thompson, mayor of the city of Chicago." The Democratic mayor of New Orleans, Arthur O'Keefe, compared Big Bill to Abraham Lincoln and Teddy Roosevelt, and the *New York Times* sardonically proclaimed Thompson, the "Master of the Mississippi." As the flood control hearings developed, the Chicago mayor's role diminished, though never entirely from the scene. Illinois Congressman Fran Reid quietly assumed authority throughout the first hearing.[98]

Coolidge was passive on the national debate about flood control. He refused to publicize policy solutions. At a mid-summer news conference, he declared that "a careful survey was being made of the flood area by three or four engineering bodies and that until their report on fact was made it would be impossible to suggest legislation."[99] In the months that followed, Coolidge repeated his stagnant position. In turn, the Lower Valley ceased its inquiries and curtailed its lobbying efforts "for fear of alienating the Administrations affections." But if the president was recalcitrant, his secretary of commerce offered a different perspective. Hoover believed that he spoke for the administration. This appealed to the Lower Valley residents. A true waterways advocate, Hoover advocated large appropriations for the Lower Valley and emerged sympathetic on the issue of local contributions. Hoover stated, "In the face of their great losses and their present destitution I do not see how the people along the river can contribute much more than the maintenance of the central works after they have been once constructed."[100]

The president broke his self-imposed silence on flood control in his State of the Union address to Congress on December 6, 1927, and touched off a firestorm. Addressing the issue in only a general way, he made clear his views on local contribution. The Mississippi Valley should, Coolidge asserted, "pay enough so that those requesting improvements will be charged with some responsibility for their cost, and the neighborhood where works are constructed have a pecuniary interest in preventing waste and extravagance and securing a wise and economical expenditure of public funds." Flood control and water ways advocates alike reacted with shock. Secretary Hoover's assurances "had lulled the fears of most people" and "were such as to furnish reasonable grounds for the belief that Hoover spoke for the President." This meant that the federal government should pay for spillways. The policy difference between Hoover and Coolidge was immense. Coolidge's recommendations created divisions within his own party and served to unify opposition against him, particularly in the Mississippi Valley and the House Flood Control Committee. This would help explain why the Lower Valley would not support a Republican candidate in 1928 and certainly not 1932.[101]

In the end, and hailed by Reid as the "greatest piece of constructive legislation ever enacted by Congress," the 1928 Flood Control Act adopted a comprehensive flood control program for the Lower Valley that authorized $325 million for the construction of two large floodways in the Tensas and Atchafalaya basins, a smaller parallel floodway at New Madrid, and a single spillway to protect the city of New Orleans. It also called for higher and stronger levees and for the establishment of a hydrology lab to bring scientific study to the management of the Lower Mississippi River. Louisiana would be the largest single beneficiary of the new law. According to the *Times-Picayune*, Mayor Arthur O'Keefe of New Orleans promptly dispatched four telegrams of congratulations, for President Calvin Coolidge, Illinois Senator Wesley Jones, Representative Frank Reid, and Mayor William Hale Thompson of Chicago.[102]

Yet there was frustration in the Lower Valley. The 1928 Flood Control Act was limited. In the wake of the 1927 flood disaster, the Democratic leadership had advocated the adoption of a comprehensive flood control plan to include tributary improvements, an extensive system of reservoirs, and federal expenditures in the neighborhood of $100 million a year. Many Southerners had also called for expanded civilian participation in the development and implementation of any plan. Coolidge ignored or refused their appeals. The final law was characterized by a weakened MRC, massive floodways, meager compensation for the use of private land, and an enfeebled engineering board.[103]

The origins of the 1928 Flood Control Act reveal that politicians rather than engineers drove the formation of federal flood control policy in the United States. This also had important implications for both the Army Corps of Engineers and the Lower Mississippi Valley. Illinois Congressman Frank R. Reid and the MRC asked for the implementation of a definite flood plan. In part, this was due to budgetary reasons. Unfortunately, the necessary technical solutions that would eventually obviate the need for one of the two major floodways in Louisiana were still several years away. That plus fiscal conservatism precluded any serious consideration of employing reservoirs as alternative floodways. This led to ten years of litigation by the residents of the Atchafalaya and Tensas basins seeking to forestall the construction of floodways and for the Army engineers, the gradual "unwinding" of the Jadwin flood control plan throughout the 1930s.[104]

By mid-century, the effects of Coolidge's conservative influence on the development of a comprehensive flood control policy had been largely mitigated, as the scale of the project grew beyond anything that even Congressman Reid or Mayor Thompson could have imagined in pre-Depression 1928. The catastrophic financial collapse of October 1929 ushered in a period of extraordinary economic hardship but also brought a dramatic expansion in the size and role of the federal government. With the Democrats back at the helm in 1931, Louisiana reestablished authority over the Mississippi River policy in Congress and directed its efforts towards amending the 1928 law. Under the vital leadership of Riley J. Wilson of New Orleans, the House Flood Control Committee ordered a thorough reexamination of the Jadwin plan.[105]

ELECTIONS

Hoover won the 1928 election with ease. But did he really win? He did not carry a single Deep Southern state, and he inherited an unresolved flood situation and an unparalleled economic crisis. He won because he was in the right place at the right time, not necessarily because he was the right man for the job. His individualism policy front would backfire severely.[106] What he got right was his initial ability to manipulate the media to his favor and capitalize on his party position. The press viewed him favorably as the right man to handle the flood crisis. Second, the Republican stranglehold over the presidency, which they held almost exclusively for sixty years, was difficult to break. Further, Hoover was in an enviable position, since the regulatory role of the federal government was in its infancy. More federal aid was needed, but it was not expected, and any blame would not link to Hoover. However, this temporary lull would be supplanted by sharp criticism from some of the most disadvantaged groups.[107] The Republican presidential nominating process gave blacks power and some of it was in the South. This was ironic since Southern states had voted for a Republican presidential candidate since Reconstruction. Few blacks voted in general elections. However, blacks still controlled the GOP in several states. This control meant little in the South itself. But Southern states comprised 30 percent of the delegates needed for the presidential nomination. A significant percentage of these delegates were black, which meant political power on which Hoover did not capitalize. Barry writes that publicity over his handling of the flood had virtually created his candidacy, but it could evaporate in a moment if the seeming triumph exploded in a scandal. And a scandal over race made both the party's Progressives and its black politicians desert.[108]

WHY HOOVER?

Hoover had a lot of experience assisting and managing social upheaval. Hoover was in London during World War I and led a relief effort in distributing supplies. His accomplishment would help give him the title of Great Humanitarian. Hoover's management approach was linked to the principle of associationism. This meant noncoercive, nonpolitical promotion of general welfare. Hoover's emphasis on volunteerism was not intended to minimize the national government but to make it more expansive. Hoover was politically deft and used the media wisely. He championed the Red Cross and spoke on NBC radio to urge public contributions and support. It worked. The broadcast brought the Red Cross's fundraising total to $17 million, more than three times the initial target. As the water finally receded, Hoover basked in another round of adoring headlines. The newsmen who had watched him work tirelessly for sixty days in the flood zone, sleeping most nights in make-shift quarters on ships and trains, were deeply impressed. The great Kentucky journalist Silas Bent wrote in *Scribner's* that "miracles are the meat this Caesar feeds on."[109]

Hoover deserves credit for lowering the death rate and preventing the spread of any catastrophic disease. He may have exaggerated the level of volunteerism, since there was a significant federal contribution of boats, aircraft, food, and other provisions. However, Hoover had little experience with the South. He was disbelieving and then offended at the report that African Americans were being mistreated by white leaders in refugee camps. Numerous reports stated blacks were forced to work on the levees at gunpoint. Hoover understood management distribution. He consulted with agriculturalists to provide instruction on how to improve their self-sufficiency by raising chickens and preserving fruit. He spoke with African American leaders about using relief funds to purchase unused feed, as well as to make the transition from sharecropper to farmer. However, Hoover underestimated the politics within the relief effort of understanding Southern ways and was overly confident on national support.[110]

The publicity value of Hoover's flood relief was incalculable. Charles Lindbergh crowded Hoover out of the headlines but not out of the news at the end of May. For three months, Hoover and the flood were a top news story; then President Coolidge wrote a few words that made Hoover a leading contender for the presidency. Warren is valuable in describing Hoover. He explains that an innate shyness caused Hoover to be ill at ease with strangers and casual acquaintances. He was described as shy, awkward, diffident, and even embarrassed in formal social intercourse; in a small circle of intimates, though, he was a lively conversationalist and a fascinating raconteur. Such a man would never be a slapper of backs, a generator of anecdotes, an arm around the good fellow's shoulder. He lacked the qualities generally ascribed to good candidates. "Yet time and again, reporters remarked on his ability to instill in those surrounding him a spirit of intense loyalty."[111]

A great ambition for himself and for his country was the force that carried Hoover into the White House. He believed firmly in the great doctrines of democracy—the fundamental law, the free but responsible individual, and the mission of America to carry democracy to the world. These beliefs were fortified by David Starr Jordan's "gospel of liberal democracy," which he heard at Stanford.[112]

On December 3, 1929, Hoover outlined to Congress his vision to prevent another macro flood. This included a trunk line system of interior water-ways with a uniform depth of nine feet. By systematic development of the Mississippi, Ohio, Missouri, Allegheny, Illinois, and Tennessee Rivers and certain canals, he would authorize a north-south trunk waterway 1,500 miles long touted with various branches, including an east-west trunk waterway of 1,600 miles. The network was to be connected with the North Atlantic by the Great Lakes and St. Lawrence System, thus providing water transport between Chicago, St. Louis, Kansas City, Omaha, Louisville, Cincinnati, Pittsburgh, Memphis, Chattanooga, Minneapolis, St. Paul, and New Orleans. The price tag at the time was $55,000,000 per annum for about five years.[113]

Four years later, the inevitable happened. A major realignment occurred, whereby the flood, abandonment of black voters, and the Great Depression came together as a perfect storm. On the one hand, the Republican Party neglected and overlooked black voters as well as flood management miscalculations. On the other hand, Democrats sought black support. In the summer of 1932, DNC secretary Bob Jackson wrote, "The current state of our economy bears heavily upon the urban negro." Unlike black Americans in the South, the "urban negro" would probably be able to vote in the November elections. Roosevelt won the election so overwhelmingly that it is impossible to say that the black vote mattered decisively. But in analyzing the results of a questionnaire, the NAACP reported that "informed Negroes" shifted to the Democrats in significant numbers. Motivated by economic conditions and depression, many black voters shed their traditional tendency to support the Republicans.[114]

According to Barry, the Great Flood would have challenged any president. But it occurred during a time when there was little expectation for federal governmental intervention. Hoover was ultimately unable to maintain long-term political momentum in managing the aftermath of the Great Flood. The case is replete with irony. As Barry states, Hoover was a brilliant fool. He was brilliant in the way his mind could seize and grapple with a problem, brilliant in his ability to accomplish a task, and brilliant in the originality, comprehensiveness, and depth of the political philosophy he developed. He was a fool because he rejected evidence and truths that did not conform to his biases, and he fooled himself about what those biases were. He was, as former president and then Chief Justice William Howard Taft described him, a dreamer with grandiose ideas.[115]

HOOVER'S PHILOSOPHY

Hoover believed in indirect governmental intervention and that more prosperous people would help those in need. In other words, he believed in aggressive and structured volunteerism. He once said that government could best serve the community by bringing about cooperation between groups. However, if that did not occur, then the federal government would need to respond. The nation's response to the flood disaster seemed to confirm his beliefs initially. Of the 33,849 people in the Red Cross flood effort, only 2,438 were paid. Ultimately, tens of millions of Americans donated money for relief. However, these rehabilitation efforts highlighted a policy hole. Refugees leaving camps were destitute and those who owned farms, rented farms, or sharecropped on plantations smaller than 200 acres were supposed to receive household and farming equipment, seed for crops, and if their home had been destroyed, tents and camp bedding. But this did not occur uniformly. Hoover also valued private credit relief. He emphasized that credit would be the driving force that would link industry and private individuals to assist in the relief effort. However, it was a trap. Farmers had mortgaged their lands but otherwise had little capital to offer as collateral to big lenders.[116]

In the end, there was little financial relief for the flood victims. This was ironic because the Treasury Department, prior to the flood, had collected a record surplus of $635 million. However, the government would not create a single loan guarantee program. Hoover's private capital campaign ultimately amounted to $20 for each victim. The media, which was initially favorable to Hoover's approach, soon became critical. In all fairness, newspapers directed their vent mostly towards Coolidge. However, Hoover took the criticism personally and responded to numerous critics by writing personalized lengthy responses that often ran as special articles.[117]

THE RED CROSS

The National Red Cross, aided by the Department of Commerce and the National Guard, had the responsibility to house flood refugees. One hundred and thirty-four relief camps were established to shelter the thousands of homeless flood refugees. However, the management of these relief camps, largely administered by Southern whites, reflected endemic racism. The National Red Cross's commitment to grassroots mobilization and voluntarism allowed southern whites to operate relief camps with almost total autonomy; the early direct input from the National Red Cross came from the few experienced Red Cross workers who were present at the site to coordinate equipment, supplies, and authority for expenditures between the Red Cross regional headquarters and the local committees. National Red Cross officials evinced little interest in the treatment of black laborers by Southern whites, proclaiming that since they did not create the social conditions in the South, it was not their function to reform them. Instead, Red Cross officials believed that their role was to relieve temporary suffering due to the disaster and not make systemic social changes. Hoover resonated with this belief, arguing, "The national agencies have no responsibility for the economic system which exists in the South or for matters which have taken place in previous years."[118]

Overt racism was rampant. The Red Cross provided for a decentralized relief infrastructure, which left the administrative role to the discretion of local Southerners. Plantation owners soon colluded with local Southern whites to ensure that black relief camps served merely as holding pens designed to ensure the retention and preservation of the Southern labor force. In the black camps, National Guard soldiers were armed and as one contemporary observed, effectively prevented entrance into the camps of any outside persons or exit from the relief camps. Black refugees could not leave the relief camps without a Red Cross approved destination. In some instances, black laborers were even forced to wear tags listing the name of the planter for whom they had previously worked. The head of one relief camp reported being instructed not to release any family or persons from the camp except at the personal or written consent of the landlord from whose plantation the laborers came.

The *Vicksburg Evening Post* reflected these labor practices by reporting that every effort was made to control and return black laborers to their prior employers. L.O. Crosby, Mississippi's regional coordinator of flood relief, reaffirmed the need to detain black laborers in the relief camps until the water receded, so they could be put to work cleaning up the flood-ravaged plantations. General Curtis Green, the National Guard Officer in charge of the four Vicksburg refugee camps, explained that regardless of what the refugees themselves wanted, Red Cross authorities were committed to returning refugees to the place from which they had been evacuated, so there would be no shortage of labor to clear lands and prepare crops.[119]

If black laborers refused to leave, they had to provide concrete proof of an alternative plan. This plan had to be presented in the form of a letter from a relative stating that the refugee could receive assistance from him or her indefinitely. Refugees who could not produce such a letter and who persisted in their refusal to leave the camp were informed that they were no longer eligible to receive Red Cross supplies. Dependent on Red Cross rations for sustenance and fearful of consequent stigmatization and abuse from the National Guard, many black laborers had no choice but to return to the plantations.[120]

This type of governing philosophy was particularly treacherous when so many lives were at stake. Barry notes that the Great Flood poured in by as much as thirty feet of water over lands where nearly a million people lived. Twenty-seven thousand square miles were inundated, roughly equal to Massachusetts, Connecticut, New Hampshire, and Vermont combined. An estimated 330,000 people were rescued from rooftops, trees, isolated patches of high ground, and levees. The Red Cross ran 134 tent cities in seven states—Kentucky, Tennessee, Missouri, Illinois, Mississippi, Arkansas, and

Louisiana. A total of 325,554 people, including many African Americans, lived in these camps for as long as four months. An additional 311,922 people outside the camps were fed and clothed by the Red Cross. Most of these were white. Of the remaining 300,000 people, most fled and a few cared for themselves, surviving on their own food and on their own property.[121]

ELECTIONS

Herbert Hoover capitalized on the Great Flood, which helped propel him into the 1928 presidency. However, it is important to assess his challengers. A composite analysis will be drawn with eight identifiable factors that offer insight towards explaining the 1928 and 1932 elections. The Great Mississippi Flood of 1927 should be appreciated in the context of understanding the Democratic challengers. Hoover's 1928 challenger was an equal enigma.

Al Smith was a career politician who worked his way up in Tammany Hall. He began his political career working at the polls for the precinct leader. In 1903, he entered the New York Assembly and championed reform measures such as workmen's compensation, equal pay for women teachers, and better care for the handicapped. As majority leader of the Assembly in 1911, he supported William F. Sheehan for U.S. senator and encountered the successful opposition of Franklin D. Roosevelt.[122]

Smith's services in the Assembly helped consolidate his Democratic position. After a term as sheriff of New York, he became president of the Board of Alderman. Elected governor in 1918, he occupied the executive mansion at Albany until 1928. Throughout his tenure as governor, Smith revealed a genuine humanitarian instinct. He supported minority rights and vetoed bills that sought to degrade education by requiring teachers to prove their Americanism. He supported freedom of speech, thought, and education, and he saw political action as a core liberty.[123]

Herbert Hoover and Alfred E. Smith had a great deal in common. They were both self-made men, proud of their rise from obscurity to eminence, and deeply devoted to the system in which they had personally experienced success. But the dissimilarities outweighed the commonalities. Hoover began as a farm boy in Iowa with a Quaker background, worked his way through college, became a mining engineer, acquired great wealth, and achieved fame as an organizer of Belgian relief during World War I and as an administrator in the Wilson, Harding, and Coolidge administrations. Smith, by contrast, was an Irish Catholic who grew up on the Lower East side, went into politics as a young man, and with the help of Tammany Hall, rose to governorship. There he gained a reputation for efficiency and social reform.[124]

There were also two Americas in 1928's candidates: city and country, East and West, Protestant and Catholic. There were two styles: Smith—informal, down to earthy, expansive, wise cracking; Hoover—austere, reserved, blunt, humorless. Or in other terms, "Al Smith as was seen with his brown derby and big cigar was 'wet' while the 'Great Engineer' with his plain dress and severe manner was 'dry.'"[125]

By the time the Republicans met in Kansas City on June 12, 1928, Hoover was a front runner. "Who but Hoover?" was a traditional campaign slogan. Hoover was teamed up with Senator Charles Curtis from Kansas and had the business community support. He demonstrated efficiency as the Commerce Department head; he also showed humanitarian and administrative competence for victims of the Mississippi Valley flooding. He called for limited governmental intervention in the economy, tax reduction, high tariffs, and full enforcement of the 18th Amendment.[126]

The Democratic platform was ambiguous, proposing tariff revision and farm relief measures. As for Prohibition, the Democrats pledged "an honest effort" toward enforcing the 18th Amendment. The 1928 convention, gathered in Houston (to please Southern Democrats) on June 26, was a sharp contrast to 1924. William McAdoo, spokesman for the rural South and West, had dropped out in 1927 "in the interest of the party unity," and the delegates in Houston resolved to submerge their rural–urban, North–South, and wet–dry differences. With McAdoo out of the running, there was only one logical candidate: Al Smith, the enormously popular and successful governor of New York.[127]

Radio had become electorally important, so Hoover had an advantage. He tended to be prolix, ponderous, and pedantic in his speech-writing and came across as a high-minded statesman. Smith was better in person but froze with the microphone. The country was still prosperous and Hoover made the most of it. Hoover said in his nomination speech, "We in America today are near to the final triumph over poverty than ever before in the history of the land." Hoover stressed the "American system" of free enterprise as the source of prosperity, and Republican orators promised a "chicken in every pot and two cars in every garage."[128]

Religion was a major issue. Smith emphasized "the absolute separation" of church and state. "I have taken an oath of office nineteen times," he declared. "Each time I swore to defend and maintain the Constitution of the United States." However, there was resistance to Smith's approach. Many Protestant ministers railed against him. One minister stated, "If you vote for Al Smith, you're voting against Christ and you'll be damned." Anti-Catholic literature dating back to the pre–Civil War know-nothing days was revived and circulated throughout the country, insisting, "A Vote for Al Smith is a Vote for the Pope," and a Smith triumph was thought to mean "Rum, Romanism, and Ruin."[129]

Prohibition was also a big issue. Hoover called Prohibition "a great social and economic experiment, noble in motive and far-reaching in purpose" and said it "must be worked out constructively." Smith, disturbed by the crime spawned by Prohibition, favored "fundamental changes in the provisions for national prohibition." He was criticized by the Anti-Saloon League, the Women's Christian Temperance Union, and other militant dry groups.[130] Smith was also hurt by his Tammany Hall connection because of its image of corruption and greed. Many people thought he would become a Tammany President.[131]

Hoover and Smith supported equality of opportunity, protection of the American home, and the welfare of American children. Both stressed the importance of developing inland waterways and conserving natural resources. Both favored better relations with Latin America, although Smith could be more forthright in denouncing current policies. An analysis of his major speeches shows that Hoover dealt too much in generalities, banalities, and exhortations.

Hoover stressed great economic gains and endorsed full employment based on sound financials buttressed by vigorous governmental cooperation to promote economic welfare. Hoover did not define sound policies or specify what the federal government could do to maintain full employment. Republicans had ended the unemployment of 1921 with "a nation-wide employment conference" and "a program for the systematic organization of the whole business community to restore employment." Labor's prosperity depended on "sound governmental policies and wise leadership." Hoover believed in these principles and announced, "Never in our history was the leadership in our economic life more distinguished in its abilities than today, and it has grown greatly in its conscientiousness of public responsibility."[132] He was ambiguous regarding federal relief for refugees and feared federal aid might lead to federal intrusion into state matters. He abhorred federal intrusion more than concentrated wealth.[133]

Hoover recognized that the public did not understand intricate economic relationships. He believed the business cycle was impacted by periods of optimism and pessimism. This may suggest why he was so placid in the public. He may have concealed his true feelings from the press and associates.[134]

The final count cast on November 6, 1928, gave Hoover 21,392,000 votes and Smith only 15,016,000, making the popular vote much closer than the electoral count of 444 to 87. Smith carried the Deep South, which was Mississippi, Alabama, Georgia, South Carolina, Arkansas, and Louisiana. He also captured Massachusetts and Rhode Island. Hoover did not capture the Deep South. It really should not have been a surprise. Coolidge had been slow to address the flood, and somehow, the state of Illinois was more aggressive in developing new flood legislation. Hoover was in the South during the crisis, but he assumed a deficit. The Deep South was already distrustful of Republican big corporate ideology, and feelings of alienation may have been accentuated due to relief lags. Blacks were already disenfranchised and lack of relief as inequality only exacerbated the situation.[135]

EIGHT-VARIABLE ANALYSIS

One of the seminal components of this study has been to gauge how the environment impacts a campaign, specifically toward the presidency. First, the Great Flood unmasked the limitations of federalism at that time. It also revealed how woefully unprepared the federal government was in addressing force majeure events like major floods. However, the environment's impact on a national campaign cannot be isolated as a cause. Therefore, in addition to the environment, an eight-step typology has been developed to further evaluate the 1928 election. The key factors are media, campaign strategies, political trust, momentum, bandwagon effect, incumbency, Rose Garden strategy, and retrospective voting. Admittedly, some of these terms are more modern day or contemporary social constructs. However, they are important in providing a composite understanding of how the Great Flood truly impacted the 1928 election.

1) Media is important, and while social media was quite different than today, it was advanced enough to portray deep unsettling images of the flood as well as the swathe of destruction. For the most part, the media was favorable enough to enable him to secure the 1928 election. However, it was myopic, and Hoover's tenure in office would be limited to one term.
2) Hoover's general campaign strategy was reflective of his experiences and personal values. He placed supreme confidence on the free market system and supported limited government more than Coolidge. He also espoused volunteerism and believed that private relief agencies would serve as the fulcrum force on mitigating the storm's impact.
3) Political trust is more of a modern construct, tightly correlated with public opinion polls. This was still a decade away. However, presidents always need public support. It appears that Hoover's initial support came from big businesses, the media, and prominent relief agencies like the Red Cross. Political trust was more fractional, with greater support in the Northeast and Western part of the United States.
4) Momentum—Hoover had momentum in his political record. He had achieved success in relieving the food famine towards the end of World War I. He also had a lot governmental experience, serving in various

capacities under Wilson, Harding, and Coolidge. The media was quick to support him.

5) Bandwagon approach—This approach is very similar to momentum, though it includes numerous stakeholders. In this case, Hoover had the Republican Party support, the media, and strong support from traditional Republican strongholds of the time: the powerful Northeast, Midwest, and West. Whether new groups suddenly supported his campaign initiative is hard to discern. It is clear that he had secured critical key stakeholders, at least enough to secure the 1928 nomination and election.

6) Incumbency—As a general rule, incumbents have political advantages. However, in this case, Hoover had modified incumbency. The Republic Party was in office, but he was a newcomer for the presidency. Party incumbency was helpful and aided his ascent to the 1928 presidency.

7) Rose Garden strategy is a modern construct that has been used to assess presidents in the latter part of the twentieth century. In short, it reflects an uncanny ability to seem natural and not weigh activity or gesture in terms of votes. Hoover was politically principled and believed in earnest in the free market system. He championed social values and equality. However, he did not likely gauge some of the social inequities associated with the flood. Particular reference to the black sharecroppers should be noted.

8) Retrospective Voting—This is also a modern term but yields important utility. It asks *What have you done for me lately?* in its approach. This concept is inherently tied to economic activity. The record was mixed here, because the economy was still strong during the 1928 election. However, there was protracted suffering and relief delay in the flood areas.

1932 ELECTION

There was an exuberant feeling among Democrats that defeating Herbert Hoover in the 1932 election would be easy. However, there were also people positioned in the far left who thought that the political opening was for candidates other than Franklin Delano Roosevelt. However, that would be a tall task. Franklin Delano Roosevelt was a great campaigner. He demonstrated deft and skill in his speeches. It was depression time and he demonstrated an air of optimism. Warren states, "He was an optimist, confident of his own ability, superbly courageous, mentally alert, and well educated. He possessed the power of leadership, and his instinctive humanitarianism which bridged the gulf between elites and the masses."[136]

President Hoover had no overpowering desire to run in 1932. The Republican Party was fracturing. There were even rumblings of party opposition to support Calvin Coolidge, William E. Borah, Hiram Johnson, and several others. When his secretary broached the subject early in the year, Hoover brusquely announced his indifference to another nomination. Part of the problem was that Hoover struggled on the national scene as a policy maker. He could not rally his party. This was somewhat unusual for the Republican Party. The last incumbent president removed by the Republican Party was Rutherford B. Hayes in 1880.

Yet President Hoover had a defeatist attitude when he began the campaign. His post-election statement reveals a somber perspective. He commented, "As we expected, we were defeated in the election." His speeches lacked enthusiasm and he was unable to take advantage of the radio medium that had presented itself as an important campaign tool. At times, he mumbled and did not clearly present the important messages that he had written. As the campaign neared its conclusion, Hoover gained self-confidence and offered a sharp rebuttal of the proposed New Deal at Madison Square Garden on October 31, 1931.[137]

Both candidates were subject to criticism. Each candidate was accused of hiding behind vague generalities, absurd promises, and irresponsible charges. Both candidates were satirized by a term called "The Drifter": "It is only a new wrapper for the old baloney. A program which doesn't mean anything can sometimes be made quite impressive if stated in twelve points, and . . . it is easy to slip in a joker somewhere among them without attracting too much attention." It is possible for Herbert Hoover to promise the farmers higher prices for their produce in nine points and in the tenth, to conclude none of the proposed methods will raise food prices. At the same time, Roosevelt can mesmerize his audience with twelve points for controlling the public utilities but not disturb private initiative and ownership.[138]

Hoover possessed encyclopedic knowledge, limitless energy, and great administrative skill. However, he was politically naïve and lacked political intelligence. He struggled in making political decisions. Yet he enjoyed publicity through extensive newspaper, magazine, and film contacts. When Will Irwin in 1928 pieced together the campaign film *The Master of Emergencies*, he had "some ten miles" of miscellaneous cinema films showing Hoover's activities dating back to 1914. "All his advertising has made him appeal to the American imagination but not to the American heart."[139]

This was a sharp rebuke for the "Great Engineer," and bitter commentary emerged about Hoover. For example, Hoover asked his secretary of treasury to lend him a nickel to buy a soda for a friend, and the latter said, "Here's a dime: Treat them all!" And a Kansas farmer declared that Hoover was the greatest engineer of the world, since "he had drained, ditched, and damned the United States in three years." Even ex-President Coolidge was depressed. "This country," he announced, "is not in good condition."[140]

Hoover acknowledged in his *Memoirs*, "General prosperity had been a great ally in the election of 1928," but general depression "was a major enemy in 1932." The Great Depression followed the devastating stock market crash of 1929. It was the worst in the nation's history and shattered the President's reputation for administrative skill and humanitarian concern. Hoover was, in fact, the first president to take positive measures to cope with an economic depression, but the action he took—expanding public works and sponsoring the Reconstruction Finance Corporation to lend money to banks, industries, and state and local governments—failed to stem the tide of disaster. By the time Americans launched the 1932 campaign season, industrial production was low, unemployment was widespread, and there were scores of farmers facing financial ruin. By 1932, millions of Americans were *damming* Hoover and the Republican Party. When the nominating conventions met in Chicago in June of 1932, the Democrats believed they could win as long as they could avoid any major errors.

Hoover felt obliged to run though it was a political trap game. Hoover wanted to vindicate himself and his policies, and a Republican denial would mean party failure. The Republican convention was subdued. Hoover and Vice President Charles Curtis were both re-nominated on the first ballots. However, there was a tempered response. There were no spontaneous demonstrations or spirited celebrations. The delegates did not even bother to post pictures of the president around the convention hall. The Republican platform praised the administration's antidepression measures, called for a balanced budget and a protective tariff, and urged repealing the 18th Amendment (Prohibition) and returning control of the liquor tariff to the states. "Surely it is astonishing," remarked columnist Walter Lipmann, "that in the midst of such great economic distress, there should be no rumbling here of social discontent."[141]

The Democratic Convention was different. Franklin D. Roosevelt, two-term governor of New York, was the front-runner; he had shown vigor and resourcefulness in meeting an economic crisis in New York and his supporters had been carefully gathering support for him. But Alfred E. Smith wanted to try again, and he had the support of party regulars, particularly in the East. John Nance Garner, speaker of the House, was also popular; he had the backing of the Texas and California delegations, and William Randolph Hearst was pushing hard for him in chains of newspapers across the country. When the delegates began voting, FDR led on the first ballot with Smith in second place and Garner trailing far behind, but he lacked the necessary two-thirds to win.[142]

Roosevelt men made a deal with Garner; if he released his delegates, he would receive second place on the ticket. Garner knew he could not win first place himself, and he was far closer in sympathies to FDR than to Smith. He was also anxious to avoid a deadlock in the convention. Hearst, who controlled the California Delegation, decided FDR was acceptable—especially since he had repudiated the League of Nations in February—and finally agreed to go along with Garner.[143]

A Roosevelt nomination was not a foregone conclusion, and there were many critics. "It's a kangaroo ticket," stated a Texas politician after Roosevelt's nomination, "stronger in the hindquarters than in the front." He was not the only person to underestimate Roosevelt. H. L. Mencken wrote, "Here was a great convention . . . nominating the weakest candidate before it." Walter Lippmann was even more disparaging. He had already dismissed FDR as "an amiable boy scout." The New York governor, he now wrote, "is no crusader. He is no tribune of the people. He is no enemy of entrenched privilege. He is a pleasant man who, without any important qualification for office, would very much like to be President."[144]

Garner and Roosevelt differed sharply in campaign strategies. Garner's *sit down, do nothing, and win the election* approach was in sharp contrast to Roosevelt. Garner gave only one radio speech. FDR disagreed. He loved campaigning and rode about 13,000 miles by train, making sixteen major addresses, each devoted to a special topic.[145]

Roosevelt also delivered conventional speeches. Surprisingly, some supporters thought he spoke in generalities like Hoover, especially when he called for government spending restraints and a balanced budget. On September 23, 1932, at the Cotton Club in San Francisco, Roosevelt presented the basic philosophy of the New Deal when he insisted that the federal government must help the business community develop "an economic constitutional order" in which there would be a fairer distribution of wealth and in which every man would be assured the right to make a comfortable living.[146]

Hoover had not planned any extensive campaigning. He remained hard at work in the White House. However, the "Hoover depression" roused his wrath. Hoover's response when he took to the stump in October of 1932 was too late. He gave nine speeches, during which he insisted the depression stemmed from World War I and originated abroad and not at home as FDR maintained. He further retorted that his measures prevented total collapse, saying, "Let no man say it could not have been worse." He reiterated his faith in individual initiative and free enterprise, accused the Democrats in Congress of blocking his efforts to restore the economy, and called FDR's proposals radical and socialistic. Hoover emphasized that there were signs of recovery and any delay was due to FDR's fear tactics.[147]

Hoover was the last president to write his own speeches. They did not instill confidence in the nation. They sounded dreary in comparison to FDR's eloquent messages. In one, he rebutted a Republican charge that he was under the influence of radical foreign notions, commenting, "My policy is as radical as American liberty, as radical as the Constitution of the United States." He wanted to make an even stronger response to allegations of un-Americanism and stated that Hoover's record as president was that of the Four Horsemen: Destruction, Delay, Despair, and Doubt.[148]

The 1932 election left little to be imagined. On November 8, 1932, some 40,000,000 people went to the polls. FDR won over 7,000,000 more popular votes than Hoover. Winning 22,821,857 (57.4 percent) to 15,781,841 (39.7 percent), he also carried 42 of the 48 states and won 472 electoral votes to Hoover's 39. The Democrats also won both houses of Congress by big majorities. However, the election was not necessarily a mandate for the New Deal; the New Deal was still rather vague in FDR's mind. But it unquestionably represented "a firm desire on part of the American people" as William Allen White stated, "to use government as an agency for human welfare."[149]

FDR'S FOCUS

The 1932 election was a critical time in American political history. Never before had the nation witnessed such a political realignment. The Republican Party lost its strongholds on the Northeast and West. The Democrats carved out new political territory. They expanded to absorb almost the entire nation in sharp contrast to a party that primarily held onto the Deep South since the end of Reconstruction. What was at stake was the financial stability of the United States as well as the legitimacy of the executive office. The New Deal was awkward and untested, and it prompted a change in federal management.

According to Lowi, the New Deal was born in 1933 and was buried at some point toward the end of 1939. During those six fateful years, the Roosevelt administration expanded the civil service from 572,000 to 920,000 employees, a rate of increase of 58,000 employees per year. The Roosevelt budget grew from $4.6 billion to $8.8 billion, a rate increase of about $700 million per year. In the four preceding years, the Hoover administration had expanded the civil service from 540,000 Coolidge employees to 572,000, an increase of about 8,000 per year. The Hoover budget had expanded from $3.1 billion to $4.6 billion, a rate increase of about half that of the six years of the New Deal prior to mobilization.[150]

However, it may not have been a fiscal revolution. In 1934, which was the first full year of the New Deal, the budget was $6.7 billion. About $2 billion was allocated to the Works Progress Administration (WPA) and $1 billion to the Public Works Administration (PWA); another half billion dollars was budgeted for the Civil Works Administration (CWA). These three programs alone accounted for nearly 53 percent of the 1934 budget, 46 percent of the 1935 budget, and 41 percent of the 1936 budget. Although these programs were proposed as recovery and relief programs, they also featured patronage. Comparable programs existed before the New Deal, including river and harbor improvements, highway construction, agricultural assistance, and other "internal improvements."[151]

The New Deal can be divided into two types. The first is regulatory policy. These resemble regulatory efforts attempted by the national government between 1887 and 1932. They are similar to policies associated with the state governments. The regulatory policies of the New Deal went beyond a narrow interpretation of interstate commerce and attempted to affect the local conditions that the Supreme Court defined as outside national government action. These new regulatory programs became known by the first letters of their official names. A cursory study of the items reveals that they are regulatory in the sense that each seeks to impose obligations directly upon citizens.[152] The national government established a direct and coercive relationship between itself and individual citizens, or in other words, manifested a function of coercive federalism. This meant that the federal government would compel states toward adhering to national standards. This was the beginning of the shift from federalism to a more top-down model.

The second type of policy was redistributive or welfare state policy. The Federal Reserve Act and the income tax are examples of this type of policy. This policy framework was what Coolidge and to a certain extent Hoover could not conceptualize to realize its potential. Still, other critical messages are revealed. First, these policies differ from traditional patronage in that societal impact is much broader. Second, redistributive policy, like regulatory policy, is coercive. However, the configuration is different. Redistributive policies do not attempt to impose direct obligations on individuals; rather, they attempt to influence individuals by manipulating the environment of conduct rather than conduct itself. They seek to create new structures, to influence people by manipulating the value of property or money, and to categorize people according to some universalized attribute such as level of income, age, or status of occupation.[153]

The Supreme Court also recognized the difference between regulatory and redistributive policies, accepting the constitutionality of regulatory policies in the famous cases of *NLRB v. Jones & Laughlin Steel Corp.* The National Labor Relations Act provided, among other things, that the National Labor Relations Board (NLRB) could forbid any person from engaging in an unfair labor practice "affecting commerce." The grievance in question originated in one of the Jones & Laughlin plants in Pennsylvania, and the constitutional issue was whether manufacturing, which is inherently local, had a sufficient effect upon interstate commerce in some cases to justify Congress's intervention.[154]

Roosevelt's policies reshaped the federal government. He never abandoned the patronage state. Instead, he built on top of it a regulatory and redistributive government. This enabled the national government to modernize. The New Deal had a far reach, ranging from the local farmer to the corporate business person. The modern welfare state was born, and while it took time to evaluate, a new social contract between state and society was created. This contract was confirmed in the Employment Act of 1946. Though the act did set up a new agency, the Council of Economic Advisers, whose function is implied by its name, it established no new programs. However, the Employment Act is a milestone in the history of American government because the national government officially and explicitly claimed responsibility for providing employment to people seeking it or other support if employment was not available. The national government would be responsible for every injurious act sustained by any individual citizen and also for providing the conditions for every individual citizen's wellbeing.[155] These changes are fundamental to the continuing legitimacy and stability of modern government. By 1946, legitimacy shifted from representation to governance and later, to the president's capacity to govern. There is a debate about whether institutional change brought on by the New Deal was inevitable.

One of the most important political changes attributable to the New Deal was President-Congress relations. A large bureaucracy was created that delegated broad powers of discretion to each of the agencies. It could be argued that early tenets of such political change, including corporate and interest group liberalism, predated the New Deal. The National Recovery Administration (NRA) was an extreme example of corporatist politics and eventually declared unconstitutional by the Supreme Court.[156] Hoover contributed to the theory as well as the practice of interest-group liberalism. However, the key was Roosevelt, whose hospitality to these ideas and practices, as well as the success of his administration in having them adopted into law, made him a stronger proponent of this approach. Roosevelt was more a broker than thinker. He was a pragmatist and improviser even if such an approach reflected inconsistencies.

And there were conflicts, sometimes between the executive office and legislative branch, as well as the between the executive office and the judiciary. Roosevelt displayed a consistent preference for writing the conflicts into legislation and providing for the group interactions to continue within the administrative process itself.[157] Hoover never reached that plateau.

EIGHT-VARIABLE ANALYSIS

There was a stark difference in approaches between Hoover and Roosevelt. The eight-variable analysis can also be applied to the 1932 election to help us understand Hoover's policy limitations.

A) Media—The media was an initial ally to Hoover with the Great Flood. However, he failed to address the black refugee crisis. The situation was compounded with the Great Depression. He had a penchant for courting the media. However, he was unable to sell himself as a problem solver for the 1932 election. He appeared maladroit and lackluster in the speeches that he delivered.

B) Campaign strategies vary. However, his strategy mirrored his political philosophy. He appeared reserved and hesitated in making extensive campaign speeches. This was a critical gap especially during such a troubling time.

C) As mentioned previously, political trust is a key variable and is used in modern polling. However, it is central here, because Hoover had the opportunity to galvanize political trust. He had extensive political experience and was the Great Humanitarian and Great Engineer. He could solve societal problems. One could argue that some of the challenges were connected to the limited role of the federal government. Yet as this study demonstrates, there were several policy gaps as well as his inability to assuage critical societal concerns. Hoover's volunteerism and limited federalism may have worked for the food famine, but it would not suffice a decade later.

D) Momentum was a critical concern for Hoover, who was in deficit for the 1932 election. He was not able to channel new ideas or instil confidence in the American public.

E) Bandwagon effect was one of the starkest components for the Hoover campaign. He had made critical errors in his flood management approach. He alienated black voters in the South and never capitalized on the cracking the Deep South for Electoral College votes. Admittedly, it was another time, as the South was beleaguered by Jim Crow. Blacks could not vote, and whites were already distrustful of the Republican Party due to Coolidge's stand-off approach during the early days of the flood's aftermath. Hoover had four years to correct that but failed to do so. This was further compounded by the economic crash leading to the Great Depression. This alienated scores of his followers, extending nationwide.

F) Incumbency would prove to be one of the most debilitating factors for the Hoover campaign. He was the sitting president for managing the Great Flood results and even more ominously the Great Depression. These factors undermined the power of incumbency and ultimately led to his defeat.

G) Rose Garden Strategy—Hoover evidenced some of these strategies by trying to appear distant yet presidential. However, the political times in the United States were changing. This meant a renewed urgency for federal involvement. Distance was not an effective strategy for a country in need.

H) Retrospective voting was another seminal concern and is fairly easy to gauge. It was hard for Hoover to overcome such challenges. It is unfair to say he was solely responsible for policy failures. But could he have done more in assuaging refugee suffering? Could he have ameliorated the living conditions in the Hoovervilles? Hoover was part of a changing American landscape. He offered valuable key approaches, but he needed to make his case, which was desperately needed in 1932. Another party did.

NOTES

1. Kenneth Whyte, *Hoover: An Extraordinary Life in Extraordinary Times* (New York: Vintage, 2017).
2. George Nash, *The Life of Herbert Hoover: Master of Emergencies, 1917–1918* (New York: Norton, 1996).
3. Nash, *The Life*.
4. Ibid.
5. Harris Gaylord Warren, *Herbert Hoover and the Great Depression* (New York: Norton, 1967).
6. Warren, *Herbert Hoover*.
7. Ibid.
8. Ibid.
9. Ibid.
10. Ibid.
11. Ibid.
12. Ibid.
13. Ibid.
14. Ibid.
15. Ibid.
16. Ibid.
17. Ibid.
18. Ibid.
19. Nash, *The Life*.
20. Ibid.
21. Ibid.
22. Ibid.
23. Ibid.
24. Ibid.
25. Ibid.
26. Ibid.
27. Ibid.
28. Ibid.
29. Ibid.
30. Ibid.
31. Ibid.
32. Ibid.
33. Ibid.
34. Ibid.
35. Ibid.

36. Ibid.
37. Warren, *Herbert Hoover.*
38. Ibid.
39. Ibid.
40. Ibid.
41. Ibid.
42. Ibid.
43. Ibid.
44. Ibid.
45. Ibid.
46. Ibid.
47. Richard M. Mizelle Jr., *Backwater Blues: The Mississippi Flood of 1927 in the African Imagination* (Minneapolis: University of Minnesota Press, 2013), 7–15.
48. David Butler, "Focusing Events in the Early Twentieth Century: A Hurricane, Two Earthquakes, and a Pandemic," in *Emergency Management: The American Experience 1900-2010*, ed. Claire B. Rubin (London: CRC Press, 2012): 13–50.
49. Butler, "Focusing Events," 13–50.
50. Ibid.
51. Ibid.
52. Ibid.
53. Ibid.
54. Ibid.
55. Ibid.
56. Ibid.
57. Ibid.
58. Ibid.
59. Ibid.
60. Ibid.
61. Gareth Davies, "The Changing Presidential Politics of Disaster: From Coolidge to Nixon," in *Recapturing the Oval Office: New Historical Approaches to the American Presidency*, eds. Brian Balogh and Bruce Schulman (Cornell University Press, 2015).
62. Davies, "The Changing Presidential."
63. Ibid.
64. Robyn Spencer, "Contested Terrain: The Mississippi Flood of 1927 and the Struggle to Control Black Labor," *Journal of Negro History* 79 (Spring 1994): 170–181.
65. Butler, "Focusing Events," 13–50.
66. Mizelle Jr., *Backwater Blues.*
67. Ibid.
68. Ibid.
69. Ibid.
70. Ibid.
71. Ibid.
72. Susan Scott Parrish, *The Flood Year 1927: a Cultural History* (Princeton, NJ: Princeton University Press, 2017), 8–29.
73. Parrish, *The Flood Year 1927.*

74. Ibid.
75. Mizelle Jr., *Backwater Blues.*
76. Ibid.
77. Ibid.
78. Richard M. Mizelle Jr., "Black Levee Camp Workers, the NAACP, and the Mississippi Flood Control Project, 1927-1933," *The Journal of African American History* 98, no. 4 (Fall 2013): 511–530.
79. Spencer, "Contested Terrain," 170–181.
80. Ibid.
81. Ibid.
82. Ibid.
83. Ibid.
84. Deborah Hopkinson, *The Great Flood of 1927*, www.scholastic.com/storywork.
85. Herbert Hoover, *The Memoirs of Herbert Hoover: The Cabinet and the Presidency 1920-1933* (Macmillan Company: New York, 1952), 1–405.
86. Hoover, *The Memoirs*, 1–405.
87. Ibid.
88. Ibid.
89. Ibid.
90. Ibid.
91. Warren, *Herbert Hoover.*
92. Mathew T. Pearcy, "After the Flood: A History of the 1928 Flood Control Act," *Journal of the Illinois State Historical Society* 95, no. 2 (Summer 2002): 172–80, www.jstor.org/stable/40193521.
93. Pearcy, "After the Flood," 172–180.
94. Ibid.
95. Ibid.
96. Ibid.
97. Ibid.
98. Ibid.
99. Ibid.
100. Ibid.
101. Ibid.
102. Ibid.
103. Ibid.
104. Ibid.
105. Ibid.
106. John Barry, *Rising Tide: The Great Mississippi Flood of 1927 and How It Changed America* (New York: Simon and Schuster, 1997), 173–179.
107. Eric Rauchway, *Winter War: Hoover, Roosevelt, and the First Clash Over the New Deal* (New York: Basic Books, 2018), 13–15.
108. Barry, *Rising Tide.*
109. Barry, *Rising Tide.*
110. Spencer, "Contested Terrain," 170–81.
111. Warren, *Herbert Hoover.*
112. Warren, *Herbert Hoover.*

113. Warren, *Herbert Hoover.*
114. Rauchway, *Winter War.*
115. Warren, *Herbert Hoover*
116. Barry, *Rising Tide.*
117. Barry, *Rising Tide.*
118. Barry, *Rising Tide.*
119. Mizelle Jr., "Black Levee," 511–30.
120. Ibid.
121. Barry, *Rising Tide.*
122. Warren, *Herbert Hoover.*
123. Ibid.
124. Ibid.
125. Ibid.
126. Ibid.
127. Ibid.
128. Ibid.
129. Ibid.
130. Ibid.
131. Ibid.
132. Ibid.
133. Ibid.
134. Ibid.
135. Ibid.
136. Ibid.
137. Whyte, *Winter War.*
138. Warren, *Herbert Hoover.*
139. Ibid.
140. Ibid.
141. Ibid.
142. Ibid.
143. Ibid.
144. Ibid.
145. Ibid.
146. Ibid.
147. Ibid.
148. Ibid.
149. Ibid.
150. Lowi, *The Personal President,* 1, 24, & 34.
151. Ibid.
152. Ibid.
153. Ibid.
154. Ibid.
155. Ibid.
156. Ibid.
157. Ibid.

Chapter 6

How Do Environmental Factors Impact a Political Campaign?

The 1927 Great Mississippi Flood was one of several factors that impacted both the 1928 and 1932 elections. If we start with the term *environmentalism*, we can see that lack of effective regulations contributed in part to the Great Flood. This had long-term implications. Displacement, despair, and dislocation were all key end products from the Great Mississippi Flood of 1927. Early optimism in the post-flood period soon gave way to disenfranchisement, unmasking the static and deplorable Jim Crow living conditions in the Deep South and revealing fractures in federal policy. The federal government needed to provide greater levels of intervention. Lack of effective management exacerbated a major social rift in the United States. The rift was widest in the industrial North and behind that, the Deep South, which had retained deep structural and social divides between blacks and whites. The Great Mississippi Flood did not create these conditions but certainly highlighted the daily living conditions. Blacks were politically disenfranchised, so it is hard to say that their votes would have changed the 1928 or 1932 elections. However, this was an epitome of a bigger issue.

The Great Depression and the need to redefine the role of the federal government were central to the election outcomes. The Great Depression was, in part, caused by a lack of federal oversight to protect banks. Unlike the Great Recession of 2009–2010, the federal government lacked safety controls to safeguard citizen deposits. As a result, a frenzied panic caused many financial institutions to fail. The central bank failure immediately following the 1929 stock market crash was also due to a limited regulatory role of the federal government. Federal anti-trust legislation in the 1890s sought, albeit weakly, to break up monopolies. The Progressive Period, 1900–1920, created an eight-hour work day and tighter food processing and packing restrictions.

Further, the federal government increased its national presence by establishing a national income tax in 1913. However, the government was slow to provide concrete regulations and restrictions on business practices. Federal environmental law was more than a half century away. Until the early part of the twentieth century, the federal government was simply not expected to be the lead supervisor in managing force majeure events.

There is ample evidence that limited federal intervention was the preferred practice. Hoover's management approach of relying on private interests and volunteerism went unchecked. Hoover was a student and perhaps a victim of a different time period. The writings of Henry James and others were slowly being supplanted by prominent public administrators like Max Weber and Frederick Taylor. The government was being asked to do more. The 1920s as a whole yielded a veil of deception because deep regulatory behavior was not fully operational. The idea that the federal government would need to take a leadership role in managing domestic affairs let alone natural disasters was hard to fathom. It was not so much that dual federalism was the daily mainstay in managing society. However, it existed and was particularly traceable to the Deep South.

Still, states could not handle the Great Flood alone. This event impacted several states. Hoover's principle of volunteerism, which worked during the famine relief effort of World War I, was not an effective solution to assuage refugee suffering. The principle of associationalism called for private capital to be lent to local farmers. However, this was a crucial error, because the farmers did not have enough credit to guarantee lending. Further, even if there had been lending, how much it would have improved the lives of black sharecroppers is unclear. The Red Cross enjoys a national prominence, and even today, they are leaders in raising funds for flood and hurricane victims. Yet the uncanny truth is at that time they were ineffective in evenly distributing relief supplies, implicitly reinforcing Jim Crow policies during and after the Great Flood. Hoover may have exacerbated the situation by not selecting NAACP members to be part of the commission reviewing black plight and suffering in the delta region.

These conditions gave way to the need for a new type of federalism, one in which central authority was both procedurally and substantively effective. In those days, the waffling and hedging by President Coolidge as well as other inopportune approaches, created a pathway from refugee tent cities to Hoovervilles. Admittedly, the Great Flood and its aftermath also created the forum for thinkers and politicians to burgeon forth the New Deal. It has been said that necessity is the mother of invention, and perhaps that was needed at the time. However, the federal government was redefined several times in a short period, first by the Great Flood, and second, by the Great Depression, as well as the political realignment of 1932. The concept of national policy has a much greater reach and understanding today.

One of the most egregious errors during the Great Flood was the government's blind devotion to a levees-only policy. This problem extended through all levels of government. The levees revealed a limited understanding of the mitigation concept. This is of particular concern because hesitancy and political intransigence can translate into a loss of land, revenue, and lives.

Conflicting interpretations about the roles of the federal government and storm management exist. According to figure 3.1, the number of presidential-issued disaster declarations has increased exponentially, especially in the twenty-first century. However, declaring a national emergency and mitigating refugee suffering is another matter.

This study originated as a way to assess the causal link between environmental factors and political campaigns. This assessment relies on our understanding and evaluation of the executive office. Some people might argue that the structural shifts in federalism have aided the president, creating additional power to manage key storms. However, this creates an uncomfortable dilemma. We expect the president to act definitively in addressing storm management, but sometimes that is not possible. Lack of information, distance, and first responders must be factored into the policy solution equation. We expect the president to visit critical impact sites, but that does not necessarily translate into immediate relief and supplies. We expect FEMA to address the most critical issues on the ground, but in proven cases like Katrina, communication technology has underperformed. New laws have been established to prevent aftershocks of future flooding. Yet disaster management issues remain. It is not enough to say that a top-down model should be adopted, whereby the president can delegate authority to the requisite relief agencies.

We must also recognize that numerous factors impact a campaign. Environmental factors are important but other elements must be recognized. In order to satisfy the requirement, this study identified eight variables impacted the 1928 and 1932 elections. Admittedly, some terms are modern constructs and have been developed well beyond the study review's time frame. However, each variable offers important explanatory utility in political insight and executive decision making. Each variable also offers depth and understanding regarding the decisions Hoover made and those that he did not.

1) Media—The media, while in its infancy, was still significant for the time and cast light on the extensive storm damage of the Great Flood.
2) Campaign strategies—This is often a misunderstood concept, but ultimately, there exist compelling campaign strategies and others that could

break a candidate. In Hoover's case, he had a penchant for interacting with the media. He was not a particularly strong speaker, which contributed to overall political challenges.

3) Political trust—This is a valuable construct that details the public's penchant for a particular candidate. Hoover was in a political quagmire after the Great Flood. He could gain the confidence of the nation from a long-term perspective.

4) Momentum—Hoover had significant momentum. However, he may have been trapped due to his own personal philosophies as well as an antiquated federal system.

5) Bandwagon effect—Hoover's best efforts were his prior political experiences. However, he did not build a strong enough coalition to address the Great Flood nor the environmental or political aftermath of the storm.

6) Incumbency—Hoover was acting secretary of commerce when he assumed control of managing the great flood. That the incumbent advantage went to the Republican Party is a plausible theory for understanding how Hoover gained the presidency in 1928 as well as why he suffered a devastating defeat four years later.

7) Rose Garden strategy—This is similar to the general campaign strategy of acting normal and not chasing an election. Hoover was not able to change voter perceptions, which is reflective of Farley's Law.

8) Retrospective voting—The Great Flood undoubtedly impacted the 1928 election, and the long-term refugee suffering contributed in part to the 1932 election outcomes.

Figure 6.1 is very informative for this study as a basic but clear assessment of the way the states voted in the 1928 and 1932 elections. Hoover carried three of the six central states impacted by the Great Flood. He won Tennessee, Missouri, and Illinois by securing, on average, 54.6 percent of the popular vote. However, Al Smith carried Louisiana, Mississippi, and Arkansas by winning, on average, 72 percent of the popular vote. This suggests that the people of Deep Democratic states at the time voted along party lines. It also infers that Hoover's positive reception by the national media was not necessarily shared by the residents directly impacted by the Great Flood. Hoover may have also received a poor policy framework from President Coolidge. Coolidge had waffled about securing aid to the flood victim regions. Hoover was appointed to lead the recovery appeared in several places. However, this may have had more to do with symbolic management than providing direct federal aid. This time lapse only served to disenfranchise people from the Republican party. Hoover would lose all of those states in the 1932 election by 76 percent voting against him and the Republican party. This was in part due to the national realignment and changing identities of the major political parties. Moving forward to the twenty-first century, the voting patterns in these states reflect the remnant of the 1932 political realignment. All of the affected states, with the exception of Illinois, have consistently voted Republican from 2000 to 2016. But in that time period, we have experienced Hurricane Katrina, Hurricane Rita, the Gulf Oil Spill, war, and terror. Yet party allegiance remains firm, which reaffirms importance of Farley's Law.

Environmentalism is a regulatory concept in directed opposition to limited federalism, and certainly dual federalism. Today it has gained greater social and political significance due to resource vulnerability like water supplies, global concerns like climate change, and global pandemics as noted with COVID-19. Environmental stewardship should encompass disaster management. This requires both adept public administration skills as well as a clear understanding of the risks and advantages of effective environmental management. Clearly identifying the problem as well as balancing both environmental and societal needs is necessary. Environmentalism also requires effective collective action. This means numerous stakeholders must agree how to develop effective management strategies. This starts with effective regulations as well as leaders with clear vision and authority. First responders must be part of the equation, since they are often the people with the best opportunity to make the greatest difference.

For Herbert Hoover, the Great Flood led to his personal damming of the presidency. Policy intransigency, stubbornness, and a limited federal government created a precarious environment in which to direct policy. Societal conditions and federal expectations were markedly different from today. This leads to a policy vortex or a catch-22 situation. We expect the president to deliver on addressing concrete solutions to force majeure events. However, the changing nature of federalism implies that effective disaster management agencies are needed at all levels of the government, extending beyond the presidency to other stakeholders. Yet if disaster management goes wrong, blame will be ascribed to the president. This, in essence, is the damning of the presidency.

Today, we expect the commander in chief to be at the helm in disaster management. Failure is not tolerated and could result in a sharp public rebuke. Yet regardless of how the future of politics transpires, the public is structurally tied to political parties and will most likely not change their party vote for the president, unless for a large calamity like the Great Depression. Therefore, environmentalism impacts a national campaign, provided that one looks at the totality of circumstances. It is certainly influential in a presidential campaign and the increasing numbers presidential issued disaster declarations continue to strengthen the nexus between environmental factors and political campaigns.

HYPOTHESES TESTING AND RESEARCH QUESTIONS

The central theories used in this study were Farley's Law and the theory of minimal change, which is inherently an offshoot of incremental policy. The data collected for this study was very straightforward. Figure 6.1 depicts the Electoral College outcomes for the state impacted by the Great Flood of 1927 and records data for voting preferences pre and post Katrina in the same deep Southern States. The data includes popular and Electoral College results from the elections of 1928 and 1932. These data are then juxtaposed with the popular and Electoral College results in storm-impacted areas pre and post Katrina, including elections results from 2004 to 2016.

According to figure 6.1, despite the great calamity caused by the Great Mississippi Flood, people's voting preferences in the 1928 election were largely unaffected. This means that flood states continued to vote Democratic in the national election. This may be noted for a variety of reasons. First, political disenfranchisement from the Republican Party existed prior to Coolidge's initial response. Second, Jim Crow policy inhibited black people from voting; and third, those who could vote were firmly connected to a specific party. People in the Deep South were determined to vote Democratic regardless of the extent of flood damage.

These findings are consistent with the elections of 2004 and 2008, where Deep Southern states voting preferences (see figure 6.1) did not change their presidential choice despite experiencing the wrath of Hurricane Katrina. The Deep Southern states supported the Republican Party in 2008. This leads to another query about the role of federalism. In the 1927 flood, federalism was in its infancy. Instead, Hoover relied on individualism and the principle of associationalism. It was an underwhelming response, but as noted with the Katrina case, federal disaster management needed to improve. Federalism is a form of shared governance. This means the response has to be a combination of federal, state, and local efforts. However, this still does not absolve the president.

In terms of hypotheses testing, the following points are realized. H_1 asks whether greater environmental events lead to greater shifts in voting in national elections alone. The answer is no. People are not likely to change their votes in a national election even if they experienced serious environmental degradation. This finding reveals how entrenched political ideology is. H_2 wonders whether increased volunteerism is an effective flood mitigation strategy. In this case, the answer is also no. Hoover miscalculated the effectiveness of his principle of volunteerism as a strategy in a number of ways. First, it is questionable even to apply his World War I volunteer approach to this flood case, as it was a completely different type of disaster management. The former was a distributional case; the Great Flood required complex mitigation management strategies. In short, there was no easy solution. Hoover's principle of association was also misguided. He assumed private interests would fill the relief void. Unlike World War I, where the driving force was the Food Administration, who would take the lead was unclear. Further, there seemed to be apparent confusion about managing local politics. This allowed Jim Crow policies to continue unabated, which only exacerbated the volunteer relief cause.

One of the study's limitations was that federalism has changed considerably. Certainly, the locus of governmental power is located at the national level. However, there is significant say at the state and local levels. H_3 asks whether increased federal intervention influences voter decision in national elections during major environmental events. The answer is, again, no. The main reason correlates back to Farley's Law and the theory of minimal returns. Figure 6.1 details vital elections when major storms occurred, and there is still no shift in state behavior, at least at the national level. The implicit finding, then, is that force majeure or major floods or hurricanes do not *directly* impact a national presidential outcome. They do reveal cracks within federalism. Also, the situation might change due to the rapid increase in presidential disaster declarations and the sudden emergence of COVID-19.

MORE FINDINGS

Several themes have been elucidated in this study. The central focus has been on the nexus between environmental factors and political campaigns. The roles of the president and challenger have been evaluated using an eight-variable analysis. We have also investigated the changing role of federalism and the rise in presidential-issued disaster declarations. A fair discussion has been evidenced about the perplexing role of the Red Cross and its treatment of African Americans in the flood affected regions in the Deep South. One of the central challenges within the study has been to qualify a comparative understanding of the different time periods and expectations.

John Barry states that the Great Flood changed the identity of the United States. This admission has a lot of veracity. The Flood also exposed in raw detail the unequal treatment of refugees and detailed the deplorable conditions that many blacks encountered. These developments may have been a precursor toward the national environmental justice movement. Environmental justice did not gain foothold as a social movement until the 1980s. Its basic premise rests upon the idea the people of color have been disproportionately exposed to environmental harms. The Great Flood justifies that concern. It was a different place and time, but living in deplorable health conditions satisfied some of the environmental justice requirements, though the anecdotal evidence is weak in assessing how poor environmental conditions and black suffering impacted the overall outcomes of the 1928 and 1932 elections. Yet it is apparent that ineffective flood management led to further disenfranchisement, which in turn, served as another catalyst component for the Republicans and Herbert Hoover to lose the 1932 presidential election, and in part a contribution to a major political realignment of 1932.

There is also the need to develop a better understanding of the policy process. Lievanos states that in order to understand how and why certain claims become policy, one should, among other things, focus on "ascertaining the institutional conditions under which . . . actors have more or less influence and understanding how political discourse affects the degree to which policy ideas are communicated and translated into practice."[1] It demands participatory justice in environmental decision-making processes in addition to pushing for distributive justice. This means each group receives the same benefits as prescribed under the law. This clearly was not the case with how the Red Cross operated in the flood-prone regions. Distributive justice seeks to redress disproportionate environmental burdens largely attributed of both governing and corporate entities. Finally, it demands that agencies "make environmental justice a part of all they do."[2]

The link between environmental factors and the political campaigns could be strengthened by understanding the importance of the precautionary principle. It states, "Where there are threats of serious or irreversible damage, the lack of full scientific certainty shall not be used as a reason for postponing cost-effective measures to prevent environmental degradation."[3] This is a sharp critique on the levees-only policy. This policy was inopportune despite becoming a vetted practice for more than half a century. Candidates and governmental agencies must be held accountable. Environmental justice utility challenges contemporary policy making. Many of the problems associated with Katrina lodged with bureaucratic inefficiency. There was adequate science through storm simulations. However, the simulations were hardly operational at the onset of the storm. The EJ framework challenges policy makers to adhere to scientific certifications and regulatory standards, as well as to provide safe environments for all people. This will greatly enhance the future disaster management policy process.

A hard glance back to the 1927 Mississippi Flood reflects these salient concerns, particularly the lack of equity in providing relief to black flood victims. Clearly, that time was encapsulated with Jim Crow policies, which creates uneasy exit strategies to avoid any blame. Environmental justice issues exist, though more research should be conducted in evaluating their impact on a national election. At the least, the status quo has been challenged. Time will tell.

A NEW MANAGEMENT APPROACH
FOR THE PRESIDENT?

One of the most glaring deficiencies within the Hoover administration was overreliance on volunteerism. It worked with the food distribution in Europe during World War I but was inadequate for addressing a macro flood. In reality, our federal system shields the president from direct responsibility for disaster management. The president should not be viewed as a first responder but should convey clarity and directives in a timely manner. However, FEMA, the main agency responsible for mitigating storm and other disaster damage, underperformed with Hurricane Katrina as well as with other recent hurricanes. This is where the conundrum lies. It has been said the strongest defense is the weakest link in a policy. An underperforming executive agency not only reflects on the specific agency but also on the entire executive branch, leading all the way back to the presidency. Therefore, new management approaches must be considered. According to Lohman and Lohman, leadership needs more discovery, better training in explaining and applying leadership skills. This may be hard to achieve in disaster management, since it is difficult to simulate such emergency situations. However, leadership training should be expansive and extend to staff members with executive, managerial, and supervisory experience.[4]

Leadership management has been depicted as a linear model. This means leadership training should be separated from machine models of organizations with emphases on command and control or rigid top-down approaches. Instead, emphasis should be placed on more rational models of organization as systems of interaction. George Terry defined management as "the activity which plans, organizes and controls the operations of the basic elements of men, materials, machines, methods, money, and markets, providing direction and coordination." It also provides leadership to achieve the key objectives. One of the trickier semantic issues is the debate between the terms administration, management, and governance.[5] The following reflects a series of management strategies that may be used in effectively treating disaster management.

1) One semantic issue is a long-standing disciplinary inconsistency in the use of the terms *business management* and *public administration*. Both terms—*social administration* and *social management*—refer to approximately the same guidance processes in commercial and public organizations, respectively.

2) There should be a greater understanding of specific management approaches such as Fayol. He was a French mining engineer who is generally credited as an originator of the classic management tradition

and the first to formulate a complete set of management principles intended to guide the practice of managers. Although Fayol's principles are commonly known, they are less clearly understood is his attempt to distinguish management processes from administration as a narrower, more specialized part of overall management. When social administration, public administration, hospital administration came into being, they tended to blur his criterion. More recently, a distinct "management" literature has emerged in several of these disciplines.[6]

In examining management, we should avoid excessive devotion to a particular method. There are hundreds of management techniques available, many with colorful and alluring names like goals analysis, time, motion study, and total quality management, with wonderful graphics as well. The certainty

	1928					1932			
	EC	winner win	lose	%	EC	winner win	lose	%
Louisiana	10 D	164,655	51,178	7628%	10 D	249,418	19,386	92.79%
Mississippi	10 D	124,539	27,153	82.10%	9 D	140,168	5,866	95.98%
Arkansas	9 D	119,196	78,497	60.29%	9 D	189,602	30,960	85.96%
Tennessee	12 R	195,388	168,085	58.22%	11 D	259,473	130,783	66.49%
Missouri	18 R	834,080	666,641	49.58%	15 D	1,025,406	584,488	63.69%
Illinois	29 R	1,769,141	1,338,348	56.93%	29 D	1,882,304	1,525,622	55.20%

2000				2004			
EC	winner win	lose	%	EC	winner win	lose	%
9 R	927,871	837,785	52.55%	9 R	1,102,169	840,937	56.72%
7 R	573,230	421,696	57.62%	6 R	684,981	467,384	59.44%
6 R	472,940	448,841	51.31%	6 R	572,898	482,047	54.31%
11 R	1,061,949	1,014,232	51.15%	11 R	1,383,336	1,051,613	56.81%
11 R	1,189,924	1,169,968	50.42%	11 R	1,455,713	1,275,651	53.30%
22 D	2,589,026	2,153,097	54.60%	21 D	2,891,550	2,382,772	54.82%

2008				2012				2016			
EC	winner win	lose	%	EC	winner win	lose	%	EC	winner win	lose	%
9 R	1,148,275	812,486	58.56%	8 R	1,152,262	841,803	57.78%	8 R	1,178,638	850,394	58.09%
6 R	687,266	531,020	56.40%	6 R	710,746	574838	55.29%	6 R	700,714	510,374	57.86%
6 R	638,017	448,600	58.72%	6 R	647,744	421724	60.57%	6 R	684,872	445,763	60.57%
11 R	1,479,178	1,122,804	56.85%	11 R	1,462,330	998,574	59.42%	11 R	1,522,925	985,102	60.72%
11 R	1,445,814	1,483,297	49.36%	10 R	1,482,440	1,281,249	53.64%	10 R	1,594,511	1,233,755	56.38%
21 D	3,419,348	2,110,831	61.83%	20 D	3,019,512	2,231,920	57.50%	20 D	3,090,729	2,504,096	55.24%

Figure 6.1   Presidential Election Results in the Deep South. *Source:* Data from www .270towin.com, last accessed 12-2-2019.

they promise can be reassuring to policy makers. However useful such techniques may be, they are merely tools, and each is based on a set of assumptions. They may be useful for certain purposes and completely inappropriate at other times. In no sense do these tools define the essential content of the practice of social administration.

Several decades ago, the philosopher of science Abraham Kaplan encouraged keeping a proper perspective on the limits of technologies with his very graphic "law of the hammer." Give a little boy a hammer, Kaplan noted, and he will find things that need pounding. The same is true of management and all methods. The caveat is to avoid a one-size-fits-all approach.[7]

Drucker states that there is a big difference in doing the right things and doing things the right way. There will always be some level of uncertainty in the policy decision-making process. Perhaps a starting point is that one cannot be correct all of the time. Administrative decisions are made in real time, and momentous choices must be made with insufficient time for full consideration or review. Under such conditions, no one should expect to always be right. The critical difference between effective and ineffective administrators is not a matter of who is right most often, but who learned to recognize, confront, and correct their mistakes. Management tools can be helpful for many things, but they can do little to eliminate an essential core of uncertainty in administrative decision making. The federal government and the presidency have a tall task ahead of them in addressing each new force majeure and critical environmental event.[8]

NOTES

1. Raoul S. Lievanos, "Certainty, Fairness, and Balance: State Resource and Environmental Justice Policy," *Sociological Forum* 27, no. 2 (2012): 481–503. https://doi.org/10.1111/j.1573-7861.2012.01327.x.

2. Lievanos, "Certainty," 481–503.

3. Ibid.

4. Roger A. Lohmann and Nancy Lohmann, *The Processes of Management*, Social Administration: Columbia University Press, 2002.

5. George R. Terry, *Principles of Management*, Irwin Series in Management, 1972.

6. Henri Fayol 2002 as cited in Lohmann and Lohmann.

7. Lohmann and Lohmann, *The Processes*.

8. Lohmann and Lohmann, *The Processes*.

Chapter 7

Conclusion

This book argued that in terms of presidential elections, the term *environmentalism* should be expanded beyond its regulatory framework. An expansive definition that includes socioeconomic factors such as race and economy is critical, making the term a more robust variable in its explanatory value of a political campaign. The Great Mississippi Flood reveals numerous fissures within American society. The flood impacted 1 percent of the nation's population. It displaced thousands, as well as disrupted the fabric of society. Governing responses were limited and even if with the best imagined plans, lack of political understanding at the regional and local levels set the course for further fracturing of the Republican Party.

Hoover believed in governing intervention for natural disasters, but his overreliance on the private sector proved problematic. He could not guarantee enough private capital to ensure a sound recovery. His principle of volunteerism, while honorable, could not overcome deeply entrenched Jim Crow policies, which proved to pronounce and prolong the refugee crisis. This, in turn, would create the pathway for blacks to shift to the Democratic Party. This shift would take time. Hoover won the 1928 presidential election convincingly, but ineffective responses to the flood victims coupled with a rapidly developing depression left little room for Hoover or for the Republican Party to overcome. Yet there is a silver lining: The federal government did create a national flood policy plan. This could be interpreted as an early manifestation of the New Deal, even though it began during the Hoover administration.

Ultimately, force majeure events are like political maelstroms. They can be difficult for any presidency. There is no one-size-fits-all management plan that can predict or best address such crises. What is clear is that policy makers need to understand an expansive definition of environmentalism

159

and recognize that governing or nongoverning agencies must not only have effective distribution plans but also understand politics at the local level. This inherently suggests that local stakeholders are essential in the decision-making process. However, unlike the Great Flood of 1927, federal oversight is necessary though it was seriously lacking at the time. Hoover capitalized on the flood by using social media and taking a "hands on" approach to help with the distribution relief effort. However, he did not understand the politics of the region, which ultimately contributed to consuming his presidential efforts.

The terms *technosphere* and *ecosphere* were important to this study because these concepts parallel the conflict between the environment and industrialization. They are inherently at odds with each other, particularly those who see environmentalism as a hindrance to the free market economy. This is a difficult debate in current political terms. Yet as Commoner states,[1] there is no such thing as a free lunch. This may be true, but whether such a debate will resonate with the national campaign agenda in 2020 or beyond is unclear.

Hence, the *Damming of the Presidency* was a study to offer a fresh interpretation about the role of the environment in national campaigns. This complex question links the term *environment* to several other critical variables such as campaigns, media, public opinion, rhetoric, federalism, and economy. The Great Mississippi Flood stands out for several reasons, but perhaps most notably because it planted the seeds for a new form of shared federalism to be implemented. It is far from perfect, but Diamond stated that democracy is the best game in town.[2] Maybe another probe would argue that shared federalism is. Then what the does damming of the presidency indicate? In many respects, it posits that complex configurations are needed to manage major storms. Like a catch-22, if the president does too much, such efforts may supplant state and local efforts. Empirical data suggests this has not happened. If the president or administrative agency does too little, they are the recipients of sharp and long-term criticism. This reproach may not impact a national election, but it certainly impacts a legacy. Which of the two is more important?

Today, environmentalism has been beleaguered and narrowly framed by federal and state regulatory capacity. This puts political parties at odds with each other, especially with key concepts like climate change. But just like Hoover, who had an opportunity to use such events as a political opportunity, today, we wait to see which party can strategically understand that environmentalism extends beyond its regulatory capacity. The Democratic Party might seem like a natural fit, but in all fairness, political opportunities are temporary and any hesitation, misinterpretation, or base reductionism can easily erase any perceived advantage. In the end, astute political policy makers must see that each action or inaction can have long-term campaign impacts.

Finally, in 2020, there has been renewed concern regarding the role of how environmental factors can impact a political campaign. The global community has faced the daunting task of addressing COVID-19. The same issues that pervaded the Great Mississippi Flood of 1927 are eerily similar today. The Great Flood evidenced unprecedented refugee suffering, the disenfranchisement of the black community in the delta region, economic dislocation, and an ambiguous federal role in addressing the situation. Today, COVID-19 is a central challenge. There have been claims that the disease disproportionately strikes people of color and that it has altered the nation's economy. Businesses across the country have had to change the way they do business, and there has been a greater shift to conduct business virtually. Equally perplexing is the role of the federal government and the presidency. The federal government has struggled to make definitive policy approaches in addressing the pandemic, and when policy decisions were made, they took several months to became operational. Today, the American public receives segmented information in how to respond to and protect against the pandemic. This includes various aspects of social distancing, such as wearing a mask and avoiding large social gatherings. However, these policies have not been uniformly practiced.

The disaster management end goal is not about who is to blame but instead, how to move forward. Significant inspection is extended towards the president. If the federal government is successful, then credit will be extended to both the governing agencies and the president. If it is not successful, criticism will be directed toward the governing agencies like FEMA and the Center for Disease and Control. The president will be held accountable.

The Damning of the Presidency then comes into greater focus. The modern president is part of a nuanced and heavily bureaucratized form of federalism. The relief agencies may even be lodged in the executive branch. These agencies have tremendous responsibilities to implement policies. However, this power has to be preestablished. Even then, each disaster strikes differently, offering various challenges. This places the president in the precarious position of lead manager. Public expectations are high and grow on a daily basis. However, not all necessary information is readily available. Hoover's central challenge was operating under governing system of limited federal intervention. Therefore, a plausible explanation was that he did not have enough room to make the necessary policy choices.

A long glance suggests that the United States has made significant strides socially, morally, and politically. In one decade, one can witness significant health and technological advancements. While there are still necessary steps to achieve full social and racial equality, Jim Crow policies have long been eliminated. The role of the federal government is much more expansive. It may not always be viewed as a protective paternalism for the states.

The government has made significant strides to provide a meaningful and pragmatic regulatory framework. Many of these strides emerged from the aftermath of the Great Flood, the Great Depression, and the numerous components of New Deal legislation. This translated into greater federal roles and expectations, which means the president must be involved in the multitiered decision-making process. However, bigger does not always mean better. There has to be skilled and effective administrators who can guide and advise the president. The success of this endeavor then depends on a sufficient number of able administrators to guide and advise the president. How will future presidents respond? And in what time frame? Disaster management leaves no room for error.

NOTES

1. Barry Commoner, *Making Peace With the Planet*, New York: The New Press, 1975, 14–15.
2. Larry Diamond, *Developing Democracy*, Baltimore, MD: Johns Hopkins Press, 2004, 2–4.

Bibliography

Agnew, John. "Waterpower: Politics and the Geography of Water Provision." *Annals of the Association of American Geographers* 101, no. 3 (2011): 463–476. http://dx.doi.org/10.1080/00045608.2011.560053.

Allen, Priscilla D., and Jennifer L. Scott. "Disaster after Disaster: Unexpected Thousand-Year Flood and Presidential Election." *Reflections* 23, no. 2 (2017): 53–59. https://reflectionsnarratives ofprofessionalhelping.org/index.php/Reflectio ns/article/view/1552/1483

Ariel, Robert A. "A Monthly Effect in Stock Returns." *Journal of Financial Economics* (1987). https://doi.org/10.1016/0304-405X(87)90066-3.

Barry, John M. *Rising Tide: The Great Mississippi Flood of 1927 and How It Changed America*. New York: Simon and Schuster, 1998.

Belli, Melvin. *Ready for the Plaintiff*. New York: Bobbs-Merrill, 1963.

Birkland, Thomas. *Lesson of Disaster*. Washington, DC: Georgetown University Press, 1997.

Birkland, Thomas, and Sarah Waterman. "Is Federalism the Reason for Policy Failure in Hurricane Katrina?" *The Journal of Federalism*, 2008.

Boettke, Peter J. "The Politics, Economics and Social Aspects of Katrina." *Southern Economic Journal* 74, no. 2 (2007). https://ssrn.com/abstract=1085631.

Bowers, John Waite. "Language Intensity, Social Introversion and Attitude Change." *Speech Monograph* 30, no. 4 (1963): 345–352. https://doi.org/10.1080/036377 56309375380.

Bradac, James, John W. Bowers, and John Courtright. "Three Language Variables in Communication Research, Intensity, Immediacy, and Diversity." *Human Communication Research* 5, no. 3 (1979): 257–269. https://doi.org/10.1111/j.1468 -2958.1979.tb00639.x.

Brown, Robert E. "Acting Presidential: The Dramaturgy of Bush Versus Kerry." *American Behavioralist Scientist* 49, no. 1 (2005): 78–91. https://doi.org/10.1177 /0002764205279397.

Bullock, Jane A., George Haddow, Damon Coppola, Erdem Ergin, Lissa Waterman, and Sarp Yeletaysi. *Introduction to Homeland Security*. Burlington, MA: Elsevier, Inc., 2006.

Bus, George W. *Decision Points*. New York: Crown, 2010.

Cable News Network (CNN). *Hurricane Charley: Two Days Later*, 15 August 2005.

Campbell, James E. *The American Campaign: U.S. Presidential Campaigns and the National Vote*. College Station: Texas A&M University Press, 2000.

Carney, James, Karen Tumulty, Amanda Ripley, and Mark Thompson/Washington. *An American Tragedy: Four Places Where the System Broke Down*. Time, 2005.

Carrns, Ann. "Army Corps Faces Scrutiny on Levee Flaws." *Wall Street Journal*. November 2, 2005.

Cassidy, John. "How Much Did Hurricane Sandy Help Obama?" *New Yorker*. November 4, 2012.

Clementson, David E., Paola Pascual-Ferra, and Michael J. Beatty. "When Does a Presidential Campaign Seem Presidential and Trustworthy? Campaign Messages through the Lens of Language Expectancy Theory." *Presidential Studies Quarterly* (2016). https://doi.org/10.1111/psq.12299.

Commoner, Barry. *Making Peace with the Planet*. New York: New Press, 1992.

Conlon, Tim. "From Cooperative to Opportunistic Federalism: Reflections on the Half-Century Anniversary of the Commission on Intergovernmental Relations." *Public Administration Review* 66, no. 5 (2006): 663–676. https://doi.org/10.1111/j.1540-6210.2006.00631.x.

Davies, Gareth. "The Historical Presidency: Lyndon Johnson and Disaster Politics." *Presidential Studies Quarterly* 47, no. 3 (2017): 529–551. https://doi.org/10.1111/psq.12384.

Day, Douglas C., and Howard Kunreuther. *The Economics of Natural Disaster: Implications for Federal Policy*. New York: Free Press, 1969.

De Alessi, L. *Property Rights, Private and Political Institutions in the Elgar Companion to Public Choice*. Northampton, MA: Edward Elgar, 2001.

Derthick, Martha. "Where Federalism Didn't Fail." *Public Administration Review* 67 (2007): 36–47. https://doi.org/10.1111/j.1540-6210.2007.00811.x.

Diamond, Larry. *Developing Democracy*. Baltimore, MD: Johns Hopkins University Press, 2004.

Edward, George III. *The Strategic President: Persuasion and Opportunity in Presidential Leadership*. Princeton, NJ: Princeton University Press, 2009.

Enns, Peter K., and Brian Richman. "Presidential Campaigns and Fundamentals Reconsidered." *The Journal of Politics* 75, no. 3 (2013): 803–820. https://doi.org/10.1017/S0022381613000522.

Excerpts from Brown Hearing. *Wall Street Journal*, 27 September 2005. http://online.wsj.com/article/SB112785315597053609.HTML.

Fayol, Henri as cited in Lohmann and Lohmann, *The Processes of Management Social Administration*. New York: Columbia University, 2002.

FEMA. *A Chronology of Major Events Affecting National Flood Insurance Program*. Washington, DC: The American Institute for Research, 2002.

Finger, Mathias, Ludivine Tamiotto, and Jeremy Allouche, eds. *The Multi-Governance of Water: Four Case Studies.* New York: State University Press of New York, 2006.

Fletcher, Michael. "President Again Takes on Role of 'Consoler in Chief.'" *Washington Post,* April 18, 2007.

Gelman, Andrew, and Gary King. "Why Are American Presidential Election Campaign Polls so Variable When the Votes Are so Predictable?" *British Journal of Political Science* 23, no. 4 (1993): 409–451. https://doi.org/10.1017/S0007123400006682.

Gerber, Brian J., and David B. Cohen. "Katrina and Her Waves. Presidential Leadership and Disaster Management in an Intergovernmental Context." In *Disaster Management Handbook,* edited by Jack Pinkowski, 51–74. New York: CRC Press, 2008.

Gertz, Bill. "Mikulski Faults FEMA Officials, Call for Probe." *Washington Times,* September 4, 1992.

Geschwind, Carl-Henry. *California Earthquakes: Science, Risk, and the Politics of Hazard Mitigation.* Baltimore, MD: Johns Hopkins University Press, 2001.

Greenberg, David. *Republic of Spin: An Inside History of the American Presidency.* New York: Norton, 2016.

Grodzins, Morton. *The American System: A New View of Government in the United States.* Edited by D. J. Elazar. Chicago, IL: Rand McNally, 1966.

Haddow, George, Jane A. Bullock, and Damon Coppola. *Introduction to Emergency Management,* 3rd ed. Boston, MA: Elsevier, 2007.

Herzik, and Mary L. Dodson. "The President and Public Expectations: A Research Note." *Presidential Studies Quarterly* 12, no. 2 (1982): 168–173. https://www.jstor .org/stable/27547802.

Holbrook, Thomas. *Do Campaigns Matter?* Thousand Oaks, CA: Sage, 1996.

Hoover, Herbert. "The Constructive Character of the Republican Party." Delivered over the television and radio networks, New York, October 18, 1952.

Hoover, Herbert. *The Memoirs of Herbert Hoover: The Cabinet and the Presidency 1920-1933.* New York: Macmillan Company, 1952.

Johnson, Robert, William Crittenden, and Gerald Jensen. "Presidential Politics, Stocks, Binds, Bills, and Inflation." *Journal of Portfolio Management* 26, no. 1 (1999): 27–31. https://doi.org/10.3905/jpm.1999.319771.

Kapucu, Naim, Montgomery Van Wart, Richard Sylves, and Farhod Yuldasheve. "U.S. Presidents and Their Role in Emergency Management and Disaster Policy: 1950-2009." *Risk, Hazards, and Crisis in Public Policy* 2, no. 3 (2011): 1–34. https://doi.org/10.2202/1944-4079.1065.

Kincaid, John. *From Cooperative to Opportunistic Federalism: Reflections on the Half-Century Anniversary of the Commission on Intergovernmental Relations.* Wiley: Public Administration Review, 1990.

Kingdon, John. *Agendas, Alternatives and Public Policies,* 2nd ed. New York: HarperCollins, 1995.

Lakonishok and Seymour Smidt. "Are Seasonal Anomalies Real? A Ninety Year Perspective." *Review of Financial Studies* 1, no. 4 (1988): 403–425. https://doi.org /10.1093/rfs/1.4.403.

Lazarseld, Paul, Bernard Berelson, and Helen Gaudet. *The Peoples' Choice.* New York: Duell, Sloane, & Pearce, 1944.

Lee, Ben Clarke. *Mission Improbable: Using Fantasy Documents to Tame Disaster.* Chicago, IL: University of Chicago Press, 1999.

Lenz, Gabriel S. "Learning and Opinion Change. Not Priming: Reconsidering the Priming Hypothesis." *American Journal of Political Science* 53, no. 4 (2009): 821–837. https://doi.org/10.1111/j.1540-5907.2009.00403.x.

Lievanos, Raoul S. "Certainty, Fairness and Balance: State Resonance and Environmental Justice Policy." *Sociological Forum* 27, no. 2 (2012): 481–503. https://doi.org/10.1111/j.1573-7861.2012.01327.x.

Lohman, Roger A., and Nancy Lohman. *The Process of Management and Social Administration.* New York: Columbia University Press, 2002.

Lohoff, Bruce A. "Herbert Hoover: Spokesman of Human Efficiency: The Mississippi Flood of 1927." *American Quarterly* 22, no. 3 (1970): 690–700. https://doi.org/10.2307/2711620.

Lowi, Theodore J. *The Personal President Power Invested Promise Unfulfilled.* Ithaca, NY: Cornell University Press, 1986.

———. "The State in Political Science: How We Become What We Study." *American Political Science Review* 86, no. 1 (1992): 1–7. https://doi.org/10.2307/1964011.

Lowry, William. *Dam Politics Restoring America's Rivers.* Washington, DC: Georgetown University Press, 2003.

May, Peter, and Walter Williams. *Disaster Policy Implementation Managing Programs under Shared Governance, Disaster Research in Practice.* New York: Plenum Press, 1986.

Maysilles, Duncan. *Ducktown Smoke the Fight over One of the South's Greatest Environmental Disasters.* Chapel Hill, NC: University of North Carolina Press, 2011.

McClurg, Scott D., and Thomas M. Holbrook. "Living in a Battleground, Presidential Campaigns and Fundamental Predictors of Vote Choice." *Political Research Quarterly* 62, no. 3 (2009): 495–506. https://doi.org/10.1017/S0022381614000413.

Melosi, Martin. "Environmental Justice, Ecoracism, and Environmental History." In *To Love the Wind and Rain,* edited by Dianne D. Glave and Mark Stoll. Pittsburgh, PA: University of Pittsburgh Press, 2006.

Mills, Nicolaus. *Herbert Hoover and Hurricane Katrina.* Dissent, Winter 2006.

Miskel, James. *Disaster Response and Homeland Security: What Works and What Doesn't.* Palo Alto, CA: Stanford University Press, 2008.

Mizelle, Richard M. Jr. "Black Levee Camp Workers, The NAACP, and the Mississippi Flood Control Project, 1927-33." *The Journal of African American History* 98, no. 4 (Spring 2013). https://doi.org/10.5323/jafriamerhist.98.4.0511.

Mark Murray. Lessons from a master of disaster. *National Journal* 33, no. 2 (2001): 133–135.

Nakamura, David. "After Aurora Shootings, Obama Again Takes on Role as Healer in Chief." *Washington Post,* July 7, 2012. https://www.washingtonpost.com/politics/after-aurora-shootings-obama-again-takes-on-role-as-healer-in-chief-in-colorado/2012/07/22/gJQAdEO92W_story.html.

Nash, George. "Herbert Hoover Versus the Great Depression." *Hoover Digest* 3, Summer 2016. https://www.hoover.org/research/hoover-vs-great-depression.
———. *The Life of Herbert Hoover Master of Emergencies, 1917-1918.* New York: Norton, 1996.
Neuman, Yair, Ophir Nave, and Eran Dolev. "Buzzwords on Their Way to a Tipping Point: A View from the Blogosphere. *Complexity* 16, no. 4 (2010): 58–68. https://doi.org/10.1002/cplx.20347.
Neustadt, Richard. *Presidential Power: The Politics of Leadership.* New York: John Wiley and Sons, Inc., 1960.
Ogden, Joseph P. "The End of the Month as a Preferred Habitat: A Text of Operational Efficiency in the Money Market." *Journal of Financial and Quantitative Analysis* 22, no. 3 (1987): 497–513. https://doi.org/10.2307/2330967.
Parry-Giles, Trevor. "Presidentialism, Political Fiction, and the Complex Presidencies of Fox's 24." *Presidential Studies Quarterly* 44 (2014): 204–223. https://doi.org/10.1111/psq.12109.
Parry-Giles, Trevor, and Shawn J. Parry-Giles. "The West Wing's Prime Time Presidentiality: Mimesis, and Catharsis in a Post-Modern Romance." *Quarterly Journal of Speech* 88, no. 2 (2002): 209–227. https://doi.org/10.1080/00335630209384371.
Patterson, Thomas E. *The Press and Its Missed Assignment in the Election of 1988.* Edited by Michael Nelson. Washington, DC: CQ Press, 1989.
Pauly, Mark. Economics of Moral Hazard: Comment. *The American Economic Review, American Economic Association* 58, no. 3, Part 1 (June, 1968): 531–537.
Pfau, Michael, and William P. Eveland Jr. "Debates versus Other Communication Sources." *Human Communication Research* 15 (1994): 91–111.
Pfiffner, James P. "Ranking the Presidents: Continuity and Volatility." *White House Studies* 3, no. 1 (2003): 23. https://doi.org/10.1080/21565503.2017.1318760.
Ponder, Daniel E. *Studies in the Modern Presidency Presidential Leverage Presidential Approval and the American State.* Palo Alto, CA: Stanford University Press, 2018.
Popkin, Samuel. *The Reasoning Voter: Communication and Perversion in Presidential Campaigns.* Chicago, IL: University of Chicago Press, 1994.
Posner, Paul. "The Politics of Coercive Federalism in the Bush Era." *Publius: The Journal of Federalism* 3 (2007): 390–412. https://doi.org/10.1093/publius/pjm014.
Powell, Richard. *Publius: The State of American Federalism.* Oxford: Oxford University Press, 2004.
Quirk, Paul J. 2009. "Politicians Do Pander: Mass Opinion, Polarization, and Law Making." *The Forum* 7, no. 4 (2009): Article 10.
Rauchway, Eric. *Winter War: Hoover, Roosevelt, and the First Clash Over the New Deal.* New York: Basic Books, 2018.
Reisner, Marc. *Cadillac Desert.* New York: Penguin, 1993.
Remnick, David. "High Water: How Presidents and Citizens Respond to Disaster." *New Yorker,* October 3, 2005. https://www.newyorker.com/magazine/2005/10/03/high-water.
Roberts, Patrick. "Our Responder in Chief." *National Affairs* 44 (2010). https://www.nationalaffairs.com/publications/detail/our-responder-in-chief.

Roll, C.W. Jr. and Albert H. Cantril. *Polls: Their Use and Misuse in Politics.* New York: Basic Books, 1972.

Rossi, Peter H., James D. Wright, and Eleanor Weber-Burdin. *Natural Hazards and Public Choice: The State and Local Politics of Hazard Mitigation.* New York: Academic Press, 1982.

Rubin, Claire. *Emergency Management: The American Experience 1900-2010.* 2nd ed. Boca Raton, FL: CRC Press, 2012.

Saldin, Robert. "William McKinley and the Presidency." *Presidential Studies Quarterly* (1986). https://onlinelibrary.wiley.com/doi/abs/10.1111/j.1741-5705. 2010.03833.x

Salmore, Barbara, and Stephen Salmore. *Candidates, Parties, and Campaigns.* 2nd ed. Washington, DC: CQ Press, 1989.

Schneider, Saundra. "Who's to Blame:(Mis) Perceptions of the Intergovernmental Response to Disasters." *Publius: The Journal of Federalism* 38, no. 4 (2008): 715–738. https://doi.org/10.1093/publius/pjn019.

Shreve, David, and Robert David Johnson, eds. *The Presidential Records: Lyndon B. Johnson: Toward the Great Society.* Vol. V. New York: Norton, 2007.

Shugart, William F. "Disaster Relief as Bad Public Policy." *Independent Institute: The Independent Review* 15, no. 4 (2011): 519–539. https://www.independent.org/ pdf/tir/tir_15_04_2_shughart.pdf.

Simon, Dennis M., and Charles Ostrom, Jr. "The Politics of Prestige: Popular Support and the Modern Presidency." *Presidential Studies Quarterly* 18, no. 4 (1988): 741–759. https://www.jstor.org/stable/40574727.

Skalaban, Andrew. "Do the Polls Affect Elections? Some 1980 Evidence." *Political Behavior* 10, no. 2 (1988): 136–150. https://www.jstor.org/stable/586330.

Sobel, R. S., and P. T. Leeson. "Government's Response to Hurricane Katrina: A Public Choice Analysis." *Public Choice* 127 (2005): 55–73. https://doi.org/10.1 007/s11127-006-7730-3.

Spencer, Robyn. "The Mississippi Flood of 1927 and the Struggle to Control Black Labor." *The Journal of Negro History* 79, no. 2 (Spring 1994): 170–181. https:// doi.org/10.2307/2717627.

Steinberg, Theodore. *Act of God: The Unnatural History of Natural Disasters in America.* New York: Oxford University Press, 2000.

Stokes, Donald E. "Same Dynamic Elements of Contests for the Presidency." *American Political Science Review* 60, no. 1 (1966): 19–28. https://doi.org/10.2307/1953803.

Storey, William K. "The 1927 Mississippi River Flood" Part 2, "The Pearly River Flood." *The Public Historian* 27, no. 1 (2005): 90–93. https://doi.org/10.1525/tph .2005.27.

Sundquist, James L. *Dynamics of the Party System: Alignment and Realignment of Political Parties in the United States.* Washington, DC: Brookings Institution, 1983.

Sylves, Richard. *Disaster Policy and Politics Emergency Management and Homeland Security.* Washington, DC: CQ Press, 2008.

Sylves, Richard, and Zoltan I. Buzas. "Presidential Disaster Declaration Decisions, 1953-2003: What Influences Odds of Approval." *State and Local Government Review* 39, no. 1 (2007): 3–15. https://doi.org/10.1177/0160323X0703900102.

Sylves, Richard T. "Federal Emergency Management Comes of Age: 1979-2001." In *Emergency Management: The American Experience, 1900-2005*, edited by C. B. Rubin. Arlington: Public Entity Risk Institute, 1997.

Terry, George R. *Principles of Management. Irwin Series in Management* (1972).

The Mississippi Flood. Society of American Military Engineers Stable. *The Military Engineer* 14, no. 76 (July–August 1922): 229–230, https://www.jstor.org/stable/44605816.

Thomas, Evan. "How Bush Blew It." *Newsweek*, September 19, 2005. https://delong.typepad.com/sdj/2005/09/evan_thomas_how.html.

Tierney, Kathleen. "The Red Pill." *Social Science Council* (2005). https://www.e-education.psu.edu/geog882/sites/www.e-education.psu.edu.geog882/files/file/The_Red_Pill_%28Tierney%29.pdf.

Tierney, Kathleen, Christine Bevc, and Erica Kuligowski. "Metaphors Matter: Disaster Myths, Media Frames, and Their Consequences in Hurricane Katrina." *Annals of the Academy of Political and Social Science* 604 (2006): 57–81. https://doi.org/10.1177/0002716205285589.

Trexler, Adam. *Anthropocene Fictions, the Novel in a Time of Climate Change*. University of Virginia Press, 2015.

Troy, Gil. *See How They Ran*. Cambridge: Harvard University Press, 1996.

Tulis, Jeffrey K. *The Rhetorical Presidency*. Princeton, NJ: Princeton University Press, 1987.

Vision Critical. *Angus Reid Public Opinion* (2011) www.angusreid.org.

Warren, Harris Gaylord. *Herbert Hoover and the Great Depression*. New York: Norton, 1967.

Webber, David. *Outstanding Environmentalists of Congress*. United States Capitol Historical Society, 2002.

White, Theodore. *The Making of the President*. New York: Antheneum, 1961.

Whyte, Kenneth H. *Hoover: An Extraordinary Life in Extraordinary Times*. New York: Vintage, 2017.

Wolak, Jennifer. "The Consequences of Presidential Battleground Strategies for Citizen Engagement." *Political Science Quarterly* 59, no. 3 (2006): 353–361. https://doi.org/10.1177/106591290605900303.

Young, Andrew. "Replacing Incomplete Markets with a Complete Mess." *International Journal of Social Economics* 35, no. 8 (2008): 561–568. https://doi.org/10.1108/03068290810889189.

Zhao, Xiaofeng, Kartono Liano, and William G Hardin III. "Election Cycles and the Turn of the Month Effect." *Social Science Quarterly* 85, no. 4 (2004): 958–973. https://www.jstor.org/stable/42956014.

https://www.270towin.com/ last accessed 31-12-2018: 1928, 1932, 2000, 2004, 2008, 2012, and 2016 elections

https://www.epa.gov/laws-regulations/summary-executive-order-12898-federal-actions-addressenvironmental-justice

https://www.chicagotribune.com/news/nationworld/politics/chi-chicagodays-deweydefeats-storystory.html (last accessed 31-12-2018)

Index

Note: *Italic* page numbers refer to figures.

National Labor Relations Board
(NLRB), 140
National Recovery Administration
(NRA), 141
National Red Cross, 129
National Research Council (NRC), 35
National Response Framework (NRF),
22, 36, 54–55, 67
National Response Plan (NRP), 22, 54
National Science Foundation, 31
National Security Decision
Memorandum (NSDM), 60
natural disaster, 4, 59, 114; intervention
for, 159
natural emergencies, 23
natural hazards, 22, 27, 29, 35, 36
NEHRA. *See* National Earthquake
Hazards Reduction Act (NEHRA)
Nelson, William, 117
neoclassical economic theory, 21
neoclassical thinking, 21
Neustadt, Richard, 79–81; *Presidential
Power,* 78
New Deal, 20, 115, 116, 136, 139, 141,
159, 162; regulatory policies of, 140
New England, floods in, 10
"New Federalism," 27
Newlands, Francis G., 122
New Republic, 104, 107
New York Times, 25, 104, 123
NIMS. *See* National Incident
Management System (NIMS)
Nixon, Richard, 55, 60, 72, 74
NLRB. *See* National Labor Relations
Board (NLRB)
NLRB v. Jones & Laughlin Steel Corp.,
140
non-campaign approach, 88
normative theory, 37
NRC. *See* National Research Council
(NRC)
NRF. *See* National Response
Framework (NRF)
NRP. *See* National Response Plan
(NRP)

NSDM. *See* National Security Decision
Memorandum (NSDM)

Obama, Barack, 24, 51, 66–67
Office of Civil and Defense
Mobilization, 58
Office of Civil Defense (OCD), 59
Ohio River flood, 10, 24–26, 114
Ohio River Valley, 25
O'Keefe, Arthur, 123, 125
one-size-fits-all management plan, 159
opportunistic federalism, 22–23
Ostrom, Charles W., Jr., 76, 80
Ostrom, Elinor, 48, 49
Oxford History of the American People
(Morison), 73

Pais, Jeremy, 35
Parrish, Susan Scott: *The Flood Year
1927: A Cultural History,* 45
partisan predisposition, 85, 91
Paulson, David, 66
Pauly, Mark V., 33
The People's Choice, 83–84
The Personal President (Lowi), 81
Peter Drucker, 157
Peterson, Brenton, 4, 83
Pfiffner, James P., 55
Philips, Brenda, 36, 37
Pittsburgh Courier, 117
"plebiscitary presidency-scale," 72
policy making, 1, 81, 154; selflessness
in, 2
policy objectivity, 2
political campaigns, 93
political leaders, 13
political trust, 134, 142, 150
politics, 48; environmental management
connecting to, 43–50; of prestige,
76–77; of region, 160
poll numbers, 92–93
Polsby, Nelson, 82
Ponder, Daniel E., 71
Popkin, Samuel, 90
post-FDR period, 77–78

About the Author

Dr. Frederick D. Gordon earned his PhD in political science from the University of Southern California and master's degree in public and international affairs from the University of Pittsburgh and BA in history from Clark University, in Worcester, Massachusetts. He is the author of *Freshwater Resources and Interstate Cooperation Strategies to Mitigate an Environmental Risk* (2008) and lead editor for *International Environmental Justice Competing Claims and Perspectives* (2012). He is currently an associate professor and MPA director at East Tennessee State University.

CPSIA information can be obtained
at www.ICGtesting.com
Printed in the USA
LVHW031527270321
682675LV00002B/28